Linearization of Chains and Sideward Movement

Jairo Nunes

The MIT Press
Cambridge, Massachusetts
London, England

This book was set in Times New Roman on 3B2 by Asco Typesetters, Hong Kong and was printed and bound in the United States of America.

Library of Congress Cataloging-in-Publication Data

Nunes, Jairo.
Linearization of chains and sideward movement / Jairo Nunes.
   p.   cm. — (Linguistic inquiry monographs ; 43)
Revision of the author's dissertation (Ph. D.)—Universidade Estadual de Campinas, 2001.
Includes bibliographical references and index.
ISBN 0-262-14085-3 (alk. paper) — ISBN 0-262-64055-4 (pbk. : alk. paper)
1. Grammar, Comparative and general. I. Title. II. Series.
P151.N86   2004
415—dc22   2003064196

To Mary Kato

Viver ... O senhor já sabe: viver é etcétera ...
Guimarães Rosa

Contents

Series Foreword

We are pleased to present the forty-third in the series *Linguistic Inquiry Monographs*. These monographs present new and original research beyond the scope of the article. We hope they will benefit our field by bringing to it perspectives that will stimulate further research and insight.

Originally published in limited edition, the *Linguistic Inquiry Monographs* are now more widely available. This change is due to the great interest engendered by the series and by the needs of a growing readership. The editors thank the readers for their support and welcome suggestions about future directions for the series.

Samuel Jay Keyser
for the Editorial Board

Acknowledgments

This monograph is an extensive revision and expansion of the ideas I advanced in my Doctoral dissertation (Nunes 1995). It was concluded in May 2000 and submitted as my "tese de livre docência" at the Universidade Estadual de Campinas in November 2001. I would first like to thank all my professors, colleagues, and friends who contributed directly or indirectly to making the journey from the dissertation to the present monograph a very enriching experience.

Different parts of the material discussed here have been presented at several conferences (I Congresso Internacional de ABRALIN, 19th Penn Linguistics Colloquium, NELS 26, International Conference on Interfaces in Linguistics, XIII Instituto da ABRALIN, Troisième Colloque International "Langues et Grammaire," the XVII Summer Courses/X European Courses, II Congresso Internacional da ABRALIN, XVLII Seminário do GEL, GLOW 2000, the Workshop on the Antisymmetry Theory, the Head Movement Workshop, and the Mayfest 2002) and universities (Michigan State University, Universidad Nacional del Comahue, Universidad del País Vasco, Universidade Estadual de Campinas, Universidade Federal do Rio de Janeiro, Universität Hamburg, Universität Konstanz, University of Connecticut, University of Maryland, University of Southern California, and the Zentrum für Allgemeine Sprachwissenschaft, Sprachtypologie, und Universalienforschung). I am thankful to the audiences at these presentations for comments and suggestions.

Special thanks to Klaus Abels, Mark Arnold, Cedric Boeckx, Željko Bošković, Noam Chomsky, Marcelo Ferreira, Charlotte Galves, Hans-Martin Gärtner, Max Guimarães, Mary Kato, Richard Kayne, David Lightfoot, Pierre Pica, Jânia Ramos, Eduardo Raposo, Cilene Rodrigues, Raquel Santos, Ellen Thompson, and Juan Uriagereka.

I would also like to express my deepest gratitude to Norbert Hornstein for his constant support and his thorough and thought-provoking discussion of the monograph.

Finally, I would like to thank Conselho Nacional de Pesquisa (grant 300897/96-0) and Fundação de Amparo à Pesquisa do Estado de São Paulo (grant 97/91180-7) for having provided partial funding for this research.

Introduction

A fundamental property of human languages is that syntactic constituents are interpreted in positions different from the ones where they are phonetically realized. In (1), for instance, *John* occupies the subject position, but is interpreted as the logical object of *kissed*.

(1) John was kissed.

Within the framework of the Principles-and-Parameters Theory (see Chomsky 1981, 1986b and Chomsky and Lasnik 1993), this "displacement property" is standardly captured in the following way: given a certain structural configuration, an element may move to a different position in order to satisfy some grammatical requirement, leaving behind a coindexed trace. A trace is a phonetically unrealized category that has the relevant interpretation properties of the moved element. The moved element and its trace(s) form a sort of discontinuous object, which is referred to as a (nontrivial) chain. The relevant structure underlying the sentence in (1) is therefore as in (2), where the chain $CH = (John_i, t_i)$ is formed.

(2) $[John_i [was [kissed t_i]]]$

A considerable amount of research within the Principles-and-Parameters Theory has been devoted to properly characterizing the properties of movement, traces, and chains. In the context of the Minimalist Program (see Chomsky 1995), all these questions arise anew, in face of the elimination of much of the rich theoretical apparatus previously available. In particular, only the interface levels LF and PF are assumed, and LF objects are taken to be built from the features of the lexical items of the array that feeds a derivation (the Inclusiveness Condition; see Chomsky 1995, 228). Under the standard theory of movement stemming from Chomsky 1973, however, traces and their indices are not part of the initial array, but are introduced in the course of the derivation. Thus, a new theory of movement operations is called for in the Minimalist Program.

Addressing similar issues, Chomsky (1993) incorporates the "copy theory of movement" into the Minimalist Program. According to the copy theory, a trace is a copy of the moved element that is deleted in the phonological component (in the case of overt movement), but is available for interpretation at LF. Under this approach, the structure underlying (1) is actually the one represented in (3).

(3) [John [was [kissed John]]]

Besides being compatible with the Inclusiveness Condition, the copy theory of movement has the advantage of allowing binding theory to be stated solely in LF terms and dispensing with the operation of reconstruction (see Chomsky 1993 and section 1.2 below for discussion). However, if no explanation is provided for why "traces" (lower copies) must be deleted in the phonological component, the notion of trace as a primitive is being reintroduced. To put it more generally, the simplest—therefore most desirable—version of the copy theory of movement should take traces and heads of chains to be subject to the same principles and be accessible to the same operations.

In this monograph, I explore this null hypothesis within the general framework of the Minimalist Program and argue that differences between heads of chains and traces indeed follow from independently motivated properties of the computational system, rather than being idiosyncratic properties of the chain links themselves. In the case of phonetic realization, for instance, I will show that given the appropriate circumstances, the tail of the chain may be phonetically realized, as illustrated in (4).

(4) *Romanian* (from Bošković 2002)
    a. Cine ce   precede?
       who what precedes
       'Who precedes what?'
    b. Ce   precede ce?
       what precedes what
       'What precedes what?'

(4a) illustrates the general multiple *wh*-fronting pattern of Romanian. On the basis of the fact that the two sentences in (4) pattern alike in terms of interpretation and that exceptional *wh*-in-situ in (4b) is contingent on certain morphophonological restrictions, Bošković (2002) argues that the *wh*-object of (4b) is in fact fronted in the same way as the one in (4a); the only difference is that in (4a), the head of the chain gets phonetically realized, whereas in (4b), it is the tail of the chain that ends up being pronounced.

In the same vein, we may even find cases where more than one chain link is phonetically realized, as illustrated by "rightward focus movement" in Brazilian Sign Language and *wh*-movement in Afrikaans.

(5) *Brazilian Sign Language* (from Nunes and Quadros, in preparation)
    a. I *CAN* GO PARTY *CAN*
       'I CAN go to the party.'
    b. I HAVE *TWO* CAR *TWO*
       'I have TWO cars.'

(6) *Afrikaans* (from du Plessis 1977)
    Met wie het jy   nou weer gesê *met wie* het Sarie gedog   *met*
    with who did you now again said *with who* did Sarie thought *with*
    wie gaan Jan trou?
    who go   Jan marry
    'Whom did you say (again) that Sarie thought Jan is going to marry?'

On the one hand, the existence of constructions like (4)–(6) is good news; they suggest that the null hypothesis under the copy theory of movement—that any chain link can in principle be phonetically realized —is on the right track, at least with respect to phonetic realization. On the other hand, they now make the problem of accounting for phonetic realization of traces under minimalist strictures much harder and, therefore, much more interesting.

I take up this challenge in chapter 1. I will show that if we keep tabs on the null hypothesis under the copy theory and also assume that every chain link should in principle be computed for linearization purposes, we will have found the key to explaining why in the general case a chain does not surface with more than one link phonetically realized. The gist of the proposal is that if the two copies of *John* in (3), for instance, count as "the same" (in a sense to be made precise), no linear order can be established in accordance with Kayne's (1994) Linear Correspondence Axiom (LCA). Given that the verb *was*, for instance, asymmetrically c-commands and is asymmetrically c-commanded by "the same" element

—namely, *John*—the LCA should require that *was* precede and be preceded by *John*, violating the asymmetry condition on linear order. Put simply, deletion of all but one link is forced upon a given chain CH in order for the structure containing CH to be linearized in accordance with the LCA. I will refer to the operation of the phonological component that deletes chain links in order to satisfy linearization requirements as *Chain Reduction*. The choice of the link to escape deletion (the higher copy of *ce* in (4a) and the lower copy in (4b), for instance) will then be shown to follow from the interaction of convergence requirements of the phonological component with general economy considerations. Finally, I will show that exceptional instances such as (5) and (6), where more than one link is phonetically realized, are possible only if Morphology renders the "repeated" links invisible to the LCA.

In chapter 2, I consider whether or not we should take traces to be accessible to the computational system, in particular with respect to the locality restrictions on movement. Again, I show that the simplest hypothesis is empirically correct. Traces are also active for syntactic computation, inducing minimality effects as heads of chains do.

The final issue that I discuss is the nature of the movement operation itself. With the development of the bare phrase structure system (see Chomsky 1994, 1995), Move is understood as an operation associated with four procedures: (i) copying of a constituent α from K, (ii) merger of the copy α with K, (iii) chain formation relating the two copies, and (iv) deletion of the lower copy of α in the phonological component (in the case of overt movement). Take the derivational step sketched in (7), for instance, where the computational system has assembled the two independent syntactic objects K and L through successive applications of Merge. According to this view of Move, the computational system then makes a copy of α, as shown in (8), merges it with K, as shown in (9), and deletes the lower copy in the phonological component after the chain CH = (α, α) is formed, as illustrated in (10).

(7)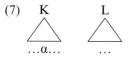

(8)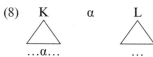

(9)

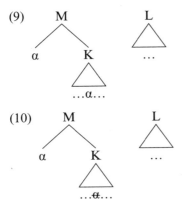

(10)

There are several conceptual inadequacies with this view. First, it cannot be the case that the phonological component blindly deletes lower copies; as mentioned above, there exist cases in which traces are phonetically realized (see (4b), (5), and (6)). Second, the system is redundant in that the notions of movement and chain capture the same relation (see Brody 1995). Finally, the stipulation that a given copy must be merged with the syntactic object that contained the "original" (see (ii) above) is still a residue of D-Structure. If a unique single-rooted object like a D-Structure representation is presented to the computational system, a moved element is bound to merge with a syntactic object that contains its trace. If no D-Structure is assumed and the computational system is allowed to resort to generalized transformations, a copied element may have choices other than a phrase containing the "original" to merge with. In other words, in a system that may operate with more than one single-rooted syntactic object at once, as assumed by Chomsky (1993, 1994, 1995, 2000, 2001), only brute force would compel movement to always target the same tree. In the case sketched above, for instance, α should also be able to merge with L at the derivational step in (8) if such merger were appropriately licensed.

Addressing these problems, I develop in chapter 3 an alternative approach in which Move is not a primitive operation of the computational system. Rather, it simply describes the interaction of the independent operations Copy, Merge, Form Chain, and Chain Reduction (deletion of chain links for linearization purposes). This alternative, which I refer to as the *Copy+Merge theory of movement*, is immune to the problems pointed out above. Deletion of chain links, for instance, does not exclusively target traces (lower copies), but is determined by convergence requirements of the phonological component and economy considerations, which leaves us some room to account for exceptional instances such as (4b), (5), and (6). The main distinctive feature of the Copy+Merge theory is that it eliminates the stipulation that a copied element must be merged with a syntactic object containing the original, allowing for constrained instances of what I have called *sideward movement*. For instance, after the derivational step in (8) is reached, α can in principle merge with L, rather than K, as illustrated in (11). Notice that under this approach, applications of Copy and Merge are not redundant with Form Chain. Under the standard assumption that chain links must be in a c-command relation, the instances of α in (11) cannot form a chain.

(11)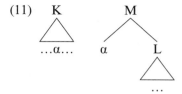

I will show that under the Copy+Merge theory, sideward movement is adequately constrained so that it not only accounts for instances of "upward" movement, but also expands the empirical coverage of standard analyses by deriving the core properties of multiple gap constructions, such as parasitic gap and across-the-board constructions, without resorting to construction-specific mechanisms or noninterface levels. I will also argue that the Copy+Merge theory provides compelling evidence for derivations in that the possibilities for a given element to undergo sideward movement change as the derivation proceeds.

By exploring the null hypothesis under the copy theory of movement, we will end up with a very different view of movement operations and the nature of the linguistic computations themselves. If the picture outlined above is on the right track, traces and Move do not have any theoretical status and there is no theoretical difference between upward and sideward movement. To the extent that it succeeds, the approach pursued here shows that minimalist parsimony may not only lead to successful reinterpretations of previous analyses on more solid grounds, but also considerably broaden the empirical coverage.

Chapter 1

Linearization and Phonetic Realization of Chains

1.1 Introduction

This monograph assumes the general framework of the Principles-and-Parameters Theory (see Chomsky 1981, 1986b and Chomsky and Lasnik 1993), with particular attention to its recent developments within the Minimalist Program, as developed by Chomsky (1993, 1994, 1995, 2000, 2001).[1] The Minimalist Program undertakes a conceptual reevaluation of the whole theoretical apparatus of the Principles-and-Parameters Theory, with the goal of explaining on more solid grounds the wealth of empirical material uncovered in the past decades. Following this approach, in this chapter and the next I submit the notion of *trace* to closer scrutiny.

Within the Principles-and-Parameters Theory, the notion of trace encompasses several types of objects that have in common the properties of being produced by a movement operation and being phonetically null. Regardless of whether traces have intrinsic features or acquire their feature specification in the course of the derivation (see Chomsky 1982, for instance), they may end up having different properties. For instance, the trace of a DP occupying an A-position is subject to the Principle A of binding theory, the trace of a DP occupying an operator position is a variable subject to Principle C, and the trace of a verb is subject to neither.[2] The distinct nature of each type of trace has been standardly captured by means of a procedure coindexing the moved element and its trace(s).

In this monograph, I propose a minimalist analysis under which traces should be treated not as grammatical formatives, but as taxonomic notions such as passive or *wh*-movement (see Chomsky 1981). My starting point will be Chomsky's (1993) revival of the "copy theory of movement," according to which a moved element leaves behind a copy that is deleted in the phonological component (in the case of overt movement), but remains available for interpretation at LF. Under this view, the sentence in (1a), for instance, has the structure represented in (1b), where the crossed-out element is not phonetically realized but may be interpreted at LF (henceforth, copies will be annotated by superscripted indices).

(1) a. John was kissed.
    b. [John^i [was [kissed ~~John^i~~]]]

Assuming that a trace is either a copy of a lexical item of the numeration or a copy of an X-bar-theoretic object built from lexical items of the numeration, the simplest—therefore most desirable—theory should take heads of chains and traces to be subject to the same grammatical principles. Eventual differences between traces and heads of chains should then be derived either from the content of the copies themselves or from properties of the computational system. A tough challenge for such a minimalist approach to movement is phonetic realization. It just seems to be a fundamental property of traces that they are not pronounced, and this property apparently cannot be derived without taking traces to be grammatical formatives.

This turns out to be only the general case, however. We may indeed find instances where the trace but not the head of the chain is phonetically realized. Consider the Serbo-Croatian sentences in (2) and (3), for instance (from Bošković 2000, 2001).

(2) *Serbo-Croatian* (from Bošković 2000, 2001)
    a. Ko šta   kupuje?
        who what buys
    b. *Ko   kupuje šta?
        who buys   what
        'Who buys what?'

(3) *Serbo-Croatian* (from Bošković 2000, 2001)
    a. *Šta šta   uslovljava?
        what what conditions
    b. Šta uslovljava šta?
        what conditions what
        'What conditions what?'

(2) illustrates the general Serbo-Croatian pattern of obligatory movement for *wh*-phrases. Following ideas by Franks (1998), Bošković (2000, 2001) argues that the unexpectedly acceptable sentence in (3b) also in-

volves overt *wh*-movement of the object *šta*, the difference between (2) and (3) being that in (3), the trace is phonetically realized (for reasons to be discussed later), rather than the head of the chain; that is, the relevant structures of (2a) and (3b) are as represented in (4).

(4) a. [ko šta^i kupuje šta^i]
    b. [šta šta^i uslovljava šta^i]

There are also cases in both spoken and signed languages where the head of the chain and (some of) its traces are phonetically realized, as illustrated by *wh*-movement in (5) and "rightward focus movement" in (6).

(5) *German* (from Fanselow and Mahajan 1995)
    Wovon glaubst Du *wovon*   sie träumt?
    what-of believe you what-of she dreams
    'What do you believe that she dreams of?'

(6) *Brazilian Sign Language* (from Nunes and Quadros, in preparation)
    I *LOSE* BOOK *LOSE*
    'I LOST the book.'

From the perspective of the simplest version of the copy theory outlined above, the existence of data such as (3b), (5), and (6) is rather welcome; it shows that traces are not different from heads of chains and can in principle be phonetically realized, as well. The problem, however, is that the task of accounting for the phonetic realization of chain links now becomes much harder. Not only does one have to explain why in the general case traces are not pronounced; one also has to handle thorny cases such as (3b), (5), and (6) in a principled manner.

In addition to the puzzling issue of phonetic realization, the simplest version of the copy theory should also cope with some theory-internal asymmetries between heads of chains and traces that have been discussed in the context of the Minimalist Program. Specifically, it has been proposed that traces are not subject to Kayne's (1994) Linear Correspondence Axiom (LCA) (see Chomsky 1995, 337) and that traces (of A-movement) are not accessible to the computational system (see Chomsky 1995, 301, 304).

Despite the clouded scenario depicted above, I show in this chapter and the next that there is hope for the simplest version of the copy theory of movement. Leaving the issue of accessibility to the computational system for chapter 2, I argue in this chapter that there is no difference between

traces and heads of chains regarding linearization. I actually propose that
the fact that traces are subject to the LCA is one of the factors that contributes to their usual lack of phonetic realization. Finally, I show that
when traces and heads of chains differ with respect to phonetic realization, this difference follows from general optimality considerations regarding deletion that do not rely on properties intrinsically assigned to
traces.

The chapter is organized as follows. In section 1.2, I discuss the general
advantages of incorporating the copy theory of movement into the Minimalist Program. In section 1.3, I point out problems for the proposals
that traces should not be subject to the LCA. In section 1.4, I present the
main theoretical issues regarding the phonetic realization of traces and
discuss some recent accounts of trace deletion. Section 1.5 is the core of
this chapter. I argue that the phonetic realization of traces follows from
the fact that traces are subject to the LCA, combined with optimality
considerations regarding deletion in the phonological component. The
specific proposal that I formulate accounts not only for standard cases
such as (1), but also for cases such as (3b), where only the trace is pronounced, and cases such as (5) and (6), where more than one chain link is
phonetically realized. In section 1.6, I show how the proposed analysis is
able to account for deletion of traces in remnant movement constructions,
as well as cases of remnant movement where more than one copy is phonetically realized. Finally, in section 1.7 I present the conclusions of the
chapter.

1.2 Advantages of the Copy Theory of Movement

Since the copy theory of movement will be the cornerstone of the proposals to be developed in this monograph, I start the discussion by examining some of its advantages from a minimalist point of view, beginning
with the ones pointed out in Chomsky 1993.

1.2.1 Elimination of Noninterface Levels

One of the main goals in the Minimalist Program is to eliminate noninterface levels of representation. As discussed in Chomsky 1993, one of
the challenges for such an approach is the existence of reconstruction
effects. Consider the sentence in (7a), for instance, which is ambiguous in
that the anaphor can be coreferential with the embedded or the matrix
subject, as represented in (7b). The reading under which the anaphor is

bound by the embedded subject appears to indicate that Principle A must be computed at a noninterface level prior to LF, before movement of the *wh*-phrase takes place.

(7) a. John wondered which picture of himself Bill saw.
    b. [John$_i$ wondered [which picture of himself$_{i,j}$]$_k$ Bill$_j$ saw t$_k$]

Chomsky (1993, 35) provides an account of the ambiguity of (7a) compatible with minimalist tenets, by resorting to the copy theory of movement. Under this approach, (7b) is to be seen as an informal abbreviation of (8), where the trace is a copy of *which picture of himself* deleted in the phonological component, but available at LF.

(8) [John wondered [which picture of himself]^i Bill saw [which picture of himself]^i]

The LF structure in (8) contains the relevant pieces of information to provide the conceptual-intentional interface with the ingredients to generate the two possible interpretations of (7a). Roughly speaking, if the lower copy of *which picture of himself* in (8) is picked up for interpretation, we obtain the reading under which the embedded subject determines the reference of *himself*; if the higher copy is interpreted, we obtain the matrix subject reading instead.[3]

Leaving aside the specific technical details of Chomsky's (1993) account of reconstruction effects, it suffices for the purposes of this section to note that the copy theory is a sound theoretical maneuver from a minimalist perspective. By allowing alternative accounts of interpretive phenomena in terms of LF, it paves the way for eliminating the noninterface levels of D- and S-Structure (see Chomsky 1993, 25).

1.2.2 Interpretation of "Discontinuous" Complex Predicates

As exemplified by (9), which allows the meaning of 'photograph' for *take pictures*, displaced elements may be understood "idiomatically" as if they had not moved from their original position.

(9) How many pictures of John did you take?

Given the proposal that D-Structure is to be abandoned for conceptual and empirical reasons (see Chomsky 1993, sec. 3), the Minimalist Program must then resort to alternative means to allow for two constituents separated by a movement operation to be interpreted as an "idiomatic" expression (in the case of (9), a complex predicate involving a light verb).

The copy theory of movement provides such means at no cost: the same copies left behind by movement that are computed for binding theory purposes may also be computed in the interpretation of complex predicates. As shown in the representation of (9) given in (10), the lower copy forms a constituent with the light verb *take* and the computation of *take pictures* as 'photograph' can proceed as if no movement had occurred. In other words, another conceptual advantage of the copy theory is that it allows compliance with minimalist desiderata by providing a standard LF analysis for apparently discontinuous complex predicates.

(10) [[how many pictures of John]^i did you take [how many pictures of John]^i]

1.2.3   Elimination of Reconstruction as an Operation

One possible way to analyze the ambiguity of (7a) that is consonant with Principle A's being an LF condition is to optionally put the *wh*-phrase back in the position of the trace in the covert component, allowing the anaphor to be bound by the embedded subject at LF (for relevant discussion, see Chomsky 1976, Hornstein 1984, and Barss 1986, among others). However, as Chomsky (1993, 34) observes, postulating such a reconstruction operation is conceptually suspicious from a minimalist perspective, because it undoes a movement that is required for convergence.

In addition, taking reconstruction to be an independent operation may lead to wrong empirical predictions. Consider, for instance, an approach that assumes reconstruction at LF in order to allow the "idiomatic" reading of *take pictures* in (9) and takes Principle A to be checked in the course of the derivation in order to account for the ambiguity of sentences such as (7a). As noted by Chomsky (1993, 39), under such an approach, the anaphor in (11) could be bound by the matrix subject prior to LF and the *wh*-phrase could be reconstructed at LF, making the "idiomatic" reading available. However, this reading is not possible in (11); the interpretation of *take picture* as 'photograph' in (11) is possible only if the anaphor is bound by the embedded subject.

(11) John wondered which picture of himself Bill took.

The impossibility of the reading described above can be accounted for under the copy theory of movement, if there is no operation of reconstruction and if the conceptual-intentional interface picks up a single chain link for computations of complex predicates and binding theory. If it picks up the higher *wh*-copy in (12), for instance, the "idiomatic" reading of *take picture* is blocked; if it picks up the lower one, the "idiomatic" reading is possible.

(12) [John wondered [which picture of himself]^i Bill took [which picture of himself]^i]

Thus, another advantage of adopting the copy theory of movement is that it allows us to eliminate reconstruction as an additional operation of the computational system.

1.2.4 Satisfaction of the Inclusiveness Condition

Still another conceptual advantage of assuming the copy theory from a minimalist perspective is that it satisfies the Inclusiveness Condition, which requires that an LF object be built from the features of the lexical items of the numeration (see Chomsky 1995, 228). The motivation underlying the Inclusiveness Condition is to restrict the reference set of derivations that can be compared for economy purposes. If the system could add material that is not present in the numeration in the course of syntactic computations, the role of the numeration in determining the class of comparable derivations would be completely undermined. Thus, given the minimalist assumption that economy matters in the computations from the numeration to LF, something like the Inclusiveness Condition must be enforced in the system.

This being so, the trace theory of movement violates the Inclusiveness Condition because traces are grammatical formatives that are not part of the initial array that feeds the computation. Under the copy theory, on the other hand, a trace is simply a copy of a lexical item of the numeration or a copy of an X-bar-theoretic object built from the items of the numeration. Put in different terms, the copy theory contributes to ensuring internal coherence in the framework.[4]

1.2.5 Shape of Phonetically Realized Traces

The copy theory of movement may also account for the fact that in languages where traces may be phonetically realized, they have the same phonetic shape as the head of the chain, as illustrated in (13) and (14).

(13) *German* (from McDaniel 1986)
   Mit wem glaubst du *mit wem* Hans spricht?
   with whom think you *with whom* Hans talks
   'With whom do you think Hans is talking?'

(14) *Romani* (from McDaniel 1986)
  Kas   misline   *kas*   o Demìri dikhlâ?
  whom you-think *whom* Demir   saw
  'Who do you think Demir saw?'

To be fair, in order for sentences such as (13) and (14) to count as empirical evidence for the copy theory of movement, one must first explain why traces (lower copies) cannot be phonetically realized in the general case. This issue is discussed in detail in section 1.5. For present purposes, it is worth observing that the phonetic shape of the apparent traces in (13) and (14) (and in (3b), (5), and (6), as well) is at least what the copy theory would lead us to expect.

1.2.6 Elimination of Traces as Grammatical Primitives

One of the most appealing features of the copy theory of movement is that it provides the means for treating the notion of trace itself as epiphenomenal. If a trace is actually a copy of a given moved element, it need not be specified as a grammatical formative in Universal Grammar (UG); it is either a lexical item (here taken to include functional heads, as well) or an X-bar-theoretic object built from lexical items. Under such an approach, we would expect the properties of different traces to follow either from the content of the copies themselves or from independently motivated properties of the computational system. The interpretation of a *wh*-trace as a variable, for instance, could be due to its intrinsic features as (a copy of) a *wh*-phrase (see Chierchia 1991 and Hornstein 1995, chap. 6, for instance), whereas the general distribution of traces in a given structure could be regulated by standard conditions on movement/chain formation or by conditions on deletion (see Lightfoot 2002).

In the following sections, I pursue this line of reasoning and investigate the apparent asymmetries between heads of chains and traces with respect to the LCA and phonetic realization. I argue (i) that heads of chains and traces are both subject to the LCA, and (ii) that the phonetic realization of both heads of chains and traces is determined by linearization of chains and optimality computations regarding deletion. To the extent that it succeeds, the analysis to be developed below takes substantial steps toward eliminating traces as grammatical formatives.

Before getting to the analysis proper, let us consider how traces have been analyzed with respect to linearization and phonetic realization within the Minimalist Program.

1.3   Traces and the Linear Correspondence Axiom

With Kayne's (1994) influential proposal that linear order is determined by hierarchical structure, as dictated by the Linear Correspondence Axiom (LCA) in (15) (see Kayne 1994, 33), an interesting question arises: are traces computed for purposes of linearization? The question is even more intriguing if one assumes that a trace is a copy of the moved element.

(15) *Linear Correspondence Axiom*
Let X, Y be nonterminals and x, y terminals such that X dominates x and Y dominates y. Then if X asymmetrically c-commands Y, x precedes y.

Kayne (1994, 10) briefly mentions the question of linearization of traces under the copy theory of movement when discussing the phrase markers in (16) and (17) with respect to the LCA. According to Kayne, (16) is a well-formed phrase marker because V asymmetrically c-commands N and therefore *see* is to precede *John*; in (17), on the other hand, V and NP c-command each other and therefore no linear order between *see* and *John* can be established.

(16)

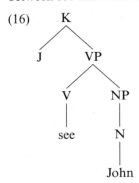

(17)

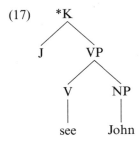

Assuming the distinction between phrase markers such as (16) and (17), Kayne considers two possibilities as to how structures containing traces may comply with the LCA:

The question arises of what happens if *John* (or any phrase) is moved. If the result of movement is that DP (or NP) dominates just a trace, then *see* and that trace will not be ordered at all with respect to one another, since the internal structure of DP (or NP), which ensured antisymmetry, will have been lost. This might conceivably be a tolerable consequence, since traces are in any event not visible. It is notable, though, that this question does not arise if movement transformations leave a copy rather than a trace. (Kayne 1994, chap. 2, n. 3)

Given his claim that the LCA is the source of the major properties of standard X-bar theory, Kayne (1994, 49) concludes that the LCA underlies the entire set of syntactic representations. This entails, however, that S-Structure and LF should not allow a structure containing a head and the trace of its complement for the same reason a structure such as (17) should not be permitted: it violates the LCA. Kayne's suggestion that the "invisibility" of traces at PF exempts them from being subject to the LCA is therefore at odds with his conceptual argument that the LCA applies to all syntactic representations, including LF (see Kayne 1994, sec. 5.2).

On the other hand, as Kayne observes, there seems to be no problem in linearizing a given head and the trace of its complement under the copy theory of movement, provided that the trace has internal structure; in other words, traces do not differ from unmoved elements with respect to linearization considerations. We may thus draw the conclusion that the copy theory of movement is indeed a necessary component in Kayne's system in order to ensure consistency with respect to the well-formedness conditions that the LCA imposes on phrase markers.

Addressing the issue of whether or not traces should be subject to the LCA under the bare phrase structure approach, Chomsky (1995, 337) suggests that "there is no reason for the LCA to order an element that will disappear at PF, for example, a trace." I disagree with this suggestion. The null hypothesis under the copy theory of movement is that all copies should be subject to the same grammatical conditions; any proposed difference between heads of chains and traces should require strong motivation. Chomsky's suggestion could perhaps be better substantiated if reasons for deletion of traces were offered. Even so, it should be observed that the logic of the suggestion confers too much power on global computations. The linearization of a given element at a given derivational step is taken to be contingent on a deletion operation targeting that element later in the derivation. If this logic were to extend to morphological operations, for instance, one could ask why Morphology should not ignore traces, allowing contraction to proceed over them, given that they will be deleted later in the derivation. Clearly, this would yield wrong results with respect to *wanna*-contraction over *wh*-traces, for instance.

To my knowledge, there appears to be only one potential problem for the null hypothesis that heads of chains and traces are both subject to the LCA. If the links of a chain are in a sense the same element (under standard assumptions, a chain is a discontinuous object), any material intervening between two links of a given chain asymmetrically c-commands and is asymmetrically c-commanded by the same element. This state of affairs, however, is not compatible with the LCA and no linear order should obtain for structures containing chains.

In section 1.5, I turn this potential problem into a virtue by using the logic of its consequences to account for deletion of traces in the phonological component. Before we get to the discussion of how linearization considerations ultimately motivate deletion of traces, let us consider what are the main theoretical and empirical issues regarding deletion of traces and how successful some current analyses have been in addressing them.

1.4   Traces and Phonetic Realization

1.4.1   The Issues
The most salient difference between heads of chains and traces is their phonetic realization: in the general case, only heads of chains are phonetically realized. Thus, any analysis that adopts some version of the copy theory of movement has to address the following questions: (i) why is it the case that (in general) a nontrivial chain cannot have all of its links phonetically realized?, and (ii) why is it the case that (in general) traces and not heads of chains are the links that are deleted? That is, given the derivation sketched in (18), for instance, why is it not possible for the structure in (18c) to yield the PF output associated with (19a) or (19b)?[5]

(18) a. $K = [_{TP} T [_{VP} was [_{VP} kissed John]]]$
     b. *Copy*
         $K = [_{TP} T [_{VP} was [_{VP} kissed John^i]]]$
         $L = John^i$
     c. *Merge*
         $[_{TP} John^i [_{T'} T [_{VP} was [_{VP} kissed John^i]]]]$

(19) a. *John was kissed John.
     b. *Was kissed John.
     c. John was kissed.

From a minimalist perspective, the unacceptability of the sentence (19a) resulting from the derivation in (18) raises an additional puzzle. The derivation of either (19b) or (19c) from (18c) presumably involves an operation eliminating one of the copies of *John*, whereas no such operation is invoked in (19a). Thus, were the derivations of (19a), on the one hand, and the derivations of (19b) and (19c), on the other, to be compared for economy purposes, the derivation of (19a) should outrank the other two because it is more economical in the number of operations that it requires. Since (19a) is unacceptable, its derivation from (18c) must then crash or be canceled,[6] thereby being irrelevant for economy computations.

Finally, as mentioned in sections 1.1 and 1.2.5, there are also languages that apparently allow traces to be phonetically realized in addition to the head of the chain, as illustrated in (20) and (21).

(20) *German* (from McDaniel 1986)
     Mit wem glaubst du *mit wem* Hans spricht?
     with whom think   you *with whom* Hans talks
     'With whom do you think Hans is talking?'

(21) *Romani* (from McDaniel 1986)
     Kas misline *kas* o Demìri dikhlâ?
     whom you-think *whom* Demir   saw
     'Who do you think Demir saw?'

Assuming that appearances are not misleading in these cases,[7] whatever the explanation is for the deletion of the trace in (18c), for instance, it should be flexible enough to allow for some phonetically realized traces in some languages, but restricted enough not to permit every trace to be phonetically realized in these languages. Languages such as German and Romani, for instance, which may allow intermediate *wh*-traces to be pronounced, as shown in (20) and (21), do not admit phonetic realization of traces of full *wh*-phrases in intermediate positions, as illustrated in (22) and (23).

(22) *German* (from McDaniel 1986)
     **Wessen Buch* glaubst du *wessen Buch* Hans liest?
     whose book think   you *whose book* Hans reads
     'Whose book do you think Hans is reading?'

(23) *Romani* (from McDaniel 1986)
   Save   chave mislinea   *save   chave* o Demìri dikhlâ?
   which boy   you-think *which boy*   Demir   saw
   'Which boy do you think Demir saw?'

Let us consider how some current approaches available within minimalism handle the conceptual and empirical questions posed above.

1.4.2   Some Approaches to Deletion of Traces in the Minimalist Program
Chomsky (1993, 35) suggests that deletion of traces in the phonological component is an obligatory variant of a more general process that converts the structure in (24a), for instance, into the sentence in (24b), by deleting E in the phonological component.

(24) a. John said that he was looking for a cat, and so did Bill [$_E$ say
        that he was looking for a cat]
    b. John said that he was looking for a cat, and so did Bill.

The main argument for claiming that (24a) is transformationally related to (24b) is that both constructions are subject to a Parallelism Requirement, which presumably holds at the conceptual-intentional interface.[8] For instance, if *he* in the first conjunct of either of the sentences in (24) is taken to refer to Tom and *a cat* is understood nonspecifically, the same interpretation will obtain in the second conjunct. One problem for this derivational approach to the pair of sentences in (24) concerns the generality of the proposed deletion operation. As pointed out by Chomsky and Lasnik (1993, 565), given the pair in (24), it is not clear why the sentences in (25), for instance, should not be derivationally related to the ones in (26), which are, however, ill formed.

(25) a. John said that he was looking for a cat, and Bill did too.
    b. John likes poetry, but not Bill.

(26) a. *John said that he was looking for a cat, and Bill did say that he
        was looking for a cat too.
    b. *John likes poetry, but not Bill likes poetry.

The derivational approach to (24) also requires unprecedented economy computations. Noting that the bracketed constituent in (24a) has a distinctive low-flat intonation, Chomsky and Lasnik (1993, 564) propose that "the deletion rule ... could say simply that material with this intonational property may optionally delete." Within the minimalist framework, optionality should arise when the same derivational cost is ascribed to different options. Clearly, deletion and lack of deletion do not have the same derivational cost; hence, Chomsky and Lasnik's proposal appears to entail that at a certain point in the derivation, deletion is as costly as low-flat intonation. These options do not form a natural class, however. In the absence of independent evidence, it does not seem plausible to take deletion and low-flat intonation to be equally costly, if comparable at all.

Even if we disregard these problems for a derivational relation between the sentences of (24), it is still possible to make the case that deletion of traces is unrelated to ellipsis. First, traces are obligatorily deleted in the general case, as opposed to other potential "ellipsis material," which may be optionally deleted. The structure in (27a), for instance, can only surface as (27c), with deletion of the lower copy; a low-flat intonation on the trace of the subject in (27b) does not make the pronunciation of the trace acceptable. Thus, without an independent explanation for the ill-formedness of (27b) with the relevant intonation, we are led to the conclusion that deletion of traces and ellipsis are different phenomena.[9]

(27) a.   [that John said he was looking for a cat]^i is believed [that John said he was looking for a cat]^i by everyone

b.   *That John said he was looking for a cat is believed that John said he was looking for a cat by everyone.

c.   That John said he was looking for a cat is believed by everyone.

It should also be noted that deletion of traces operates with copies, elements that are not distinguished in the initial numeration; by contrast, the alleged deletion in the mapping from (24a) to (24b) operates with elements that are morphologically identical but distinctively specified in the numeration (the numeration underlying (24a) presumably contains two instances of *he*), or even with lexical items that are not identical at all (*say* is allegedly deleted in (24a) on the basis of its relation to *said*).[10] This is therefore another reason not to take deletion of traces to be a subcase of ellipsis.

Chomsky (1995, 252–253) takes the opposite view of the relation between ellipsis and deletion of traces, suggesting that it is ellipsis that is a subcase of deletion of traces:

At some point in the derivation [from (24a) to (24b)], the bracketed element must be marked as "subject to parallelism interpretation." Assume that this takes place before Spell-Out [endnote omitted]. The marking could be removal of the distinctions indicated by numeration, in which case the bracketed element is in a certain sense nondistinct from the phrase it "copies" (the latter still marked by the numeration). Such a configuration might be interpreted at PF as assigning copy intonation to the bracketed expression, and at LF as imposing the parallelism interpretations. . . . Suppose that numeration markings on the copy are changed to those of the first conjunct instead of being deleted. Then the antecedent and its copy are strictly identical and constitute a chain, if a chain is understood as (constructed from) a pair of terms (α_1, α_2) that are identical in constitution. It will follow, then, that the copy deletes, by whatever mechanism deletes traces in the phonological component. At LF the two kinds of constructions will be very similar, though not quite identical. (Chomsky 1995, 252–253)

This suggestion attempts to unify ellipsis and deletion of traces, but it ends up stressing their differences. First, "ellipsis chains" do not satisfy conditions that apply to regular chains such as c-command or Last Resort, for instance. Second, even if we assume that the operation that changes numeration markings to form "ellipsis chains" can be independently motivated, it is not obvious how this operation works in instances of "ellipsis chains" formed in discourse, as illustrated in (28). At any rate, it should be observed that deletion of traces remains unexplained under this approach.

(28) A: John said that he was looking for a cat.
     B: So did Bill.

The discussion above therefore shows that even if the problems for a derivational approach to the pair of sentences in (24) are overcome, it does not seem plausible to subsume deletion of traces under ellipsis or ellipsis under deletion of traces. The conceptual and empirical questions raised in section 1.4.1 remain virtually untouched.

Other recent implementations of the copy theory have also been unable to successfully account for the issues raised in section 1.4.1. The approaches surveyed in (29)–(32), for instance, in one way or another incorporate a variant of Chomsky's (1993) stipulation that traces must be deleted in the phonological component.[11]

(29) *Transparency* (Brody 1995, 106)
     "[I]f all chain members c-commanded by the contentive element are copies of the contentive, then it must be the case that only the highest member of such a set of copies (i.e., the contentive itself) is visible for SPELLOUT."

(30) *Form Chain* (Groat and O'Neil 1996, 135)
     "[F]orming a chain results in copying all syntactic features of the category moved, but does not copy the category's phonological matrix: it either moves it to the new position or fails to move it."

(31) *Speak Up* (Bobaljik 1995b, 350)
Pronounce the topmost/leftmost copy of each element.

(32) *Silent Trace* (Pesetsky 1997, 153; 1998, 361)
Don't pronounce the traces of a moved constituent.

Here I will not discuss the different degrees of success of each individual proposal in (29)–(32).[12] For present purposes, it suffices to focus on their common stipulative trait.[13] Since they impose lack of phonetic realization on traces in an ad hoc fashion, it is unclear how they could be amended to provide a principled account for cases like (33), for example, where more than one copy is phonetically realized.

(33) *Afrikaans* (from du Plessis 1977)
Met wie het jy   nou weer gesê *met wie* het Sarie gedog   *met*
with who did you now again said *with who* did Sarie thought *with*
wie gaan Jan trou?
who go   Jan marry
'Whom did you say (again) that Sarie thought Jan is going to marry?'

Let us then consider an alternative approach within the confines of the null hypothesis regarding the copy theory of movement, namely, that heads of chains and traces should both be subject to phonetic realization and that any difference between them should be derived from independent properties of the computational system.

1.5 Linearization of Chains and Phonetic Realization of Chain Links

1.5.1 Nondistinctiveness of Copies
Once the copy theory of movement is assumed, one needs to determine whether two terms with the same set of features are to be interpreted as distinct elements or copies. Consider the structure in (34), for example. If the pair (*John, John*) of (34) were to form a chain, it would satisfy both the Minimal Link Condition and Last Resort; actual chain formation thus depends on whether or not the two instances of *John* are nondistinct copies or elements distinctively specified in the numeration.[14]

(34) [$_{TP}$ John was [$_{vP}$ kissed John]]

I will follow Chomsky's (1995, 227) proposal that two lexical items l and l' selected from a numeration should be marked as distinct for the computational system if they are accessed by distinct applications of Select.[15] As for phrasal objects, I assume that their labels encode the relevant piece of information regarding distinctiveness; the DP [the man], for instance, is to be represented in bare phrase structure terms as $K = \{the^i, \{the^i, man^k\}\}$. Given that Copy just replicates the targeted material and does not alter distinctiveness markings, it is possible to determine, at any point in a given derivation, whether two terms with identical sets of features are to be interpreted as copies or distinct constituents.

The notion of (non)distinctiveness of constituents clearly plays no role at the PF level and at the articulatory-perceptual interface. Questions arise, however, about whether it is relevant for early computations of the phonological component when syntactic structure is still available. Consider the structure in (35), for example, which was built from a numeration containing two instances of *John*, as indicated by the indices.

(35) [$_{TP}$ John^i T [$_{vP}$ John^i [$_{v'}$ said [$_{CP}$ that [$_{TP}$ John^k was [$_{vP}$ kissed John^k]]]]]]

Let us make the natural assumption that PF should reflect the number of occurrences of each lexical item specified in the initial numeration.[16] If so, the PF output of (35) should contain only two instances of *John* and the other two should be deleted. The question is what is the criterion for choosing which of the four instances of *John* in (35) to delete. If deletion were sensitive only to identity of phonological features, (35) could in principle surface as any of the sequences in (36), contrary to fact (see note 3).

(36) a.   John said that John was kissed.
     b.   *John John said that was kissed.
     c.   *John said that was kissed John.
     d.   *Said that John was kissed John.

The fact that the only possible PF output for (35) is (36a), in which the trace of each chain is deleted, shows that the phonological component applies the deletion operation (for reasons yet to be determined) to members of a chain and not simply to terms with identical sets of phonological features. This in turn indirectly suggests that the phonological component takes the notion of nondistinctiveness of terms into account when performing deletion.

Let us explore the consequences of this conclusion for the linearization computations of the phonological component.

1.5.2 Linearization of Nontrivial Chains

If the notion of nondistinctiveness is available for early computations of
the phonological component while syntactic structure is still present, it
must certainly be available at the point where the system employs the
operation *Linearize*, which I take to be the procedure that maps a given
syntactic structure into a sequence of terminals, in compliance with the
LCA. Assuming this to be so, let us consider the asymmetric c-command
relations in (37), in order to determine how this structure should be linearized in accordance with the LCA.[17]

(37) [John^i [was [kissed John^i]]]

   Take the relation between the two copies of *John* and the copula *was*,
for instance. Since the upper copy of *John* asymmetrically c-commands
was, we should obtain the order $\langle John^i, was \rangle$, according to the LCA;
likewise, since the copula asymmetrically c-commands the lower copy of
John, the order $\langle was, John^i \rangle$ should be derived. Combining these two
results, we should obtain the partial sequence $\sigma = \langle John^i, was, John^i \rangle$.
Were the two instances of *John* distinct, σ would be a well-formed linear
order, with the copula following an occurrence of *John* and preceding a
different occurrence of *John*, as in (36a). However, since the two instances
of *John* in (37) are nondistinct, *was* is required to precede and be preceded
by the same element, *John*. σ is therefore not a linear order because it
lacks asymmetry (if α precedes β, then it must be the case that β does not
precede α).

   The structure in (37) also violates the irreflexivity condition on linear
order (if α precedes β, then it must be the case that $\alpha \neq \beta$). Since the
upper copy of *John* asymmetrically c-commands the lower one, the for-
mer should precede the latter in accordance with the LCA. Given that the
two copies of *John* in (37) are nondistinct, that would amount to saying
that *John* should precede itself.

   Failure to yield a linear order thus provides a straightforward account
of the fact that the structure in (37) cannot surface as the sentence in
(38a); the attempted derivation of (38a) from (37) is canceled, because
Linearize yields no output and no PF object is formed. To put it in general terms, if the links of a chain count as nondistinct for linearization
purposes, we have an explanation for why a chain (in standard cases)
cannot surface at PF with more than one link overtly realized: the syntactic object containing such a chain cannot be linearized.

(38) a. *John was kissed John.
     b. John was kissed.

    This is a welcome result. Recall that the derivations of (38a) and (38b) from (37) should be prevented from being compared for purposes of economy; if they were compared, the derivation of (38a) would incorrectly outrank the derivation of (38b) because it is more economical in not employing an application of deletion (see section 1.4.1). If the derivation of (38a) from (37) is canceled because it cannot be linearized, no questions of convergence or economy can be raised.[18]

    I propose that deletion of chain links is thus required for a structure containing nontrivial chains to be linearized in accordance with the LCA. This proposal has the welcome conceptual advantage that it takes both heads of chains and traces to be subject to linearization. What is required at this point is an independent motivation for why deletion generally targets traces and not heads of chains and an account of how the presence of multiple copies may circumvent the LCA in some cases. These are the topics of the next sections.

1.5.3 Deletion of Chain Links and Optimality Considerations

1.5.3.1 Full versus Scattered Deletion Consider the simplified structure in (39), in which the embedded object DP raises to the matrix subject position, leaving two copies behind.

(39) [TP[DP the [NP tall man]]^i appears [TP[DP the [NP tall man]]^i to have been kissed [DP the [NP tall man]]^i]]

As discussed in section 1.5.2, such a structure cannot be linearized as is. The highest copy of *the tall man* asymmetrically c-commands the verb *appears*, for instance, which in turn asymmetrically c-commands the other two copies. Given that these three copies are nondistinct, no linear order between *the tall man* and *appears* can be established in accordance with the LCA. Thus, Linearize yields no output for further computations in the phonological component when applying to (39) and the derivation is canceled because no PF object is formed.

    I proposed in section 1.5.2 that deletion may allow a structure containing nontrivial chains to be linearized by eliminating "repeated" material that induces lack of asymmetry and irreflexivity in the intended linear order. Nothing that has been said so far, however, prevents deletion from applying within the different links of a chain, in what may be called *scattered deletion*. For instance, deletion could in principle target different constituents in each of the links of the DP chain in (39), yielding a structure such as (40).

(40) [$_{TP}$[$_{DP}$ the [$_{NP}$ ~~tall man~~]]^i appears [$_{TP}$[$_{DP}$ ~~the~~ [$_{NP}$ tall ~~man~~]]^i to have been kissed [$_{DP}$ ~~the~~ [$_{NP}$ ~~tall~~ man]]^i]]

Although the coindexed DPs in (39) are nondistinct, the constituents that survive deletion in (40) are distinct. (40) should then be linearized in accordance with the LCA, yielding the sentence in (41), which is, however, unacceptable.

(41) *The appears tall to have been kissed man.

I propose that although the derivation of (41) converges at PF, it is not the most economical derivation starting from (39). To put it more broadly, scattered deletion does not yield an optimal derivation in the general case. Take (39), for example. Under the assumption that deletion for purposes of linearization only targets constituents (one constituent per application), the derivation of (40) from (39) requires that deletion apply (at least) five times, targeting the following constituents: the NP of the chain link in the matrix subject position, the constituents *the* and *man* of the link in the intermediate subject position, and the constituents *the* and *tall* of the link in the object position. However, three other derivations starting from (39) that employ "full deletion" of chain links are more economical; if deletion targets the whole DP of two links of the chain in (39), the structures in (42) will be derived.

(42) a. [$_{TP}$[$_{DP}$ the [$_{NP}$ tall man]]^i appears [$_{TP}$[$_{DP}$ ~~the~~ [$_{NP}$ ~~tall man~~]]^i to have been kissed [$_{DP}$ ~~the~~ [$_{NP}$ ~~tall man~~]]^i]]

  b. [$_{TP}$[$_{DP}$ ~~the~~ [$_{NP}$ ~~tall man~~]]^i appears [$_{TP}$[$_{DP}$ the [$_{NP}$ tall man]]^i to have been kissed [$_{DP}$ ~~the~~ [$_{NP}$ ~~tall man~~]]^i]]

  c. [$_{TP}$[$_{DP}$ ~~the~~ [$_{NP}$ ~~tall man~~]]^i appears [$_{TP}$[$_{DP}$ ~~the~~ [$_{NP}$ ~~tall man~~]]^i to have been kissed [$_{DP}$ the [$_{NP}$ tall man]]^i]]

Each structure of (42) can be linearized in accordance with the LCA, yielding the sentences in (43). Given that the derivation of any of the sentences in (43) employs only two applications of deletion, the derivation of (41), which requires (at least) five applications, is correctly blocked.

(43) a. The tall man appears to have been kissed.
   b. *Appears the tall man to have been kissed.
   c. *Appears to have been kissed the tall man.

Under the assumption that deletion targets one constituent per application, economy considerations concerning the number of applications of deletion thus block scattered deletion in the general case, favoring full deletion of chain links. I refer to the operation of the phonological component that converts (39), for instance, into structures such as (40) or (42) as *Chain Reduction* (see Nunes 1995, 279).

(44) *Chain Reduction*
   Delete the minimal number of constituents of a nontrivial chain CH that suffices for CH to be mapped into a linear order in accordance with the LCA.

Although I will assume the formulation in (44) for expository purposes, it is actually unnecessary to specify that Chain Reduction delete the *minimal number* of constituents; that is, Chain Reduction need not count. Economy considerations regarding the length of a derivation may indirectly determine the number of elements to be deleted, by enforcing the minimal number of applications of deletion. All things being equal, a short derivation should block a longer derivation (see Chomsky 1995, 314, 357); hence, a derivation in which constituents are unnecessarily deleted is longer, therefore less economical, than a competing derivation where no such deletion occurs.

For instance, if Chain Reduction had deleted each of the three links of the DP chain in (39), forming the object in (45a), the problem of lack of asymmetry and irreflexivity would be circumvented and (45a) could be linearized in accordance with the LCA, eventually yielding the sentence in (45b). The derivation of (45a) from (39), where the deleted material is nonrecoverable, is not optimal, however. Chain Reduction in this derivation employs (at least) three applications of deletion, when only two applications would suffice for the structure containing the DP chain to be mapped into a linear order, as shown in (42). In other words, recoverability of deletion in the case of Chain Reduction can be ensured by economy considerations regarding the length of derivations.

(45) a. [TP[DP the [NP tall man]]^i appears [TP[DP the [NP tall man]]^i to
        have been kissed [DP the [NP tall man]]^i]]
     b. *Appears to have been kissed.

Note that the derivations of (41) and (45b) from the structure in (39) were ruled out on the basis of *economy*, rather than convergence considerations. The system proposed here actually allows instances of scattered deletion if full deletion of chain links does not yield a convergent derivation. For instance, if a derivation crashes because full deletion leads to violations of other constraints of the phonological component, it will not compete with corresponding derivations involving scattered deletion.

A rather persuasive example of this possibility is found in Bošković's (2001) analysis of the contrast between Macedonian and Bulgarian with respect to the location of clitics, as illustrated in (46) and (47).

(46) *Macedonian* (from Rudin et al. 1999)
    a. Si mu   (gi)   dal li parite?
          are him-DAT them given Q the-money
    b. *Dal li si   mu   (gi)   parite?
          given Q are him-DAT them the-money
          'Have you given him the money?'

(47) *Bulgarian* (from Rudin et al. 1999)
    a. *Si mu   (gi)   dal li parite?
          are him-DAT them given Q the-money
    b. Dal li si   mu   (gi)   parite?
          given Q are him-DAT them the-money
          'Have you given him the money?'

Bošković argues that in both languages the complex head [si+mu+gi+dal] left-adjoins to the interrogative particle *li*, leaving a copy behind, as represented in (48).

(48) [si+mu+gi+dal]^i+li ... [si+mu+gi+dal]^i

Deletion of the lower copy of [si+mu+gi+dal], as shown in (49), yields a well-formed result in Macedonian (see (46a)), because in this language pronominal clitics are proclitic and *li* is enclitic. The unacceptability of (46b) then follows from the general ban on scattered deletion imposed by economy considerations regarding the number of applications of deletion.

(49) [si+mu+gi+dal]^i+li ... [s̶i̶+̶m̶u̶+̶g̶i̶+̶d̶a̶l̶]^i

In Bulgarian, on the other hand, both *li* and the pronominal clitics are enclitics; thus, deletion of the lower copy of the complex head does not lead to a convergent result (see (47a)). Bošković argues that the system then resorts to scattered deletion, as shown in (50), allowing the chain to be linearized yet at the same time satisfying the additional requirements of the phonological component.

(50) [s̶i̶+̶m̶u̶+̶gi+dal]^i+li ... [si+mu+gi+d̶a̶l̶]^i

Another potential instance of scattered deletion motivated (in part) by phonological considerations involves split constituents in Germanic and Slavic languages. Ćavar and Fanselow (1997) argue that the Croatian sentence in (51), for instance, is derived along the lines shown in (52).

(51) *Croatian* (from Ćavar and Fanselow 1997)
Na kakav   je Ivan krov bacio loptu?
on what-kind-of be Ivan roof throw ball
'On what kind of roof did Ivan throw the ball?'

(52) a. [[$_{PP}$ na [kakav krov]]^i je Ivan [$_{PP}$ na [kakav krov]]^i bacio loptu
[$_{PP}$ na [kakav krov]]^i]
  b. [[$_{PP}$ na [kakav ~~krov~~]]^i je Ivan [$_{PP}$ ~~na~~ [~~kakav~~ krov]]^i bacio loptu
~~[$_{PP}$ na [kakav krov]]^i~~]

The PP [na kakav krov] 'on what-kind-of roof' moves first to a Focus position and then to a Topic position, as shown in (52a). Assuming that elements bearing topic and focus features must be realized in the checking domain of the relevant heads, Ćavar and Fanselow show that the usual deletion of traces cannot license the realization of both topic and focus features. The system then resorts to scattered deletion within the higher links along the lines shown in (52b), allowing both requirements to be met. From the perspective of the economy approach explored here, the elimination of the lower copy of PP in (52b) for purposes of linearization should, by contrast, be obtained with a single application of deletion targeting the whole PP.

Yet another example of scattered deletion may involve some cases of extraposition, under the assumption that it is to be analyzed as the output of leftward movement, as argued by Wilder (1995). The sentence in (53) is analyzed by Wilder (1995, 292) in the following way: the PP [about the claim that Mary will hire Peter] is generated to the right of the temporal adverb and moves to some higher position, as shown in (54a). The structure in (54a) is then subject to an operation that Wilder calls Chain-Internal Selective Deletion (see Hinterhölzl 1999 for discussion), according to which phonological deletion can remove part of the antecedent and the complementary part of the trace, as illustrated in (54b).

(53) We talked about the claim yesterday that Mary will hire Peter.

(54) a. [we talked [$_{PP}$ about [$_{DP}$ the [$_{NP}$ claim [$_{CP}$ that Mary will hire Peter]]]]^i yesterday [$_{PP}$ about [$_{DP}$ the [$_{NP}$ claim [$_{CP}$ that Mary will hire Peter]]]]^i]

b. [we talked [$_{PP}$ about [$_{DP}$ the [$_{NP}$ claim [$_{CP}$ ~~that Mary will hire Peter~~]]]]^i yesterday [$_{PP}$ ~~about~~ [$_{DP}$ ~~the~~ [$_{NP}$ ~~claim~~ [$_{CP}$ that Mary will hire Peter]]]]^i]

According to the proposal in section 1.5.2 regarding nondistinctiveness and linearization, the complementary deletion operations of Wilder's Chain-Internal Selective Deletion are required by linearization considerations: if some constituent of the PP chain in (54a) appears in both links, the structure cannot be linearized in accordance with the LCA and the derivation is canceled. The fact that scattered deletion may be preferred to full deletion in this case is presumably due to other properties of the phonological component. Suppose, for instance, that the CP complement of *claim* in (54a) can be optionally marked as constituting an independent prosodic domain. In case it is so marked, deletion of the lower PP will not yield a licit prosodic structure because the adverb *yesterday* will be left "dangling." Once full deletion does not lead to convergence, the system then resorts to scattered deletion along the lines of (54b), yielding a linearizable structure compatible with the relevant prosodic requirements.

To summarize, by taking the number of applications of deletion under Chain Reduction to be determined by economy considerations, we can account for (i) why scattered deletion within chains is in general not an optimal option (it employs more applications of deletion than necessary); (ii) why convergence requirements may override the preference for deletion of entire chain links (only convergent derivations count for economy computations); and (iii) why deletion does not apply to every chain link, resulting in unrecoverable deletion (it also employs more applications of deletion than required).

1.5.3.2 Deletion of Traces versus Deletion of Heads of Chains We are still left with a problem from section 1.5.3.1: the derivations that convert a structure such as (55) into the PF output associated with any of the sentences in (56) were taken to be equally economical, for they employ the same number of applications of deletion under Chain Reduction; however, the only derivation that yields an acceptable sentence is the one in which both traces are deleted.

(55) [$_{TP}$[$_{DP}$ the tall man]^i appears [$_{TP}$[$_{DP}$ the tall man]^i to have been kissed [$_{DP}$ the tall man]^i]]

(56) a.   The tall man appears to have been kissed.
     b.   *Appears the tall man to have been kissed.
     c.   *Appears to have been kissed the tall man.

I show below that the choice among the links to be deleted is contingent on the elimination of formal features in the phonological component. But first, let us review Chomsky's (1995) proposal regarding the deletion of formal features in a derivation, starting with the computation from the numeration to LF.

Formal features may or may not be assigned an interpretation at the conceptual-intentional interface, depending on their type and on the category they are associated with. For instance, a Case-feature presumably does not receive an interpretation at the conceptual-intentional interface, whereas φ-features (gender, number, and person) receive an interpretation if they are part of a noun, but not if they are part of a verb. In case formal features are uninterpretable at the conceptual-intentional interface, they must be eliminated by LF, in order for the derivation to converge. Chomsky (1995) proposes that deletion of uninterpretable features takes place under feature checking, where *deletion* is taken to render a given feature "invisible at LF but accessible to the computation" (Chomsky 1995, 280).[19] Since interpretable features need not be deleted, they are always accessible to the computational system and may participate in more than one checking relation; uninterpretable features, on the other hand, cannot enter into a checking relation once checked.[20]

In addition to being relevant for LF computations, formal features are arguably relevant for morphological computations in the phonological component. Thus, Spell-Out must allow formal features to feed both the covert and the phonological component. The problem, however, is that formal features are not legible at the PF level (only phonological features are); if shipped to the phonological component, they should then lead the derivation to crash at PF. Dealing with this problem, Chomsky (1995, 230–231) proposes that there must be an operation of the phonological component applying after Morphology that eliminates formal features that are visible at PF. Let us call this operation *FF-Elimination* and take it to proceed along the lines of (57) (see Nunes 1995, 231), where deletion targets a single feature per application.[21]

(57) *Formal Feature Elimination (FF-Elimination)*
     Given the sequence of pairs $\sigma = \langle (F, P)_1, (F, P)_2, \ldots, (F, P)_n \rangle$ such
     that σ is the output of Linearize, F is a set of formal features, and

P is a set of phonological features, delete the minimal number of features of each set of formal features in order for σ to satisfy Full Interpretation at PF.

The difference between the head of a chain and its traces regarding phonetic realization now follows from the number of checking relations a given copy is associated with. The discussion of the relation between interpretability of formal features and checking theory has so far been restricted to the mapping from the numeration to LF: checking operations render uninterpretable features invisible at LF, eventually allowing the derivation to meet Full Interpretation and converge at this level. A natural extension of this approach is to take checking operations to render uninterpretable features invisible at PF as well; after all, no formal feature is interpreted at the articulatory-perceptual interface.[22] Assuming this extension of Chomsky's (1995) checking theory, let us reconsider the derivation of (55), repeated in (58) with the relevant Case-features represented (unchecked features are in bold and checked/deleted features are subscripted).

(58) $[_{TP}[_{DP}$ the $[_{NP}$ tall man$]]^i$-$_{CASE}$ appears $[_{TP}[_{DP}$ the $[_{NP}$ tall man$]]^i$-**CASE** to have been kissed $[_{DP}$ the $[_{NP}$ tall man$]]^i$-**CASE**$]]$

After being assembled and merged with the verb *kissed*, the DP *the tall man* raises to the specifier of each T head in order to check their strong D-features; in addition, the Case-feature of the topmost copy of *the tall man* enters into a checking relation with the Case-feature of the matrix T. Since Case is an uninterpretable feature, this checking relation renders the Case-feature of the highest copy of *the tall man* invisible at LF and, according to the extension of the checking theory proposed above, invisible at PF as well. The Case-features of the lower copies of *the tall man*, on the other hand, are unaffected by the Case-checking relation involving the highest copy.[23]

Let us then see how the DP chain of (58) is to be reduced. As discussed in section 1.5.3.1, the optimal reduction of this chain involves only two applications of deletion targeting any two of its links, as shown in (59).

(59) a. $[_{TP}[_{DP}$ the $[_{NP}$ tall man$]]^i$-$_{CASE}$ appears $[_{TP}[_{DP}$ ~~the~~ $[_{NP}$ ~~tall man~~$]]^i$-**~~CASE~~** to have been kissed $[_{DP}$ ~~the~~ $[_{NP}$ ~~tall man~~$]]^i$-**~~CASE~~**$]]$
   b. $[_{TP}[_{DP}$ ~~the~~ $[_{NP}$ ~~tall man~~$]]^i$-$_{CASE}$ appears $[_{TP}[_{DP}$ the $[_{NP}$ tall man$]]^i$-**CASE** to have been kissed $[_{DP}$ ~~the~~ $[_{NP}$ ~~tall man~~$]]^i$-**~~CASE~~**$]]$

c. [~~TP[DP the [NP tall man]]~~^{i}-~~CASE~~ appears [~~TP[DP the [NP tall man]]~~^{i}-~~CASE~~ to have been kissed [DP the [NP tall man]]^i-CASE]]

If the DP chain of (58) is reduced as in (59a), no further application of FF-Elimination is required to delete the Case-feature of *the tall man* in order for Full Interpretation to be satisfied; this feature has been deleted and is therefore invisible at PF. The PF output in (56a) is then derived after further applications of phonological rules. By contrast, if the DP chain is reduced as in (59b) or (59c), the convergent PF outputs in (56b) and (56c) are obtained only if FF-Elimination deletes the unchecked Case-feature of the copy that survives. Thus, the derivation in (59a), in which the head of the chain survives Chain Reduction, ends up being more economical than the derivations in (59b) and (59c), in which other links survive Chain Reduction, because it requires fewer applications of deletion by FF-Elimination—hence the pattern of acceptability in (56).[24,25]

Exploring the null hypothesis regarding the copy theory of movement, the above proposal thus takes the position that both heads of chains and traces should in principle be subject to phonetic realization. According to the logic of the proposal, there is nothing intrinsic to lower copies that prevents them from being pronounced. If Chain Reduction proceeds in such a way that only a trace survives, the derivation may eventually converge at PF. The fact that in most cases such a derivation yields unacceptable sentences is taken to follow from *economy* considerations, rather than convergence at PF. Since the highest chain link is engaged in more checking relations, it will require fewer application of FF-Elimination than lower chain links, thereby being the optimal candidate to survive Chain Reduction and be phonetically realized, all things being equal.

Things are not equal, however, if the phonetic realization of the head of the chain violates other well-formedness conditions of the phonological component. One such scenario is discussed by Franks (1998) in precisely these terms. Given the paradigm in (60), which shows that clitics in Serbo-Croatian generally appear in second position, Franks addresses the problem of exceptional placement triggered by prosodic considerations, as illustrated in (61a) with an appositive clause and in (61b) with contrastive focus.[26]

(60) *Serbo-Croatian* (from Franks 1998)
    a. Zoran *mi*   stalno   kupuje knjige.
        Zoran *me-DAT* constantly buys   books

b. *Zoran stalno   *mi*   kupuje knjige.
   Zoran constantly *me-DAT* buys   books
   'Zoran is constantly buying me books.'

(61) *Serbo-Croatian* (from Franks 1998)
   a. Ja, tvja mama, obeçala *sam*   *ti*   sladoded.
      I   your mother promised *AUX-1SG* you-DAT ice cream
      'I, your mother, promised you ice cream.'
   b. Javili   su   nam   da prije nekoliko dana na toj   liniji
      announced AUX-3PL us-DAT C ago several   days on that line
      voz *je*   kasnio tri   sata.
      train *AUX-3SG* was-late three hours
      'They announced that, several days ago, on that line, the train
      was three hours late.'

Assuming that second position clitics move overtly to the highest functional head available and leave copies at all the intermediate sites, Franks
(1998, sec. 2.6.2) proposes that "the puzzle of clitic placement reduces to
the issue of which copy is the one pronounced." More specifically, he
summarizes his proposal in the following way (see p. 31): (i) "Deletion of
all but the highest copy does not occur if retention of the highest copy
would result in a PF crash"; and (ii) "Economy considerations then dic-
tate that the next highest copy is pronounced, unless again the result fails
to converge." Under this view, the apparently exceptional sentences in
(61) are derived from the representations in (62) (Franks's (78) and
(79a)), where "#" indicates an intonational phrase boundary.

(62) a. [ja #tvja mama# [*sam ti*]^i obeçala [*sam ti*]^i obeçala sladoded]
   b. [. . . da *je*^{i} #prije nekoliko dana# *je*^{i} na toj liniji# *je*^{i} voz *je*^{i}
      kasnio tri sata]

Given that Serbo-Croatian clitics are enclitics, the intonational boundary induced by the appositive *tvja mama* in (62a) blocks left-adjunction of
the adjacent copy of the clitic cluster *sam ti*. If the lower copy of the clitic
cluster were deleted, as in standard cases, then the higher copy would not
be prosodically licensed, leading to a derivational crash at PF; the higher
copy is then deleted and the lower copy phonologically attaches to the
element to its left, yielding the sentence in (61a). Similar considerations
apply to the chain involving the clitic in (62b), with four copies of the
clitic *je*. The intonational boundaries set off by the contrastively focused

constituents in (62b) prevent left-adjunction of the copies after *dana* and *liniji*; as for the copy after *da*, Franks (p. 32) assumes that there is a constraint in Slavic against clitics—even enclitics—immediately preceding an intonational boundary. Thus, since the copy after *voz* is the only one in (62b) that can comply with prosodic requirements, all the other copies are deleted and the sentence in (61b) is generated.

Bošković (2000, 2002) extends Franks's (1998) analysis to apparent exceptions to obligatory *wh*-movement. Consider the Serbo-Croatian sentences in (63) and (64), for instance. (63) is representative of the general paradigm in Serbo-Croatian, with movement of all *wh*-phrases, whereas (64b) apparently shows an exceptional instance where a *wh*-phrase is prohibited from moving.[27]

(63) *Serbo-Croatian* (from Bošković 2000, 2002)
    a. Ko šta   kupuje?
        who what buys
    b. *Ko kupuje šta?
        who buys   what
        'Who buys what?'

(64) *Serbo-Croatian* (from Bošković 1999, 2002)
    a. *Šta šta   uslovljava?
        what what conditions
    b. Šta   uslovljava šta?
        what conditions what
        'What conditions what?'
    c. Šta   neprestano šta   uslovljava?
        what constantly what conditions
    d. *?Šta neprestano uslovljava šta?
        what constantly conditions what
        'What constantly conditions what?'

Given that the exceptional pattern in (64b) arises only when the sentence resulting from obligatory *wh*-movement involves adjacent occurrences of *šta*, as shown by the contrast between (64c) and (64d), and that the interpretation of (64b) does not differ from that of (64c) in the relevant respects, Bošković (2000, 2002) argues that the unexpectedly acceptable sentence in (64b) also involves overt movement of the object *wh*-phrase; however, a morphological restriction blocking adjacency of identical *wh*-words prevents the phonetic realization of the upper copy of the object chain, and the lower copy is realized instead, as represented in (65).[28]

(65) [šta šta^i uslovljava šta^i]

Bošković (2002) presents compelling evidence for this approach by showing that comparable instances of "exceptional" *wh*-in-situ in Romanian, as illustrated in (66b), are able to license parasitic gaps, as shown in (67). Under the standard assumption that in-situ arguments do not license parasitic gaps (see section 3.4.2 for discussion), the acceptability of (67) can be accounted for if the *wh*-object actually moves overtly, licensing the parasitic gap, and the trace is phonetically realized instead of the head of the chain.

(66) *Romanian* (from Bošković 2002)
    a. *Ce   ce   precede?
       what what precedes
    b. Ce   precede ce?
       what precedes what
       'What precedes what?'

(67) *Romanian* (from Bošković 2002)
    Ce   precede ce   fara   sa   influenteze?
    what precedes what without SUBJ.PRT influence-3P.SG
    'What precedes what without influencing?'

Golston (1995) proposes that restrictions against adjacent homophones, which he calls Antihomophony, is motivated by the Obligatory Contour Principle.[29] One of the many interesting cases of Antihomophony discussed by Golston involves center embedding of genitive phrases in Ancient Greek. Consider (68a) and (68b), for instance, which show that genitive DPs in Ancient Greek could either follow or precede the noun they were related to.

(68) *Ancient Greek* (from Golston 1995)
    a. [[hee   tólma]   [tóon   legóntoon]]
       the-NOM courage-NOM the-GEN speaking-GEN
       'the courage of those speaking'
    b. [[hee   [tóu   himatíoon] ergasías]
       the-NOM the-GEN crowd-GEN rule-NOM
       'the rule of the crowd'

Given the frequent alternation between structures like the ones in (68) in Ancient Greek, one would expect that the alternation in (69) (Golston's (32) and (33)) should also be attested. Golston conducted a computer search spanning over 500 years of Ancient Greek literature, but did not find any instance such as (69b), where center embedding results in two adjacent homophonous determiners. Golston then concludes that the impossibility of cases like (69b) follows from Antihomophony. That being so, there should in principle be two derivational sources for a DP such as (69a), from the perspective of our current discussion: either the embedded genitive DP is generated to the right of the relevant noun, as in (69a), or it moves and its trace is phonetically realized.

(69) a. [[[tóon   oikeíoon] tinàs]   [tóon   ekeínoon]]
        the-GEN slaves-GEN some-GEN the-GEN those-GEN
     b. *[[tóon   [tóon   ekeínoon] oikeíoon] tinàs]
        the-GEN the-GEN those-GEN slaves-GEN some-GEN
        'some of the slaves of those [people]'

By showing that both traces and heads of chains are in principle equally pronounceable, Franks's (1998) analysis of exceptional clitic placement and its extension by Bošković (2000, 2002) to exceptional lack of *wh*-movement provide compelling empirical evidence for the null hypothesis under the copy theory of movement.[30] The only piece missing in Franks's analysis is an independent explanation for why the best candidate for pronunciation is the *highest* chain link if possible, then the second *highest*, and so on.[31]

Under the approach developed in this section, however, this hierarchy is what we should expect. The ranking of best candidates for pronunciation from the highest to the lowest chain link follows from economy considerations regarding checking relations in overt syntax and applications of FF-Elimination in the phonological component. Since syntactic objects keep checking their features as they move, the higher a given chain link is, the fewer its unchecked features that FF-Elimination must delete. In other words, if a higher link survives Chain Reduction, the applications of FF-Elimination are minimized.

To sum up, lack of phonetic realization is not an intrinsic property that should characterize traces as grammatical primitives. Traces may indeed be phonetically realized if the pronunciation of the head of the chain causes the derivation to crash at PF. The fact that traces in the general case are not phonetically realized follows from the interaction of two independent factors: (i) since nontrivial chains induce violations of the LCA, they must undergo Chain Reduction; and (ii) the choice of the link to survive Chain Reduction and be phonetically realized is determined by economy considerations regarding the number of applications of FF-Elimination: given that the head of a chain participates in more checking relations than its trace(s), it will require fewer applications of FF-Elimination, becoming the optimal option for phonetic realization.

1.5.3.3 Phonetic Realization of Multiple Copies In this section, I examine some chains that have more than one full link phonetically realized and discuss why they do not cause problems for linearization.

1.5.3.3.1 Wh-*Elements* As mentioned in sections 1.1 and 1.4.1, some languages may allow *wh*-traces to be phonetically realized in addition to the head of the *wh*-chain. The sentences in (70)–(74) exemplify this phenomenon.

(70) *Afrikaans* (from du Plessis 1977)
      Met wie het jy   nou weer gesê *met wie* het Sarie gedog   *met*
      with who did you now again said *with who* did Sarie thought *with*
      wie gaan Jan trou?
      who go   Jan marry
      'Whom did you say (again) that Sarie thought Jan is going to marry?'

(71) *German* (from McDaniel 1986)
      Wen   glaubt Hans *wen* Jakob gesehen hat?
      whom thinks Hans *wen* Jakob seen   has
      'Who does Hans think Jakob saw?'

(72) *Romani* (from McDaniel 1986)
      Kas   misline   *kas*   o Demìri dikhlâ?
      whom you-think *whom* Demir   saw
      'Who do you think Demir saw?'

(73) *Frisian* (from Hiemstra 1986)
      Wêr tinke jo *wêr*'t   Jan wennet?
      where think you *where*-that Jan lives
      'Where do you think that Jan lives?'

(74) *English child grammar* (from Thornton 1990)
      Who do you think really *who*'s in the can?

At first sight, these sentences constitute counterevidence to my proposal that deletion of chain links is triggered by linearization considerations (see section 1.5.2): if the *wh*-phrases of each of the sentences are nondistinct copies, they should prevent their structures from being linearized and cause the derivation to be canceled.[32] I show below that when closely inspected, these sentences actually provide additional evidence in favor of the proposal regarding linearization of chains pursued in this chapter. Before getting into the analysis proper, let us consider two other kinds of data that show that the phenomenon illustrated in (70)–(74) is very restricted in these languages.

The first thing to note is that in languages that allow multiple *wh*-copies, phonetic realization of traces is restricted to intermediate traces, as shown by the contrast between (75) and (76), for instance. In both sentences, three *wh*-copies are phonetically realized. The difference between them is arguably due to the fact that in (75), only the intermediate *wh*-traces are realized, whereas in (76), the tail of the *wh*-chain is realized as well.

(75) *German* (from Fanselow and Mahajan 1995)
    Wen denkst Du *wen* sie meint   *wen* Harald liebt?
    who think you *who* she believes *who* Harald loves
    'Who do you think that she believes that Harald loves?'

(76) *German*
    *Wen glaubt Hans *wen* Jakob *wen* gesehen hat?
    whom thinks Hans *whom* Jakob *whom* seen   has
    'Who does Hans think Jakob saw?'

Second, as mentioned in section 1.4.1, the intermediate trace cannot contain a full *wh*-phrase, as illustrated by the German and Romani sentences in (77) and (78), which should be contrasted with (71) and (72).

(77) *German* (from McDaniel 1986)
    *Wessen Buch glaubst du *wessen Buch* Hans liest?
    whose book think   you *whose book* Hans reads
    'Whose book do you think Hans is reading?'

(78) *Romani* (from McDaniel 1986)
    *Save chave mislinea *save chave* o Demìri dikhlâ?
    which boy you-think *which boy* Demir   saw
    'Which boy do you think Demir saw?'

In order to account for the whole paradigm described above, I will rely on a suggestion by Chomsky (1995, 337) regarding the linearization of two heads in a relation of mutual c-command, as illustrated in (79), under the bare phrase structure approach. Since the bare phrase structure system does not allow vacuous projections, neither m nor p in (79) asymmetrically c-commands the other and no linear order between them can be established in consonance with the LCA.

(79)   L

A derivation containing a structure such as L in (79) should therefore be canceled, unless, as Chomsky (1995, 337) suggests, "the structure $N = [_L \ m \ p]$ has changed by the time the LCA applies so that its internal structure is irrelevant; perhaps N is converted by Morphology to a 'phonological word' not subject internally to the LCA, assuming that the LCA is an operation that applies after Morphology."[33] The suggested morphological reanalysis may be implemented in terms of the operation *fusion* of Distributed Morphology (see Halle and Marantz 1993), which takes two terminal heads that are sisters under a single category node and fuses them into a single terminal node, reducing the number of independent morphemes in a structure.

Assuming Chomsky's (1995, 337) proposal that the LCA does not apply word-internally, the data in (70)–(78) can then be accounted for if (i) successive-cyclic *wh*-movement in these languages may proceed by adjunction to an intermediate C^0, as schematically represented in (80);[34] and (ii) Morphology in these languages may convert the adjunction structure $[_{C^0} \ WH \ [_{C^0} \ C^0]]$ in (80) into a single terminal element, along the lines suggested by Chomsky with respect to $[_L \ m \ p]$ in (79). That is, once the intermediate *wh*-copy and C^0 undergo morphological fusion, the *wh*-element becomes part of the single terminal element dominating C^0 and therefore invisible to the LCA. The order of the reanalyzed *wh*-element with respect to the other elements of (80) is then indirectly determined by the position of C^0, very much the way a morpheme or a consonant is indirectly ordered with respect to the other elements of the structure containing them, based on the position of the terminal element that contains them.

(80)

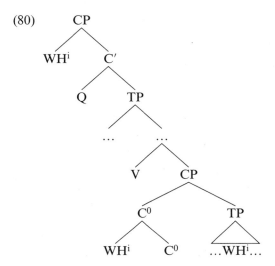

Bearing these considerations in mind, let us examine the possible outputs of (80) given in (81), after Morphology fuses the structure [$_{C^0}$ WH [$_{C^0}$ C^0]] into a single terminal element (as represented by "# ... #").

(81) a. *[$_{CP}$ WH^i ... [$_{CP}$ #[$_{C^0}$ WH^i [$_{C^0}$ C^0]#] [$_{TP}$ ... WH^i ...]]]
   b. *[$_{CP}$ WH^i ... [$_{CP}$ #[$_{C^0}$ W̶H̶^{i} [$_{C^0}$ C^0]#] [$_{TP}$ ... W̶H̶^{i} ...]]]
   c. *[$_{CP}$ W̶H̶^{i} ... [$_{CP}$ #[$_{C^0}$ WH^i [$_{C^0}$ C^0]#] [$_{TP}$ ... WH^i ...]]]
   d. [$_{CP}$ WH^i ... [$_{CP}$ #[$_{C^0}$ WH^i [$_{C^0}$ C^0]#] [$_{TP}$ ... W̶H̶^{i} ...]]]

According to the proposals made in section 1.5.2, a structure containing a nontrivial chain cannot be linearized in accordance with the LCA; since the chain links are nondistinct, they induce violations of the asymmetry and irreflexivity conditions on linear order. By deleting chain links, Chain Reduction circumvents this problem and allows structures containing chains to be properly linearized. Recall, however, that the number of applications of deletion of constituents by Chain Reduction is determined by general economy conditions regarding derivational length (see section 1.5.3.1); thus, all things being equal, Chain Reduction employs deletion as little as possible. In (81a), for instance, the intermediate link becomes invisible to the LCA after morphological fusion and need not be deleted. The other two links, however, remain visible for the LCA and prevent the whole structure from being linearized—hence the unacceptability of sentences such as (76), where all the links of the *wh*-chain are realized. In turn, (81b) is excluded by economy: since the intermediate link is invisible to the LCA, it need not—therefore, must not—be deleted by Chain Reduction; in other words, since Chain Reduction can allow the linearization of (80) with a single application of deletion, as shown in (81c) and (81d), further applications are blocked. Finally, the choice between (81c) and (81d) is the familiar one regarding deletion of heads of chains versus deletion of traces. Assuming that the head of the *wh*-chain participates in more checking relations, it requires fewer applications of FF-Elimination in the phonological component and becomes the optimal candidate for phonetic realization (see section 1.5.3.2)—hence the choice of (81d), empirically illustrated in (70)–(74).

In turn, contrasts such as the one between (71) and (72), on the one hand, and (77) and (78), on the other, are due to the fact that morphological fusion deals with heads, but not with maximal projections.[35] If Morphology is in general unable to deal with nonminimal maximal projections adjoined to heads (see Chomsky 1995, 319), *wh*-movement involving full phrases must then proceed through the intermediate Spec,CP rather than adjoining to C^0, as illustrated in (82).

(82) $[_{CP}[_{wh} \ldots]^i [_{C'} Q \ldots [_{CP}[_{wh} \ldots]^i [_{C'} C^0 [_{TP} \ldots [_{wh} \ldots]^i \ldots]]]]]$

Once all copies of the full *wh*-phrase in (82) are visible to the LCA, Chain Reduction must delete all but one link—hence the unacceptability of (77) and (78), for instance.[36]

Independent evidence for the proposed morphological restructuring of $[_{C^0}$ WH $[_{C^0} C^0]]$ as a single terminal element is provided by the dialect of German spoken in the Berlin-Brandenburg area, which, according to Fanselow and Mahajan (1995, 152–153), distinguishes multiple copies of regular PPs, as in (83a), from multiple copies of PPs that involve incorporation and independently function as simple morphological words, as in (83b).

(83) *German* (from Fanselow and Mahajan 1995)
    a. *An wen   glaubst Du *an wen*   sie denkt?
       of whom believe you *of whom* she thinks
       'Who do you believe that she thinks of?'
    b. *Wovon* glaubst Du *wovon* sie träumt?
       what-of believe you *what-of* she dreams
       'What do you believe that she dreams of?'

From the perspective explored here, dialectal and idiolectal variation in this regard (see note 35) is due not to syntactic computations proper, but to the degree of permissiveness of a given dialect or idiolect with respect to morphological reanalysis. As a rule, the more complex a constituent, the smaller the likelihood that it will undergo morphological reanalysis and become invisible to the LCA. The impossibility of a morphological reanalysis involving the higher complementizer in (80), for instance, is arguably due to its [+wh] feature, which makes it morphologically heavy in the relevant sense; in other words, only [−wh] C^0s are light enough to permit morphological reanalysis and render an adjoined *wh*-element invisible to the LCA.

In the next sections, we will see more examples of this correlation between morphological complexity and phonetic realization of multiple copies.

1.5.3.3.2 Clitics Another interesting case of morphological restructuring exempting copies from being deleted is illustrated by clitic duplication in some dialects of Argentinean Spanish.[37] The data in (84) illustrate the general pattern of clitic placement in Spanish, with the object clitic preceding a finite form or following a nonfinite form. What is relevant for our discussion is that in one dialect of Argentinean Spanish, which I refer to as dialect I, clitic duplication may be allowed, but only if the higher copy is enclitic, as illustrated in (85). Interestingly, as (86) shows, this pattern does not change even if the higher verb is in the subjunctive mood, which generally requires proclisis.

(84) *Spanish*

a. *Nos* vamos acostumbrando   a este pais   poco a   poco.
   us_{Cl} go-1PL getting-accustomed to this country little by little
   'We are getting accustomed to this country little by little.'

b. Vamos acostumbrándo*nos*   a este pais   poco a   poco.
   go-1PL getting-accustomed/us_{Cl} to this country little by little

(85) *Argentinean Spanish* (dialect I)

a. Vámo*nos*   acostumbrándo*nos*   a este pais   poco a
   go-1PL/us_{Cl} getting-accustomed/us_{Cl} to this country little by
   poco.
   little

b. *Nos* vamos acostumbrándo*nos*   a este pais   poco a
   us_{Cl} go-1PL getting-accustomed/us_{Cl} to this country little by
   poco.
   little

(86) *Argentinean Spanish* (dialect I)
    a.   para que vayámo*nos*   acostumbrándo*nos*   a este
         for   that go-SUBJ-1PL/*us$_{Cl}$* getting-accustomed/*us$_{Cl}$* to this
         pais
         country
         'in order for us to get accustomed to this country'
    b.   *para que *nos* vayamos   acostumbrándo*nos*   a este
         for   that *us$_{Cl}$* go-SUBJ-1PL getting-accustomed/*us$_{Cl}$* to this
         pais
         country

Under the approach developed in this section, the correlation between exceptional enclisis and clitic duplication receives a straightforward account. Let us assume that when the clitic climbs, it adjoins to the left of a functional category F with the finite verb adjoined to it, as represented in (87) (see Kayne 1991 and Uriagereka 1995, for instance).

(87)

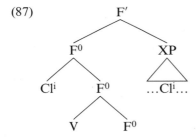

As is, the structure in (87) cannot be linearized because the two copies of the clitic induce violations of the asymmetry and irreflexivity conditions on linear order—hence the unacceptability of sentences such as (85b) and (86b). Applied to the clitic chain in (87), Chain Reduction must delete one of the copies, yielding the sentences in (84).[38] I propose that what distinguishes dialect I from other Spanish dialects is that Morphology can reanalyze the structure $[_{F^0}$ Cl $[_{F^0}$ V $[_{F^0}$ F^0]]] in (87) as a single terminal element, along the lines of the reanalysis of $[_{C^0}$ WH $[_{C^0}$ C^0]] examined in section 1.5.3.3.1, rendering the adjoined clitic invisible to the LCA. Taking enclisis to be the reflex of such morphological restructuring in this dialect, we would expect clitic duplication to always co-occur with exceptional enclisis.[39] After the three-segment F^0 in (87) is restructured as a single terminal element, the only copy of the clitic that is visible to the LCA is the lower one and it need not (therefore, must not) be deleted by Chain Reduction—hence the contrasts in (85) and (86).[40]

In another dialect of Argentinean Spanish, which I will refer to as dialect II, duplication does not correlate with exceptional enclisis and keeps the general pattern of proclisis to finite forms, as illustrated in (88).[41]

(88) *Argentinean Spanish* (dialect II)
    Yo *lo* iba   a hacer*lo*.
    I   *it$_{Cl}$* went to do-*it$_{Cl}$*
    'I was going to do it.'

If clitic duplication is a by-product of morphological restructuring, as argued above, reanalysis must have also applied in constructions such as (88), despite appearances to the contrary. The relevant difference between dialects I and II should thus be treated in terms of the order of the output of reanalysis (enclisis or proclisis), rather than in terms of application or lack of application of reanalysis. Two pieces of evidence indicate that this is indeed the case. Consider the data in (89).

(89) *Argentinean Spanish* (dialect II)
    a. Yo *se*   *lo* iba   a decir.
        I   *him$_{Cl}$* *it$_{Cl}$* was-going to say
        'I was going to say it to him.'
    b. Yo iba   a decir*selo*.
        I   was-going to say-*him$_{Cl}$*-*it$_{Cl}$*
    c. *Yo *se*   *lo* iba   a decir*selo*.
        I   *him$_{Cl}$* *it$_{Cl}$* was-going to say-*him$_{Cl}$*-*it$_{Cl}$*

The data in (89a) and (89b) show that a clitic cluster also falls under the standard pattern of clitic placement seen in (84), with proclisis to the finite auxiliary or enclisis to the nonfinite verb. Given that dialect II also allows duplication with proclisis, as seen in (88), we should in principle expect duplication of the cluster *se lo* in (89c), as well. The unexpected unacceptability of (89c) can, however, be accounted for if reanalysis fails to apply and the copies of the cluster prevent the structure from being linearized. The reason why reanalysis is impossible in (89c) can arguably be attributed to the morphological complexity of the clitic cluster. As discussed in section 1.5.3.3.1, the more complex an element is, the less likely it is to undergo morphological reanalysis. In (89c), the morphological heaviness of *se lo* presumably blocks morphological restructuring, which entails that all of the links of the clitic cluster chain are visible with respect to the LCA and must undergo Chain Reduction. Lack of Chain Reduction then prevents the structure that could yield (89c) from being linearized.

The second piece of evidence that morphological reanalysis also applies to dialect II has to do with the correlation between clitic climbing and duplication. As shown in (90), contexts where clitic climbing is not possible may allow clitic duplication.[42]

(90) *Argentinean Spanish* (dialect II)
    a. *Lo odio   hacer.
       it$_{Cl}$ I-hate do
       'I hate to do it.'
    b. *Lo* odio   hacer*lo*.
       it$_{Cl}$ I-hate do-*it$_{Cl}$*

Details of technical implementation aside, the contrast in (90) suggests that the morphological restructuring involving the higher copy of the clitic in (90b) exempts it from being computed not only with respect to the LCA, but also with respect to whatever is responsible for preventing clitic climbing in (90a). If this description is correct, the contrast in (91) can now be accounted for if the proposed morphological reanalysis must involve a finite verb. In (91a), the restructuring verb *intentar* 'try' allows clitic climbing and the higher copy of the clitic undergoes morphological reanalysis and becomes invisible to the LCA. In (91b), on the other hand, reanalysis of the upper copy does not void climbing barrierhood induced by the nonrestructuring verb *odiar* 'hate', and the sentence should be ruled out along the lines of (90a).

(91) *Argentinean Spanish* (dialect II)
    a. *Lo* iba   a intentar hacer*lo*.
       it$_{Cl}$ I-was-going to try   do-*it$_{Cl}$*
       'I was going to try to do it.'
    b. *Lo iba   a odiar hacer*lo*.
       it$_{Cl}$ I-was-going to hate do-*it$_{Cl}$*
       'I would hate to do it.'

To sum up, the instances of clitic duplication in both dialects I and II are possible only if a morphological reanalysis renders one of the copies invisible to the LCA. Chain Reduction then is not forced to delete the clitic below the word level, and we obtain a chain with more than one link phonetically realized.

1.5.3.3.3 ***Verbs*** Predicate clefting constructions in Vata (see Koopman 1984) present another case where phonetic realization of more than one copy is contingent on morphological factors.[43] As discussed in detail by Koopman (1984), a focused verb in Vata appears sentence-initially and is doubled by an identical verb in the regular positions occupied by verbs.[44]

(92) *Vata* (from Koopman 1984)

    a. *lī*   à   *lī*-dā   zué   sáká
       eat we *eat*-PAST yesterday rice
       'We ATE rice yesterday.'

    b. *lī*   Ò   dā   sáká   *lī*
       eat she/he PERF-AUX rice   *eat*
       'She/He has EATEN rice.'

Reinterpreting Koopman's discussion of Vata predicate clefting in terms of the analysis of phonetic realization of multiple copies entertained here, I assume that verb focusing involves verb movement to a Focus projection preceding TP, as shown in (93), with subsequent morphological reanalysis of $[_{Foc^0} \; V \; [_{Foc^0} \; Foc^0]]$ as a single terminal element, rendering the moved verb invisible to the LCA.[45]

(93)

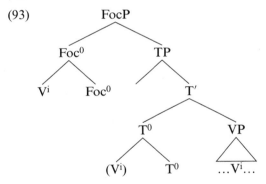

As illustrated in (92), the main verb may or may not move to T^0 depending on whether or not an auxiliary is present (see Koopman 1984, 42). If the verb moves to T^0, we obtain the chain CH_1, with three links; if it does not, we obtain the chain CH_2, with two links.[46] After the highest link of either chain undergoes morphological reanalysis with Foc^0, it will be disregarded by Chain Reduction. Applying to CH_1, Chain Reduction then takes into consideration the two lower links of CH_1 and deletes the lowest link, as in standard instances of movement, yielding constructions such as (92a). As for CH_2, it has only one link visible to the LCA and therefore does not trigger Chain Reduction; in other words, CH_2 behaves like a trivial chain for purposes of Chain Reduction and the two links are phonetically realized, as illustrated in (92b).

Evidence for the proposed reanalysis of $[_{Foc^0}$ V $[_{Foc^0}$ Foc$^0]]$ in Vata comes from our now familiar considerations regarding morphological complexity. According to Koopman (1984, 156), none of the particles that occur in I may appear with the fronted verb, whether negation or any tense particle, as illustrated in (94a) and (94b), respectively.

(94) *Vata* (from Koopman 1984)
    a. *(*nà`)* *lē* wà *ná`-lē*-kā
       (*NEG) eat they *NEG-eat*-FT
       'They will not EAT.'
    b. *lī (*wa)* wà *lī-wa*   zué
       eat(*TP) they *eat(*TP)* yesterday
       'They ATE yesterday.'

Given that predicate clefting in Vata must involve verb duplication, not allowing a gap in the position of the trace of the verb (see Koopman 1984, 162), it must be the case that the Foc head obligatorily triggers morphological reanalysis. If so, copying the negation or the tense particle in (94) arguably renders the verbal form complex enough so that reanalysis does not take place and the derivation does not converge.[47]

The most interesting indication that this approach is on the right track is the list of verbs that cannot undergo clefting. Koopman (1984, 157) shows that verb clefting is a very pervasive construction in Vata, being possible for basically all kinds of verbs. According to her, the exceptions include auxiliaries, the defective verb *na/la/lO* 'to say', and the verbs *lÈ* 'to be' and *kà* 'to have'. The crucial common property among these verbs is that none of them can be the input for morphological processes that apply to other verbs (see Koopman 1984, 158). If these verbs cannot participate in any morphological process, they certainly should not be able to undergo the proposed morphological reanalysis with Foc^0 and should not be allowed in predicate clefting constructions.

Verb clefting in Vata therefore provides very compelling evidence for the proposal that multiple copies are allowed to surface just in case morphological reanalysis renders some copies invisible to the LCA.[48,49]

1.5.3.3.4 Postpositions Dourado (2002) argues that the approach sketched above provides a straightforward account of postposition duplication in Panara (a Brazilian indigenous language), which is illustrated in (95).

(95) *Panara* (from Dourado 2002)

    a. ka hẽ Ø-ka-ra-*hɔw*-pĩaseri   prĩara *hɔw*
        you ERG REAL.TR-2SG.ERG-3PL.ABS-*with*-fight children *with*
        'You argued with the children.'

    b. ka   ka-ti-ra-*kõ*-kui   ĩkyẽ *kõ*
        you.ABS IRR-2SG.NOM-1SG.ABS-*with*-go 1SG.ABS *with*
        'You will go with me.'

Dourado has found that the possibility of postposition duplication in Panara is contingent on the possibility of standard incorporation (with deletion of the trace), as sketched in (96).

(96) *Panara* (adapted from Dourado 2002)

	Incorporation	Duplication
Instrumentative *hɔw* 'with'	*	*
Comitative *hɔw* 'with'	OK	OK
Ablative *pe* 'from'	*	*
Malefactive *pe* 'from'	OK	OK
Locative *kõ* 'with'	*	*
Comitative *kõ* 'with'	OK	OK

The cases listed in (96) are especially interesting because they involve ambiguous postpositions. Dourado proposes that in Panara, the syntactic object resulting from adjoining a postposition to a verb may optionally undergo morphological reanalysis. If reanalysis takes place, the moved element becomes invisible to the LCA and both copies are phonetically realized; if reanalysis does not take place, the two copies are visible to the LCA and the lower copy is deleted for the usual reasons, yielding a case of regular incorporation.[50]

Dourado provides independent evidence for the proposed morphological reanalysis when postposition duplication takes place, based on the presence of agreement morphology on the verb. The absolutive agreement morpheme that appears adjacent to the verbal root in constructions without incorporation remains unaltered in standard incorporation constructions, as illustrated in (97a) and (97b), for instance. By contrast, the corresponding construction with postposition duplication requires deletion of this agreement morpheme, as shown in (97c). Dourado interprets such deletion as a reflex of the morphological reanalysis that renders the incorporated postposition invisible to the LCA.

(97) *Panara* (from Dourado 2002)
    a. kamɛra   yɨ-ra-**ria**-tẽ   ĩkyẽ *hɔw* kri   tã
       you.PL.ABS REAL.TR-1SG.ABS-**2PL.ABS**-go I   *with* tribe to
       'You will go with me to the tribe.'
    b. kamɛra   yɨ-ra-*hɔw*-**ria**-tẽ   ĩkyẽ kri   tã
       you.PL.ABS REAL.TR-1SG.ABS-*with*-**2PL.ABS**-go I   tribe to
    c. kamɛra   yɨ-ra-*hɔw*-tẽ   ĩkyẽ *hɔw* kri   tã
       you.PL.ABS REAL.TR-1SG.ABS-*with*-go I   *with* tribe to

As for the impossible cases of postposition duplication, Dourado shows, on the basis of independent agreement and relativization diagnostics, that their structural configuration does not allow incorporation of the postposition, which in turn eliminates the possibilities for duplication.

1.5.3.3.5 Summary To summarize, the data involving phonetic realization of more than one chain link discussed above, rather than being counterexamples, count as further evidence for the proposal that phonetic realization of chain links is (in part) determined by linearization considerations (i.e., heads of chains and traces are both subject to the LCA). As the analysis proposed in this chapter predicts, only when chain links become invisible to the LCA can a nontrivial chain surface with more than one link phonetically realized.[51]

1.6   Remnant Movement

1.6.1   Linearization of Chains and Remnant Movement
Let us take a closer look at the formulation of Chain Reduction in (44), repeated here.[52]

(98) *Chain Reduction*
    Delete the minimal number of constituents of a nontrivial chain
    CH that suffices for CH to be mapped into a linear order in
    accordance with the LCA.

As stated, Chain Reduction of a nontrivial chain CH deletes some constituents of CH so that *the surviving constituents of CH* can be mapped into a linear order in accordance with the LCA. That is, Chain Reduction proceeds in a "local" fashion, focusing only on CH without taking into consideration how the whole structure containing CH can be linearized. The intuition behind this formulation is that by forming a given chain CH in overt syntax, the computational system already provides the phonological component with the information that the links of CH will make it impossible for a linear order to obtain, regardless of the structure containing CH. Let us see why this is so, by examining a derivation in which the computational system forms the chain $CH = (\alpha^i, \alpha^i)$ in overt syntax.

Under the natural assumption that an element cannot check its features against itself, Last Resort excludes a syntactic object such as $K = [\alpha^i \ \alpha^i]$, where α has merged with a copy of itself and the two copies stand in a mutual c-command relation. In other words, the standard c-command condition on chain formation is actually an *asymmetric* c-command condition; the links of the chain $CH = (\alpha^i, \alpha^i)$, for instance, must be in a structural configuration such that one asymmetrically c-commands the other. Since the LCA maps asymmetric c-command into precedence, one of the links of CH should therefore precede the other; however, given that the links are nondistinct copies, that leads to the contradiction that α should precede itself (see section 1.5.2).

The relevant point here is that the system need not inspect the whole structure to determine whether or not applications of Chain Reduction are required, because a chain contains in itself the relevant pieces of information regarding the potential problems for linearization. If the system strives to reduce computational complexity (see Chomsky 2000 for discussion), we should then expect the phonological component to make use of the information already made available by chain formation; that is, deletion of nondistinct constituents for purposes of linearization should proceed "locally," taking into consideration only the chain links themselves and not the whole syntactic structure. If so, for any nontrivial chain CH formed before Spell-Out, Chain Reduction simply deletes constituents of CH in such a way that the irreflexivity condition on linear order is satisfied: either the surviving constituents of each chain link are distinct or only one (visible) chain link survives (scattered and full deletion, respectively; see section 1.5.3).

There are empirical reasons to assume that deletion for linearization purposes does indeed operate locally, as in (98). Suppose, for instance, that after assembling K and L in (100) from the simplified numeration N in (99), the computational system makes a copy of the pronoun and merges it with *bought*, as shown in (101). Delaying extensive discussion until chapter 3, let us assume for current purposes that such "sideward movement" of *it* in (100)–(101) is a licit operation. Further computations finally form the structure (102).

(99) $N = \{\text{John}_1, \text{bought}_1, \text{it}_1, \text{before}_1, \text{Mary}_1, \text{saw}_1\}$

(100) a. $K = [\text{before Mary saw it}]$
      b. $L = \text{bought}$

(101) a. $K = [\text{before Mary saw it}^i]$
      b. $M = [\text{bought it}^i]$

(102) $[\text{John } [[\text{bought it}^i] [\text{before Mary saw it}^i]]]$

If deletion for linearization purposes should consider the whole syntactic structure and delete nondistinct terms, it should delete either of the copies of the pronoun in (102), yielding the sentences in (103), which are nonetheless unacceptable.

(103) a. *John bought it before Mary saw.
      b. *John bought before Mary saw it.

On the other hand, if deletion for purposes of linearization only targets chain members, as the formulation of Chain Reduction in (98) dictates, it cannot apply to either copy of *it* in (102), because the two copies do not form a chain. Once Chain Reduction is inapplicable, the nondistinct copies of *it* in (102) prevent the structure from being linearized and the derivation is canceled;[53] hence, neither of the unacceptable sentences of (103) can be generated through a derivation along the lines of (99)–(102). By applying in a local fashion (within chains), deletion for purposes of linearization therefore correctly rules out the unwanted instance of sideward movement above (see chapter 3 for detailed discussion).

Despite its conceptual attractiveness in reducing computational complexity and empirical adequacy in ruling out the sentences in (103) under the derivation in (99)–(102), Chain Reduction appears to be unable to properly handle cases of remnant movement such as (104), as pointed out by Gärtner (1998, 20) in a review of Nunes 1995. Assuming that the derivation of (104) unfolds along the lines in (105) (numbered copies are used for purposes of exposition), the chain $CH_1 = (\text{John}^2, \text{John}^1)$ is formed after the object moves to Spec,TP, and the chain $CH_2 = (VP^k, VP^k)$ is formed after the whole VP is fronted to the specifier of some functional projection XP. The question is how these chains can be reduced and allow the structure in (105c) to be linearized as in (104).

(104) ... and elected John was.

(105) a. [$_{TP}$ was [$_{VP}$ elected John]]
  b. [$_{TP}$ John^2 [$_{T'}$ was [$_{VP}$ elected John^1]]]
  c.

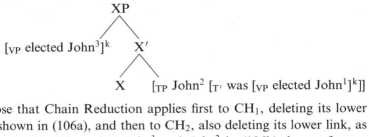

Suppose that Chain Reduction applies first to CH$_1$, deleting its lower link, as shown in (106a), and then to CH$_2$, also deleting its lower link, as shown in (106b). Given that *John^3* and *John^2* in (106b) do not form a chain, Chain Reduction cannot apply to them. Since these copies are nondistinct, they induce violations of the asymmetry and irreflexivity conditions on linear order, preventing the whole structure in (106b) from being linearized.[54] The problem is the same if Chain Reduction applies to CH$_2$ first; since the lower link of CH$_1$ is within the lower link of CH$_2$, deletion of the lower link of CH$_2$ also eliminates the lower link of CH$_1$, again resulting in the nonlinearizable structure in (106b).

(106) a. [$_{XP}$[$_{VP}$ elected John^3]^k [$_{X'}$ X [$_{TP}$ John^2 [$_{T'}$ was [$_{VP}$ elected John^1]^k]]]]
  b. [$_{XP}$[$_{VP}$ elected John^3]^k [$_{X'}$ X [$_{TP}$ John^2 [$_{T'}$ was [~~$_{VP}$ elected John^1~~]^k]]]]

We therefore appear to face a paradox: on the one hand, we want deletion for linearization purposes to proceed in a local fashion, only targeting chain members, to rule out the sentences in (103) under the derivation in (99)–(102); on the other hand, deletion seems to be required to apply in a global fashion, targeting nondistinct terms regardless of chain membership, to permit deletion of *John^3* in (106b) and derive the remnant movement construction in (104). I argue below, however, that the paradox is only apparent and that it is due to the informal notation used to characterize chains so far.[55]

As discussed by Chomsky (1995, 300), the representation of a chain such as CH = (α, α) should be seen as a notational abbreviation of CH = ((α, K), (α, L)), where K and L are each the sister of one occurrence of α. In other words, a chain can be conceived of as multiple occurrences of the same constituent occupying different structural positions; the individual links of a chain must then be identified not only in terms of their content, but also in terms of their local structural configuration.

Bearing this in mind, let us reconsider the chains formed in (105). After *John* moves to the subject position, the chain CH_1 in (107a) is formed; the notation in (107a) encodes the information that one nondistinct occurrence of *John* is the sister of T′ and the other occurrence is the sister of *elected*. Movement of VP to Spec,XP then yields the chain CH_2 in (107b), which encodes the information that one chain link is the sister of X′ and the other is the sister of *was*.

(107) a. $CH_1 = ((John^i, T′), (elected^m, John^i))$
    b. $CH_2 = (([elected^m John^i]^k, X′), (was, [elected^m John^i]^k))$

Let us now examine in detail the inner workings of deletion under Chain Reduction. Applying to CH_1 in (107a), Chain Reduction instructs the phonological component to delete the occurrence of *John* that is sister of *elected^m*. Interestingly, there are two elements in (105c) that satisfy this description, namely, *John^1* and *John^3*. In fact, these two copies are technically identical: they are nondistinct in terms of the initial numeration, they have participated in no checking relations, and their sisters are nondistinct. Assuming that the phonological component blindly scans the structure to carry out the deletion instructed by Chain Reduction, it ends up deleting the two copies that satisfy the instruction, as represented in (108a); Chain Reduction of CH_2 then proceeds as illustrated in (108b), and the sentence in (104) is derived.[56]

(108) a. $[_{XP}[_{VP}$ elected ~~John^3~~$]^k$ $[_{X′}$ X $[_{TP}$ John^2 $[_{T′}$ was $[_{VP}$ elected ~~John^1~~$]^k]]]]$
    b. $[_{XP}[_{VP}$ elected ~~John^3~~$]^k$ $[_{X′}$ X $[_{TP}$ John^2 $[_{T′}$ was ~~$[_{VP}$ elected John^1~~$]^k]]]]$

Nothing changes regarding the sentences in (103), which are still predicted to be unacceptable. Since the two copies of *it* in (102) do not form a chain, Chain Reduction is inapplicable and neither copy can be targeted for deletion; the structure therefore cannot be linearized and the derivation is canceled.

Notice that, instead of using the elementary relation of sisterhood, the system could perfectly well distinguish *John^1* from *John^3* in (105c) by resorting to nonlocal structural relations such as the set of nodes dominating each copy, for instance. The interesting empirical point is that if that were the case, it would be impossible for a remnant movement construction to be derived. The existence of this kind of construction shows that in its search for computational simplicity in the identification of chain links, the system ends up paying the price of being "fooled" by structures such as (105c), where two copies located in different structural configurations are taken to be identical for purposes of Chain Reduction.

As discussed in the next section, this approach has interesting empirical consequences when we combine it with the earlier proposal that morphological reanalysis may render a copy invisible to the LCA.

1.6.2 Remnant Movement and Phonetic Realization of Multiple Copies

Let us consider the abstract representation of the output of remnant movement as illustrated in (109), where α moves from within Y, forming the chain $CH_1 = (\alpha^2, \alpha^1)$, followed by movement of Y to some higher position, forming the chain $CH_2 = (Y, Y)$. Thus far, we have considered cases of remnant movement in which reduction of CH_1 in (109) ends up deleting α^1 and α^3. Suppose now that α^2 has been morphologically reanalyzed, becoming invisible to the LCA. According to what we saw in section 1.5.3.3, that would entail that α^2 would not have to be deleted by Chain Reduction, which would then apply only to CH_2, deleting its lower link, as represented in (110). In other words, the output of such a derivation should surface with both α^3 and α^2 phonetically realized.

(109)

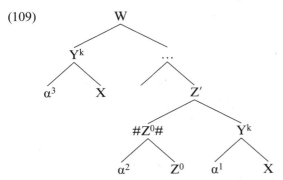

(110) $[_W [_Y \alpha^3 X]^k \ldots [_{Z'} \#[_{Z^0} \alpha^2 [_{Z^0} Z^0]]\# \overline{[_Y \alpha^1 X]^k}]]$

Predicate clefting in Korean and Japanese, exemplified in (111) and (112), can be taken to illustrate this logic.[57]

(111) *Korean* (from Nishiyama and Cho 1997)
John-i   computer-lul *sa-ss*-ki-nun *sa-ss*-ta
John-NOM computer-ACC *buy-T*-KI-CON *buy-T*-MOOD
'Indeed, John bought a computer, (but ...)'

(112) *Japanese* (from Nishiyama and Cho 1997)
    John-ga   computer-o   *kat-ta*-koto-wa   *kat-ta*
    John-NOM computer-ACC *buy-T*-KOTO-CON *buy-T*
    'Indeed, John bought a computer, (but . . .)'

Nishiyama and Cho (1997) propose that the sentences in (111) and (112) are derived through movement of TP to the specifier of a Focus phrase, followed by interspersed applications of Spell-Out and head movement. The Korean sentence in (111), for instance, is derived in the following way: given the structure in (113), the VP inside the trace of TP is spelled out as V and head-adjoins to T; the complex T head is then spelled out as V-T and adjoins to Mood, yielding a construction in which the TP is followed by V-T-Mood.

(113)

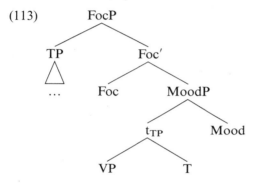

Although I follow Nishiyama and Cho (1997) in assuming that the sentences in (111) and (112) involve movement of TP, I will outline an alternative approach that overcomes the complexity and lack of generality of their proposal. More specifically, I propose that predicate clefting in Japanese and Korean involves movement of the T head (with the verb adjoined to it) to some higher projection (perhaps a Focus head), followed by remnant movement of TP, as sketched in (114).[58]

(114)

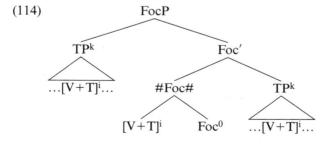

Assuming the two-segment Foc^0 in (114) is reanalyzed as a single terminal element by Morphology, the copy of $[V+T]^i$ adjoined to Foc^0 becomes invisible to the LCA and the chain $CH_1 = ([V+T]^i, [V+T]^i)$ need not be reduced, for it will have just one link visible to the LCA (see the discussion in section 1.5.3.3). Reduction of the TP chain then deletes the lower copy of TP, yielding sentences like (111) and (112), where the complex V+T appears duplicated.

Nunes and Quadros (in preparation) extend this approach to cases of duplication of focalized elements in Brazilian Sign Language (LSB; see Quadros 1999) and American Sign Language (ASL; see Petronio 1993, Petronio and Lillo-Martin 1997). Consider the LSB examples in (115), for instance, where capital letters in the glosses mark focus.

(115)   *Brazilian Sign Language* (from Nunes and Quadros, in
        preparation)
        a. (YESTERDAY) JOHN BUY CAR YESTERDAY
            'John bought a car YESTERDAY.'
        b. (WHO) LIKE BANANA WHO?
            'WHO likes bananas?'
        c. I (LOSE) BOOK LOSE
            'I LOST the book.'

(115) shows that in LSB, a focalized constituent appears in the rightmost position of the sentence and may optionally be accompanied by a double in the position where it would appear in neutral sentences. According to Nunes and. Quadros's proposal, these sentences are actually remnant movement constructions, which may optionally undergo morphological reanalysis. The sentences in (115c), for instance, are derived along the lines of (116), where the verb *LOSE* adjoins to a Focus head, as shown in (116b), and the whole TP then moves to Spec,FocP, as shown in (116c).

(116) a. $[_{FocP}$ Foc $[_{TP}$ I LOSE BOOK$]]$
      b. $[_{FocP}$ LOSE^i+Foc $[_{TP}$ I LOSE^i BOOK$]]$
      c.

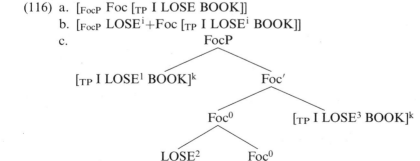

As discussed above, deletion of the trace of the chain $CH_1 = (LOSE^2,$ $LOSE^3)$ in (116) has the effect of eliminating both *LOSE^1* and *LOSE^3*, as illustrated in (117a); reduction of $CH_2 = ([_{TP}$ I LOSE^1 BOOK$]^k$, $[_{TP}$ I LOSE^1 BOOK$]^k$) then yields (117b), which surfaces as (115c) without duplication.

(117) a. $[_{FocP}[_{TP}$ I ~~LOSE^1~~ BOOK$]^k$ $[_{Foc'}$ LOSE^2+Foc $[_{TP}$ I ~~LOSE^3~~ BOOK$]^k]]$

     b. $[_{FocP}[_{TP}$ I ~~LOSE^1~~ BOOK$]^k$ $[_{Foc'}$ LOSE^2+Foc ~~$[_{TP}$ I LOSE^3 BOOK$]^k$~~$]]$

The derivation of (115c) with duplication can be accounted for if the structure $[_{Foc^0}$ LOSE $[_{Foc^0}$ Foc$^0]]$ in (116c) is morphologically reanalyzed as a single terminal element, rendering *LOSE^2* invisible to the LCA (see section 1.5.3.3). Since in these circumstances only the lower link of $CH_1 = (LOSE^2, LOSE^3)$ is visible to the LCA, Chain Reduction need not—therefore, must not—delete it. Applying only to CH_2, Chain Reduction then deletes the lower copy of TP, yielding the structure in (118), which surfaces as the duplication version of (115c).

(118) $[_{FocP}[_{TP}$ I LOSE^1 BOOK$]^k$ $[_{Foc'}$ #LOSE^2+Foc# ~~$[_{TP}$ I LOSE^3 BOOK$]^k$~~$]]]$

Given the discussion in section 1.5.3.3 regarding the correlation between morphological complexity and the possibility of reanalysis, we should expect that if the focalized element adjoined to Foc^0 is complex enough to prevent morphological reanalysis, all links of the relevant chains should be visible to the LCA and Chain Reduction should apply to both of them, as in (117). In other words, the prediction is that the more complex a focalized element, the lower the possibility of duplication. The unacceptability of the duplication constructions in (119) confirms this prediction.[59]

(119) a. (*NEXT MONTH) I WILL-GO ESTRELA NEXT MONTH
     'I will go to Estrela NEXT MONTH.'

     b. (*WHAT MAN OF-THEM) YOU LIKE WHAT MAN OF-THEM?
     'WHICH OF THOSE MEN did you like?'

     c. JOHN (*$_a$LOOK$_b$) MARY $_a$LOOK$_b$
     'John LOOKED AT Mary.'

Of special interest here is the contrast between the possible duplication of *LOSE* in (115c) and the impossible duplication of $_aLOOK_b$ in (119c), which indicates that agreeing morphology on 'look' (represented by indices) renders a verb morphologically complex enough so that reanalysis is blocked.

The analysis of phonetic realization of multiple copies in remnant movement constructions proposed above is extended by Ferreira (1999) to cases of topic duplication in a dialect of Brazilian Portuguese. In this dialect, a topicalized pronoun may appear duplicated at the end of the sentence, as illustrated in (120).

(120) *Brazilian Portuguese* (from Ferreira 1999)
    a. Ele caiu ele.
       he fell he
       'As for him, he fell down.'
    b. Eu fiz o   trabalho eu.
       I   did the work   I
       'As for myself, I did the work.'

Ferreira argues that a construction such as (120b), for instance, is derived along the lines of (121): the pronoun *eu* 'I' moves and adjoins to a Topic head, as shown in (121a), and the TP undergoes remnant movement, as shown in (121b). Assuming that the two-segment Top is reanalyzed as a single terminal, the copy adjoined to Top becomes invisible to the LCA and is not deleted by Chain Reduction. Applying to the TP chain, Chain Reduction deletes the lower copy, yielding (121c), which surfaces as (120b).

(121) a. $[_{\text{TopP}} \text{eu}^i + \text{Top} [_{\text{TP}} \text{eu}^i \dots]]$
    b. $[[_{\text{TP}} \text{eu}^i \dots]^k [_{\text{TopP}} \text{eu}^i + \text{Top} [_{\text{TP}} \text{eu}^i \dots]^k]]$
    c. $[[_{\text{TP}} \text{eu}^i \dots]^k [_{\text{TopP}} \#\text{eu}^i + \text{Top}\# [_{\text{TP}} \text{eu}^i \dots]^k]]$

Evidence for taking the element in the final position to be a topic comes from the interpretation restrictions related to topicalized pronouns. As shown in (122a) and (122b), the pronoun *ele* inside TP can refer to either an animate or an inanimate subject; if the pronoun is topicalized, however, only the animate interpretation obtains, as shown in (122c) (see Cardinaletti and Starke 1999 and Britto 1997 for relevant discussion). The fact that the pronoun of the sentence in (120a) is also subject to this animacy restriction, as the gloss indicates, suggests that (120a) is derivationally related to (122c).

(122) a. O João, ele caiu.
       the João he fell
       'As for João, he fell down.'

   b. O copo, ele caiu.
      the glass it   fell
      'As for the glass, it fell down.'
   c. Ele,   ele   caiu.
      he/*it he/*it fell
      'As for him/*it, he/*it fell down.'

As we should by now expect, if constructions such as those in (120) actually involve syntactic copies that underwent morphological reanalysis, they should exhibit morphological restrictions. (123) shows that this expectation is met: topic duplication cannot involve either full DPs or coordinated pronouns.

(123) a. *Os meninos comeram a   pizza os meninos.
       the boys   ate   the pizza the boys
       'The boys ate the pizza.'
    b. *Ela e   ele comeram todo o   pão ela e   ele.
       she and he ate   all the bread she and he
       'As for her and him, they ate all the bread.'

To the extent that phonetic realization of multiple copies in remnant movement constructions is subject to the same kind of morphological restrictions associated with standard movement, the analysis that Chain Reduction disregards word-internal copies gains further conceptual and empirical support.

1.6.3 Remnant Movement and Scattered Deletion

Let us now take a closer look at the inner workings of Chain Reduction by comparing the derivations of constructions involving remnant movement and scattered deletion. Given a remnant movement construction like the one represented in (124a), Chain Reduction applies to $CH_1 = ((\alpha, Z'), (\alpha, X^m))$ and instructs the phonological system to delete the copy of α that is the sister of X^m. Since α^3 and α^1 both meet this description, both of them are deleted, as represented in (124b). Finally, reduction of $CH_2 = (Y, Y)$ yields (124c).

(124) a. $[_W [_Y \alpha^3 X^m]^k \ldots [_{ZP} \alpha^2 [_{Z'} Z^0 [_Y \alpha^1 X^m]^k]]]$
     b. $[_W [_Y \cancel{\alpha^3} X^m]^k \ldots [_{ZP} \alpha^2 [_{Z'} Z^0 [_Y \cancel{\alpha^1} X^m]^k]]]$
     c. $[_W [_Y \cancel{\alpha^3} X^m]^k \ldots [_{ZP} \alpha^2 [_{Z'} Z^0 \cancel{[_Y \alpha^1 X^m]^k}]]]$

Let us now consider the structure in (125a). As discussed in section 1.5.3.1, if deletion of the higher or the lower link of the chain CH =

$(([_L \alpha^i \beta^m]^k, X'), (Z, [_L \alpha^i \beta^m]^k))$, as shown in (125b) or (125c), violates some requirement of the phonological component, Chain Reduction may resort to scattered deletion, deleting different constituents in each link of CH, as illustrated in (125d).

(125) a. $[_{XP}[_L \alpha^i \beta^m]^k [_{X'} X [_{YP} \ldots [_{ZP} Z [_L \alpha^i \beta^m]^k]]]]$
       b. $[_{XP}[_L \alpha^i \beta^m]^k [_{X'} X [_{YP} \ldots [_{ZP} Z [_{\overline{L} \, \overline{\alpha^i} \, \overline{\beta^m}]^k}]]]]$
       c. $[_{XP}[_{\overline{L} \, \overline{\alpha^i} \, \overline{\beta^m}]^k} [_{X'} X [_{YP} \ldots [_{ZP} Z [_L \alpha^i \beta^m]^k]]]]$
       d. $[_{XP}[_L \alpha^i \overline{\beta^m}]^k [_{X'} X [_{YP} \ldots [_{ZP} Z [_L \overline{\alpha^i} \beta^m]^k]]]]$

Given that I have proposed that the system is fooled in cases such as (124a) and ends up deleting α^1 and α^3, one wonders why the system should not also be fooled by the instruction to delete α in (125a) and incorrectly delete both copies of α.[60] The two cases are not identical, as they may seem at first sight, however. In the case of remnant movement sketched in (124b), Chain Reduction uses the information regarding the structural configuration of the relevant copy of α, namely, sister of X^m, and instructs the phonological component to scan the structure and delete the elements that match that description. In cases of scattered deletion like (125d), on the other hand, the system has more pieces of information available and the search space is in a sense more limited. Chain Reduction first uses the sisterhood information to identify the relevant link of CH (a copy of $[_L \alpha^i \beta^m]^k$) and then instructs the phonological component to delete constituents within that link. For instance, applying to CH $=$ $(([_L \alpha^i \beta^m]^k, X'), (Z, [_L \alpha^i \beta^m]^k))$ in (125a), Chain Reduction instructs the system to get the copy of L that is sister to Z and delete the copy of α within that copy of L. Thus, the phonological component does not even consider the copy of α that is within the higher link of CH and only the lower copy of α is deleted.

1.6.4 Summary

Remnant movement constructions are adequately handled in the system proposed in this chapter under the assumptions that (i) deletion for linearization purposes takes nontrivial chains into consideration, and not simply nondistinct copies; and (ii) chain identification proceeds locally, taking only the sister of a given copy into account. The analysis developed here was able to account not only for deletion of traces in standard remnant constructions, but also for duplication of focalized elements in Japanese, Korean, ASL, and LSB, and for topic duplication in a dialect of Brazilian Portuguese.

From the perspective of the present system, standard remnant movement constructions arise when the local identification of chain links tricks the system into deleting an extra copy that is not a member of the chain undergoing reduction. An important aspect of the analysis of remnant movement proposed above is that the relevant "unbound trace" need not be obligatorily deleted because of its trace nature; in fact, the unbound trace may be phonetically realized if the circumstances for phonetic realization of traces are met, as discussed in the case of focus and topic duplication. Rather than being counterevidence for the analysis developed here, remnant movement constructions actually end up further confirming the null hypothesis that every chain link can in principle be subject to phonetic realization.

1.7   Conclusion

In this chapter, I have argued that the reason why traces usually are not phonetically realized follows from the interaction between the fact that traces are subject to the LCA and economy considerations concerning the number of applications of deletion to eliminate unchecked formal features in the phonological component (the FF-Elimination operation). A syntactic object containing a nontrivial chain CH in principle cannot be linearized in accordance with the LCA; since the links of CH are nondistinct, they induce violations of the asymmetry and irreflexivity conditions on linear order, canceling the derivation because no PF object is formed. In order to prevent this state of affairs, the phonological component can resort to the operation Chain Reduction, which in the general case deletes all but one link of a nontrivial chain.

Assuming that a given head only checks the relevant features of the chain link that is in its checking domain, the head of a chain CH will always have fewer unchecked formal features to be deleted by FF-Elimination than the lower links of CH. Thus, a derivation in which Chain Reduction deletes all the links except the head of the chain is in principle more economical than a derivation in which Chain Reduction deletes all of the links of the chain except for one trace. However, if the pronunciation of the head of the chain violates other well-formedness conditions of the phonological component, leading to a derivational crash at PF, the head of the chain is deleted and a trace is pronounced instead.

The analysis developed here also accounts for cases where more than one chain link is phonetically realized. The additional possibilities are tied to the possibility of morphological restructuring. Assuming that the LCA does not apply word-internally (see Chomsky 1995, 337), if a trace is reanalyzed by Morphology as part of a single terminal element, it becomes invisible to the LCA and need not—therefore, must not—be deleted by Chain Reduction. The economy considerations that prevent all chain links from being deleted (the issue of recoverability of deletion) are thus the same as the ones allowing multiple copies when morphological reanalysis takes places: deletion should be employed as little as possible.

Finally, by taking deletion of copies for purposes of linearization to be restricted to nontrivial chains (the operation of Chain Reduction) and by relying on a local specification of chain links in terms of sisterhood, the analysis proposed in this chapter was able to account for deletion of traces in standard instances of remnant movement constructions, as well as cases where more than one copy is phonetically realized.

Overall, then, compelling evidence of different kinds supports the null hypothesis concerning the copy theory of movement in the minimalist framework, namely, that traces do not have distinct intrinsic properties that would characterize them as grammatical primitives. In particular, I have shown that traces do not intrinsically differ from heads of chains with respect to linearization or phonetic realization.

Chapter 2

Traces, Uninterpretable Features, and Accessibility to the Computational System

2.1 Introduction

Once the copy theory of movement is assumed, it must be ensured that in a convergent derivation, no "traces" have uninterpretable features; otherwise, Full Interpretation will not be met at LF. With this in mind, let us reconsider the derivation proposed in chapter 1 for the sentence in (1), as sketched in (2).

(1) John was kissed.

(2) a. K = [$_{TP}$ T [$_{VP}$ was [$_{VP}$ kissed John-**N-CASE**]]]

   b. *Copy*
     K = [$_{TP}$ T [$_{VP}$ was [$_{VP}$ kissed John^i-**N-CASE**]]]
     L = John^i-**N-CASE**

   c. *Merge and Check/Delete*
     [$_{TP}$ John^i-$_{N\text{-}CASE}$ [$_{T'}$ T [$_{VP}$ was [$_{VP}$ kissed John^i-**N-CASE**]]]]

   d. *Optimal Chain Reduction*
     [$_{TP}$ John^i-$_{N\text{-}CASE}$ [$_{T'}$ T [$_{VP}$ was [$_{VP}$ kissed ~~John^i-**N-CASE**~~]]]]

A copy of *John* merges with K in (2a) to check the EPP-feature (the strong D-feature of T), also allowing the Case-feature of the higher copy to be checked against the Case-feature of T, as shown in (2c). Since the Case-feature of the higher copy is uninterpretable at both LF and PF, it is then deleted (rendered invisible) with respect to both levels; the categorial feature, on the other hand, is deleted only with respect to PF, because it is interpretable at LF (see chapter 1, note 25). Finally, the chain CH = (John^i-$_{N\text{-}CASE}$, John^i-**N-CASE**) undergoes Chain Reduction in an optimal way and the structure in (2d) is derived.

Since Chain Reduction takes place in the phonological component, the structure that feeds the covert component is the one in (2c), not the one in (2d). As is, the structure in (2c) should cause the derivation to crash at LF because of the undeleted uninterpretable Case-feature of the lower copy of *John*. The analysis developed in chapter 1 must therefore be supplemented with some means to eliminate uninterpretable features within traces, in order to allow the relevant derivations to converge at LF.

This specific problem does not seem to arise in Chomsky's (1995) system, according to which "the features of a chain are considered a unit: if one is affected by an operation, all are" (Chomsky 1995, 381 n. 12). Thus, if the Case-feature of the higher link of (2c) is deleted and erased (see chapter 1, note 20), the Case-feature of the trace is also deleted and erased and the derivation is correctly predicted to converge at LF. Pushing this approach further, Chomsky (1995, 304) proposes that traces (of A-movement) are inaccessible to the computational system.

At first sight, Chomsky's "chain-checking" approach and the "link-checking" approach developed in chapter 1 have the same theoretical cost. The chain-checking approach is able to prevent uninterpretable features of traces from causing undesirable Full Interpretation violations at LF, but has to stipulate that traces cannot be phonetically realized. Under the link-checking approach, on the other hand, the asymmetry between heads of chains and traces regarding checking relations provides an independent basis for heads to be phonetically realized instead of traces; however, the theoretical apparatus must be enriched to prevent uninterpretable features in trace positions from inducing Full Interpretation violations at LF.

In this chapter, I argue that the theoretical cost between the two approaches is actually not the same; to handle more complex data, the chain-checking approach also requires amendments similar to the ones required under the link-checking approach (see section 2.2.1). As an alternative, I propose an analysis that takes the elimination of uninterpretable features in trace positions to be contingent on a well-formedness condition on the feature composition of chains (see section 2.2.2). Finally, I show that Chomsky's (1995) proposal that traces are inaccessible to the computational system leads to wrong empirical results; traces are shown to be accessible to the computational system and able to yield minimality effects in the same way heads of chains do (see section 2.3).

2.2   Traces and Uninterpretable Features

2.2.1   Chomsky's (1995) Approach

Chomsky (1995, 381 n. 12) proposes that feature checking should be computed with respect to the whole chain, and not only with respect to the chain link that is in the checking domain of the relevant head; that is, if a feature of a chain link is affected by an operation, the corresponding feature of the other links of the same chain is also affected.[1] Thus, under Chomsky's (1995) analysis, after *John* in (3a) moves overtly and enters into a checking relation with the T head, the Case-features of both links of the DP chain are deleted and erased, as shown in (3b). Since the DP chain has no uninterpretable feature, it satisfies Full Interpretation at LF. As for computations in the phonological component, Chomsky (1993, 1995) stipulates that traces must be deleted (see the discussion in section 1.4.2); hence, the structure in (3b) surfaces as the sentence in (3c).

(3) a. $[_{TP}$ T $[_{VP}$ was $[_{VP}$ kissed John^i-**CASE**$]]]$
    b. $[_{TP}$ John^i $[_{T'}$ T $[_{VP}$ was $[_{VP}$ kissed John^i$]]]]$
    c. John was kissed.

In chapter 1, we saw that there are not only conceptual but also empirical reasons for not taking lack of phonetic realization as an inherent property of traces; when convergence and economy requirements demand it, traces may indeed be phonetically realized (see section 1.5.3). In this section, I will put the issue of phonetic realization aside and focus on problems regarding Chomsky's (1995) chain-checking approach.

Let us examine constructions involving successive DP-raising under this approach. If every movement operation forms a new chain, the derivation of (4a), for instance, involves the formation of the three chains given in (5), where the superscripted indices annotate the position of the copies in (4b).

(4) a. John seems to be likely to be kissed.
    b. $[_{TP}$ John^4 seems [John^3 to be likely [John^2 to [be kissed John^1$]]]]$

(5) a. $CH_1 = ($John^2, John$^1)$
    b. $CH_2 = ($John^3, John$^2)$
    c. $CH_3 = ($John^4, John$^3)$

The first two movements of *John* in (4b) only check EPP-features; hence, the Case-features of CH_1 and CH_2 remain intact at the derivational step where the intermediate clause is assembled. The next movement of *John* to the matrix subject position allows its Case-feature to be checked against the Case-feature of the T head. Under Chomsky's (1995) chain-checking approach, the Case-features of both links of CH_3, namely, *John*^{4} and *John*^{3} (which is also the head of CH_2), should then be deleted and erased, as shown in (6).

(6) [$_{TP}$ John^4 seems [John^3 to be likely [John^2-**CASE** to [be kissed John^1-**CASE**]]]]

Given that the chains CH_1 and CH_2 in (6) still have Case-features, they should induce a Full Interpretation violation at LF and the sentence in (4a) should be incorrectly ruled out. To prevent this undesirable result, Chomsky (1995, 300) first assumes that the tail of a chain formed by raising the head of a nontrivial chain $CH = (\alpha, t)$ is the trace t rather than α. If so, the relevant chains in (4b) should be the ones in (7), rather than the ones in (5). Since the head of CH_3 in (7c) has its Case-feature deleted and erased, the chain-checking approach requires that the same happen with its tail, *John*^{1}, as illustrated in (8).

(7) a. $CH_1 = (John^2, John^1)$
    b. $CH_2 = (John^3, John^1)$
    c. $CH_3 = (John^4, John^1)$

(8) [$_{TP}$ John^4 seems [John^3-**CASE** to be likely [John^2-**CASE** to [be kissed John^1]]]]

This reinterpretation of the notion of chain tail is, however, insufficient to ensure that all uninterpretable features are eliminated; the Case-feature of the heads of CH_1 and CH_2 in (8) still remain active and should induce a Full Interpretation violation. To cope with this issue, Chomsky (1995, 301) admittedly stipulates that if an element heading the A-chain $CH = (\alpha, t)$ raises, the formal features of the trace created by this operation are deleted and erased.[2] Thus, when *John* in (4b) moves from the most embedded to the intermediate subject position, and from there to the matrix subject position, the formal features of the traces left behind (*John*^{2} and *John*^{3}, respectively) are erased and the chains CH_1 and CH_2 of (7) should no longer violate Full Interpretation.

Besides reintroducing the notion of a trace as a grammatical primitive, these questionable amendments suggested by Chomsky (1995, 300–301) are still insufficient to account for other instances of overlapping chains.[3] Take the verb movement structure in (9), for instance, which is formed after a main verb V adjoins to a light verb v, yielding the chain $CH_1 = (V^2, V^1)$, and the complex verbal head adjoins to T, yielding the chain $CH_2 = ([_{v^0} V^3 + v], [_{v^0} V^2 + v])$.

(9)

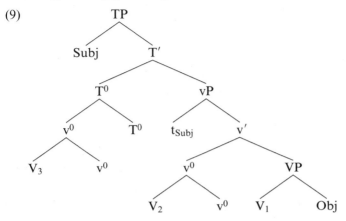

Under Chomsky's (1995, 312) analysis, checking relations and θ-relations are in complementary distribution; hence, the (trace of) the subject in Spec,vP in (9) does not enter into a checking relation with the verbal complex and the uninterpretable φ-features of V must be checked against the subject in Spec,TP.[4] After such checking, the φ-features of both links of $CH_2 = ([_{v^0} V^3 + v], [_{v^0} V^2 + v])$ should be deleted and erased under Chomsky's chain-checking approach, but not the φ-features of the lower link of $CH_1 = (V^2, V^1)$. Crucially, the tail of CH_2 is different from the head of CH_1; hence, Chomsky's proposal revising the notion of chain/ trace and the stipulated erasure of formal features of intermediate links are inapplicable to the verb movement illustrated in (9). The presence of visible uninterpretable φ-features in V^1 should then yield a Full Interpretation violation at LF, incorrectly ruling out standard instances of verb movement to T.

A similar problem arises with respect to the derivation of a sentence such as (10a).

(10) a. What did John see?
    b. [what-**CASE** did+Q [$_{TP}$ John [$_{vP}$ see what-**CASE**]]]
    c. [what-**CASE** did+Q [$_{TP}$ John [$_{vP}$ FF(what-**CASE**)+see what-**CASE**]]]
    d. [what-**CASE** did+Q [$_{TP}$ John [$_{vP}$ FF(what)+see what]]]

Overt movement of *what* in (10b) only checks the strong *wh*-feature of the interrogative complementizer and does not allow the Case-feature of either link of $CH_1 = (what\text{-}\mathbf{CASE}, what\text{-}\mathbf{CASE})$ to be checked. In the covert component, the formal features of the lower copy of *what* raise to check Case, yielding the chain $CH_2 = (FF(what), FF(what))$, as shown in (10c). Under Chomsky's chain-checking approach, the checking relation involving the head of CH_2 should delete and erase the Case-feature of both links of CH_2; since the lower link of CH_2 is within the lower link of CH_1, this checking operation ends up eliminating the Case-feature of the lower link of CH_1, as well, as shown in (10d). However, since the Case-feature of the upper link of CH_1 has not been eliminated, it should induce a violation of Full Interpretation at LF, incorrectly ruling (10a) out.

Noting the problem posed by sentences such as (10a), Chomsky (1995, 303) further adds that "[a] convention is then needed requiring erasure of F throughout the array of chains containing F, so that no −Interpretable feature remains in the operator position." In the next section, I propose an implementation for this convention and show that it is sufficient to account for the problematic cases discussed here.

2.2.2   An Alternative Approach

2.2.2.1   The Feature Uniformity Condition   Suppose that at LF, all links of a chain must be uniform in terms of feature composition, as stated in (11) (see Nunes 1995, 221).

(11) *Feature Uniformity Condition*
      Given a chain $CH = (\alpha_1, \ldots, \alpha_n)$, every α_i $(1 \leq i \leq n)$ must have the same set of features visible at LF.

Let us now reconsider the structure in (12), under the approach explored in chapter 1, which does not make use of erasure and takes traces to be immune to the operations affecting heads of chains (see section 1.5.3.2).

(12) [John-N-ϕ-$_{CASE}$ T [was kissed John-N-ϕ-$\mathbf{CASE}$]]

In the covert component, both links of $CH = (John\text{-}N\text{-}\phi\text{-}_{CASE}, John\text{-}N\text{-}\phi\text{-}\mathbf{CASE})$ in (12) have the same semantic features and no phonological features. They differ, however, with respect to formal features visible at LF: all the formal features of the lower link are visible, whereas the Case-feature of the upper link was checked and deleted with respect to both PF and LF.[5] As it stands, the chain CH = (John-N-ϕ-$_{\text{CASE}}$, John-N-ϕ-**CASE**) in (12) should therefore violate the Feature Uniformity Condition in (11).

In principle, there are two possible ways for CH to become uniform: either its head somehow gains an unchecked Case-feature, or the Case-feature of the trace is eliminated. The first possibility can be easily discarded, for gaining an uninterpretable feature is at odds with one of the main purposes of the mapping from the numeration to LF, which is to eliminate uninterpretable features. Exploring the second possibility, we can formalize the convention suggested by Chomsky (1995, 303) in connection with (10) along the lines of (13) (see Nunes 1995, 222), where deletion targets a single feature per application.

(13) *Chain Uniformization*
      Delete the minimal number of features of a nontrivial chain CH in order for CH to satisfy the Feature Uniformity Condition.

If Chain Uniformization deletes the Case-feature of the tail of CH = (John-N-ϕ-$_{\text{CASE}}$, John-N-ϕ-**CASE**) in (12), CH complies with the Feature Uniformity Condition. Furthermore, since no uninterpretable feature survives at LF, Full Interpretation is satisfied and the derivation converges, as desired. Notice that if Chain Uniformization had deleted all the semantic features of CH in addition to the unchecked Case-feature, CH would also satisfy the Feature Uniformity Condition. However, this undesirable result does not arise; as stated in (13), Chain Uniformization resorts to the fewest possible applications of deletion. If a single application of deletion allows CH to comply with the Feature Uniformity Condition, economy considerations block further applications.[6]

Let us now consider the linked chain CH$_4$ = (John^4-N-ϕ-$_{\text{CASE}}$, John^3-N-ϕ-**CASE**, John^2-N-ϕ-**CASE**, John^1-N-ϕ-**CASE**) in (14), which is obtained by linking the chains in (5), formed by the successive raising of *John* in (4) (see Chomsky and Lasnik 1993, 563).

(14) [$_{\text{TP}}$ John^4-N-ϕ-$_{\text{CASE}}$ seems [John^3-N-ϕ-**CASE** to be likely [John^2-N-ϕ-**CASE** to [be kissed John^1-N-ϕ-**CASE**]]]]

The links of CH$_4$ in (14) differ in that the head of the chain does not have a Case-feature visible at LF, whereas the other three links do. Thus, in order for CH$_4$ to satisfy the Feature Uniformity Condition, Chain Uniformization employs three applications of deletion, each targeting an

unchecked Case-feature, yielding the structure in (15). After these operations, CH_4 in (15) satisfies not only the Feature Uniformity Condition,
but also Full Interpretation, because no uninterpretable feature is visible
at LF; hence, the derivation converges at LF.

(15) [$_{TP}$ John^4-**N**-ϕ-$_{CASE}$ seems [John^3-**N**-ϕ-$_{CASE}$ to be likely [John^2-**N**-
ϕ-$_{CASE}$ to [be kissed John^1-**N**-ϕ-$_{CASE}$]]]]

Let us now return to the chains $CH_1 = (V^2$-ϕ, V^1-$\phi)$ and $CH_2 =$
$([_{v^0} V^3$-$_\phi$+v], [$_{v^0} V^2$-ϕ+v])$ of the problematic case of verb movement
in (9), repeated in (16).

(16) [$_{TP}$ Subj$_i$ [[$_{v^0}$ V^3-$_\phi$+v]+T] [$_{vP}$ t$_i$ [$_{v'}$[$_{v^0}$ V^2-ϕ+v] [$_{VP}$ V^1-ϕ Obj]]]]

In order for CH_2 to satisfy the Feature Uniformity Condition, Chain
Uniformization deletes the ϕ-features of V^2, as shown in (17a); as a by-
product of this deletion, CH_1 becomes nonuniform because V^2 is a link of
CH_1. Chain Uniformization then deletes the ϕ-features of V^1, as shown in
(17b), allowing CH_1 to satisfy the Feature Uniformity Condition, as well.
After these two applications of Chain Uniformization, there remain no
uninterpretable ϕ-features that could incorrectly induce a Full Interpretation violation.[7]

(17) a. [$_{TP}$ Subj$_i$ [[$_{v^0}$ V^3-$_\phi$+v]+T] [$_{vP}$ t$_i$ [$_{v'}$[$_{v^0}$ V^2-$_\phi$+v] [$_{VP}$ V^1-ϕ Obj]]]]
     b. [$_{TP}$ Subj$_i$ [[$_{v^0}$ V^3-$_\phi$+v]+T] [$_{vP}$ t$_i$ [$_{v'}$[$_{v^0}$ V^2-$_\phi$+v] [$_{VP}$ V^1-$_\phi$ Obj]]]]

The sentence involving overt *wh*-movement in (10a) receives a simi-
lar account. After overt movement of *what* and covert movement of
FF(what), we obtain the structure in (18a), with the uniform chain
$CH_1 = (what^1$-**CASE**, what^2-**CASE**)$ and the nonuniform chain $CH_2 =$
$(FF(what^1$-$_{CASE}), FF(what^1$-**CASE**))$. Chain Uniformization deletes the
Case-feature of the lower link of CH_2, as shown in (18b), and, as a consequence, CH_1 becomes nonuniform. Chain Uniformization then applies
to CH_1, deleting the Case-feature of the upper link, yielding the structure
in (18c). Since every Case-feature of (18c) is eliminated, the derivation
converges at LF, as expected.

(18) a. [what^2-**CASE** did+Q [$_{TP}$ John [$_{vP}$ FF(what-$_{CASE}$)+see
          what^1-**CASE**]]]
     b. [what^2-**CASE** did+Q [$_{TP}$ John [$_{vP}$ FF(what-$_{CASE}$)+see
          what^1-$_{CASE}$]]]
     c. [what^2-$_{CASE}$ did+Q [$_{TP}$ John [$_{vP}$ FF(what-$_{CASE}$)+see
          what^1-$_{CASE}$]]]

2.2.2.2 Preventing Overgeneration   Consider the chain CH = (Bill, Bill) in (19b). The categorial feature of the upper copy of *Bill* is deleted with respect to PF, but not with respect to LF (see section 1.5.3.2); hence, the two copies remain identical at LF. Although CH satisfies the Feature Uniformity Condition, the derivation crashes at LF, because both copies in (19b) have an unchecked Case-feature and there is no available Case checker (the two main verbs are passive and the matrix T checks the Case-feature of the expletive).

(19) a. *It was believed Bill to be often kissed.
       b. [it was believed [Bill-**CASE** to [be often kissed Bill-**CASE**]]]

If Chain Uniformization deleted the unchecked Case-features of CH, the Feature Uniformity Condition would be satisfied and the derivation in (19b) would be incorrectly allowed to converge. However, this incorrect result does not arise, because Chain Uniformization does not apply to chains that are already uniform with respect to feature composition. The important thing to keep in mind is that, as stated in (13), deletion of features by Chain Uniformization is triggered by the Feature Uniformity Condition, not by Full Interpretation at LF. This is a natural assumption to make: if Full Interpretation at LF could simply trigger deletion of uninterpretable features, no movement operation would ever be necessary.[8]

Let us finally reconsider the structure in (20).

(20) [John-$_{CASE}$ was kissed John-**CASE**]

I have been tacitly assuming that Chain Uniformization applies in the covert component. If Chain Uniformization applied to the DP chain in (20) in overt syntax and deleted the Case-feature of the lower copy of *John*, Full Interpretation would be satisfied at LF and the two copies would be identical with respect to FF-Elimination in the phonological component. In the context of the proposal advanced in section 1.5.3.2, that would incorrectly predict that phonetic realization of either copy in (20) should be possible. Given that the Uniformity Condition on the mapping from the numeration to LF makes the same set of operations available in the covert component and in overt syntax (see Chomsky 1995, 229), the task then is to prevent Chain Uniformization from applying overtly, without intrinsically ordering the applications of the computational system.

I propose that although available throughout the mapping from the numeration to LF, economy considerations block applications of Chain Uniformization in overt syntax. The intuition is that the system need not care about the feature composition of chains in overt syntax, because chains are not PF objects; in other words, overt syntax only cares about what is relevant to both PF and LF. I will technically implement this intuition by comparing Chain Uniformization and Spell-Out for economy purposes. Consider the derivational step after the structure in (20), for instance, is assembled, where the computational system may either apply Chain Uniformization to the DP chain or spell out the whole structure. According to the notion of derivational cost proposed by Chomsky (1995, 226) (see chapter 1, note 24), Spell-Out is costless because it is required for a derivation to be generated: if it does not apply, no pair (PF, LF) obtains; Chain Uniformization, on the other hand, is derivationally costly because it is related to a convergence condition (the Feature Uniformity Condition). Since Spell-Out is more economical than Chain Reduction, it ships the structure in (20) to the phonological component and the DP chain is uniformized in the covert component. Independent economy considerations may therefore ensure that Chain Uniformization applies only in the covert component, without violating the Uniformity Condition (see Nunes 1999b for further discussion).

2.2.3 Summary

We have seen that both Chomsky's (1995) chain-checking approach and the link-checking approach explored in chapter 1 must be supplemented with additional means in order to eliminate uninterpretable features of traces. The question is what is the best way to achieve such elimination.

As seen in section 2.2.1, Chomsky's (1995) proposal in this regard involves (i) a revision of the notion of chain for cases of successive-cyclic movement (see Chomsky 1995, 300), (ii) a stipulation forcing erasure of formal features of intermediate traces of A-chains (see Chomsky 1995, 301), and (iii) a convention requiring erasure of a feature F throughout the array of chains containing F if F is erased in some chain (see Chomsky 1995, 303).

In section 2.2.2, I have proposed instead that the implementation of Chomsky's (1995, 303) convention in (iii) in terms of the Feature Uniformity Condition and Chain Uniformization is sufficient to account for the instances of overlapping chains discussed in section 2.2.1, with no need to revise the notion of chain tail or stipulate the elimination of interpretable features of intermediate traces. It should be noted that the Feature Uniformity Condition is a natural well-formedness condition on chains, and Chain Uniformization is constrained enough so that it does not overgeneralize and its application in the covert component may be independently ensured by economy computations.

The alternative approach proposed in section 2.2.2 is not only simpler and conceptually sound, but is also consistent with the relevance of intermediate traces for binding and scope (see note 3). More importantly, it differs from Chomsky's in that it does not ascribe special properties to (intermediate) traces; it continues to subscribe to the most desirable version of the copy theory of movement, by taking traces and heads of chains to be subject to the same grammatical conditions.

In the next section, we will see that the simpler approach is also the one that makes the correct empirical predictions regarding traces and intervention effects.

2.3 Traces and Accessibility to the Computational System

As discussed in section 2.2.1, Chomsky's (1995) approach to the elimination of uninterpretable traces is based on the following assumptions: (i) if a feature of a chain link is affected by an operation, the corresponding feature of the other links of the same chain is also affected; and (ii) the formal features of intermediate traces of A-chains are erased. Chomsky (1995) extends the second assumption to traces of A-movement generally, claiming that they are inaccessible to the computational system and, in particular, should yield no violation of the Minimal Link Condition.

In this section, I focus on the empirical consequences of this extension. I will show that, contrary to Chomsky's claim, traces of A-movement are indeed accessible to the computational system and do induce minimality effects. Furthermore, I show that the approach outlined in section 2.2.2 provides a straightforward account of the data.

2.3.1 Expletive Constructions
Let us consider the structure in (21).

(21) [there$_i$ seem [t$_i$ to be believed [t$_i$ to be many books out of place]]]

The expletive has been inserted in the most embedded clause, checking the strong D-feature of T, and raises twice, checking the strong D-feature of the intermediate and the matrix T heads. In the covert component,

FF(many books) adjoins to [FF(seem)+T], checking its Case against T and checking the φ-features of FF(seem) (see Chomsky 1995, 275). Taking (21) to be the only instance in which a trace of an expletive could induce a Minimal Link Condition violation, Chomsky (1995, 302) concludes that "the trace of an expletive does not enter into the operation Attract/Move; it is immobile and cannot bar raising."

In fact, (21) does not shed light on the issue of the accessibility of expletive traces, because neither trace of *there* should prevent movement of FF(many books); presumably, they only have a D-feature (see Chomsky 1995, 287), and no checking relation between FF(many books) and [FF(seem)+T] involves D-features. There are, however, other constructions in which not only does the issue arise, but a trace of an expletive is shown to induce a Minimal Link Condition violation. Consider, for instance, a derivational step in which a structure such as (22) has been assembled.

(22) [$_{TP}$ T seems [$_{CP}$ that it was told John [$_{CP}$ that he was fired]]]

Discussing structures such as (22), Chomsky (1995, 295) claims that no convergent derivation arises from inserting the expletive *it* in the subject position of the embedded clause. The reasoning is as follows. Raising of *John* to the matrix clause to check the strong D-feature of T, as shown in (23a), violates the Minimal Link Condition, because the expletive is a closer element that can check this feature.[9] Hence, the sentence in (23b) is unacceptable.

(23) a. [$_{TP}$ John$_i$ T seems [$_{CP}$ that it was told t$_i$ [$_{CP}$ that he was fired]]]
     b. *John seems that it was told that he was fired.

In turn, Chomsky argues, if the expletive of (22) raises to the matrix subject position in compliance with the Minimal Link Condition, as illustrated in (24a), it will be able to check the strong feature of T, but not the Case-feature of T or the φ-features of [FF(seems)+T]; since the Case- and φ-features of *it* are uninterpretable, they were erased in the previous checking relation in the embedded subject position. Given that the Case-features of T and *John* and the φ-features of [FF(seems)+T] remain unchecked at LF, the derivation violates Full Interpretation and crashes— hence the unacceptability of (24b).

(24) a. [$_{TP}$ it$_i$ T seems [$_{CP}$ that t$_i$ was told John [$_{CP}$ that he was fired]]]
     b. *It seems that was told John that he was fired.

Therefore, according to Chomsky's reasoning, the only convergent alternative to (24a) is to move *John* to the embedded subject position and insert the expletive in the subject position, as illustrated in (25a), yielding the acceptable sentence in (25b). Recall that the option of moving *John* to the embedded subject position, which violates Procrastinate, is not to be compared with the option of inserting *it* for purposes of economy, because the latter does not lead to a convergent derivation.

(25) a. [TP it T seems [CP that John$_i$ was told t$_i$ [CP that he was fired]]]
     b. It seems that John was told that he was fired.

There is one problem with Chomsky's analysis of the derivation of (24b), however (see Nunes 1995, 2000 for discussion). In Chomsky's (1995) system, when the expletive enters into a checking relation with the embedded T in (22), its Case- and φ-features are deleted and erased. Its D-feature, on the other hand, is just deleted; if it were erased, the whole category would be erased, violating the additional condition that whole constituents cannot erase (see Chomsky 1995, 281). Although invisible at LF, the deleted D-feature of the expletive is accessible to the computational system in Chomsky's (1995) system; hence, it could raise and check the strong D-feature of the matrix T, as illustrated in (24a). In the covert component, FF(John) should then be able to raise and adjoin to [FF(seems)+T], checking the Case-feature of T and the φ-features of FF(seems); crucially, the trace of the expletive cannot block this movement because its Case- and φ-features were erased. According to this analysis, the derivation in (24a) should therefore converge and be compared with (25a) for purposes of economy. At the point where the strong feature of the intermediate T is checked, (25a) violates Procrastinate, but (24a) does not; hence, (24a) should incorrectly block (25a).

Chomsky's (1995) analysis of checking in terms of deletion and erasure therefore incorrectly predicts that (25b) should be unacceptable and that (24b) should be acceptable. A plausible way to prevent this undesirable result is to allow the trace of *it* in (24a) to block raising of FF(John) at LF. If such an approach proves successful in accounting for the unacceptability of (23b) and (24b) and for the acceptability of (25b), we will have evidence against Chomsky's (1995) proposal that traces of A-movement are inaccessible to the computational system.

The system I proposed in section 2.2.2 provides a straightforward account of the sentences in (23)–(25). I have assumed that a checking operation merely renders an uninterpretable feature invisible at LF (deletion), with no resort to the additional process of erasure (see chapter 1, note 20). Thus, if the expletive is inserted in the subject position of the structure in (22), its Case- and ϕ-features will be rendered invisible at LF by entering into a checking relation with [was+T], but they remain present in the structure, as illustrated in (26a). However, its D-feature may remain visible after checking the strong feature of the intermediate T head and is able to check the strong feature of the matrix T in (26b) (see section 1.5.3.2).

(26) a. [$_{TP}$ T seems [$_{CP}$ that it-$_\phi$-$_{CASE}$ was told John [$_{CP}$ that he was fired]]]
    b. [$_{TP}$ it^i-$_\phi$-$_{CASE}$ T seems [$_{CP}$ that it^i-$_\phi$-$_{CASE}$ was told John [$_{CP}$ that he was fired]]]

In the covert component, the Case-features of *John* and T and the ϕ-features of *seems* in (26b) still need to be checked in order for the derivation to converge. However, movement of FF(John) to check them violates the Minimal Link Condition: the trace of the expletive, which also has Case- and ϕ-features, is closer to [FF(seems)+T] than *John* is. Hence, no convergent derivation can obtain if the expletive is inserted in the intermediate subject position; this in turn prevents (26b) from being compared for economy purposes with (25a), repeated in (27), yielding the correct results.

(27) [$_{TP}$ it T seems [$_{CP}$ that John$_i$ was told t$_i$ [$_{CP}$ that he was fired]]]

I have shown that upon close inspection, Chomsky's (1995) checking theory in terms of deletion and erasure makes wrong predictions about the status of the sentences in (24b) and (25b) (see Nunes 2000 for further discussion). Furthermore, I argued that the contrast between these two sentences can be accounted for if traces are accessible to the computational system and therefore are able to block movement across them, yielding Minimal Link Condition violations. As noted at the outset, this is a sound result from a conceptual point of view. Once the copy theory of movement is adopted, there is no principled reason to expect lower chain links to be inherently different from the head of the chain in terms of accessibility to the computational system.

2.3.2 Raising Constructions

Another piece of data that apparently bears on the issue of accessibility of traces to the computational system is related to raising constructions. Chomsky (1995, 305) takes the contrast between the French sentences in (28) as evidence that traces do not block movement.

(28) *French*
    a. *[Jean$_i$ semble à Marie [t$_i$ avoir   du   talent]]
       Jean seems to Marie   have-INF PART talent
       'Jean seems to Marie to be talented.'
    b. [Jean$_i$ lui$_j$ semble t$_j$ [t$_i$ avoir   du   talent]]
       Jean 3SG.DAT.CL seems   have-INF PART talent
       'Jean seems to him/her to be talented.'

Raising of *Jean* to check the strong feature of the matrix T in (28a) is presumably ruled out by the Minimal Link Condition: *Marie* could check the strong feature of T, and it c-commands the embedded subject. Assuming that the clitic in (28b) adjoins to the T head, *Jean* is allowed to cross both the clitic and its trace, without yielding a Minimal Link Condition violation: the clitic does not prevent this movement because it is in the same minimal domain as the moved subject (see Chomsky 1995, 356), and the trace of the clitic does not block this movement because its formal features have been erased.

Before we examine Chomsky's analysis of the contrast in (28), let us consider the English counterpart of (28a), given in (29). The same reasons that rule out (28a) should in principle apply to (29). Chomsky (MIT lectures, fall 1994) suggests that raising of the embedded subject in cases such as (29) may be accounted for if inherently Case-marked elements do not count for the purposes of the Minimal Link Condition. Thus, if *Mary* receives an inherent Case from *seems* in (29), it will not be able to block raising of an embedded element to the subject position and the derivation can converge, as desired.

(29) [John$_i$ seems to Mary [t$_i$ to be talented]]

If (29) can be analyzed along these lines, we are then not forced to take (28b) as evidence that traces do not block movement. Suppose that raising verbs in French assign inherent Case to dative clitics. If so, the trace of the clitic would not prevent movement in (28b) for the same reasons that *Mary* does not in (29).

Evidence that this suggestion might be on the right track comes from the unacceptability of the sentence in (30).

(30) *French*
    *[[à Marie]$_i$ semble t$_i$ [Jean avoir   du   talent]]
    to Marie   seems   Jean have-INF PART talent
    'Jean seems to Marie to be talented.'

If *Marie* blocks the movement of *Jean* in (28a) because it can check the EPP-feature of the matrix clause, it should in principle be able to move to the matrix subject position, as shown in (30). The Case-feature of *Marie* should then be checked against the preposition, and the remaining unchecked Case-features of *Jean* and the matrix T should be checked against each other. If traces do not block movement owing to the erasure of their formal features, the trace of *à Marie* in (30) should not prevent movement of FF(Jean) to check its Case-feature against T, yielding a convergent derivation. Given that (30) has the relevant properties of (28b) but does not yield an acceptable sentence, it is unlikely that the acceptability of (28b) is due to the alleged inaccessibility of traces to the computational system.

Under the checking theory I have adopted here, the Case-feature of the trace of *à Marie* in (30), even if checked, is not erased and prevents movement of FF(Jean) for Case reasons, in the same way the D-feature of *à Marie* in (28a) prevents *Jean* from checking the strong feature of the matrix T head. The absence of a Minimal Link Condition violation in (28b) must then be a reflex of the properties of inherently Case-marked elements, also present in (29), rather than a reflex of the properties of traces (see Ausin and Depiante 1999 and Boeckx 2000 for further discussion).

2.3.3 Covert Movement

The last piece of evidence that Chomsky (1995) presents in favor of the idea that traces of A-movement do not block movement is related to how the T head should look at LF if we assume that "interpretive operations at the interface should be as simple as possible," which in turn demands that "forms that reach the LF level must be as similar as typological variation permits—unique, if that is possible" (Chomsky 1995, 359).

Under this view, the T head of languages in which both subject and object move overtly should be as simple as (31), where Vb is the verbal complex formed by adjoining the main verb to the light verb. In order to maximize similarity, Chomsky (1995, 360) then proposes that in languages in which only the subject moves overtly, the formal features of the object adjoin directly to T, as shown in (32).

(31)

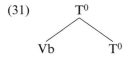

(32)

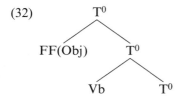

What is relevant for our discussion is that in order for FF(Obj) to adjoin to T in (32), it must cross the intervening trace of the subject in Spec,vP, as shown in (33).

(33) $[_{TP}$ Subj $[_{T'}[_{T^0}$ FF(Obj) $[_{T^0}$ Vb $[_{T^0}$ T]]] $[_{vP}$ t_{Subj} $[_{v'}$ t_{Vb} $[_{VP}$ t_V Obj]]]]]

This movement is allowed, given Chomsky's (1995, 304) assumption that the formal features of traces of A-movement are deleted and erased. We have seen in the previous sections that empirical data do not warrant such an assumption. The contrast in (34) (from Chomsky 1995, 274) suggests that this assumption also makes wrong empirical predictions regarding the proposed adjunction of FF(Obj) to T.

(34) a.   There arrived three men (last night) without identifying themselves.
     b.   *I met three men (last night) without identifying themselves.

The (marginal) acceptability of (34a) is interpreted as showing that in the covert component, FF(three men) raises and adjoins to T, whence it can control PRO in the adjunct clause and indirectly license the anaphor. Thus, if FF(Obj) adjoined to T in English as in (32), it should also be able to control PRO and license the anaphor in (34b), contrary to fact.

Another problem for Chomsky's approach was brought to my attention by Marcelo Ferreira (personal communication). If FF(Obj) can freely cross the trace of the subject, the system overgenerates. Consider the structure in (35), for instance, which is derived under Chomsky's approach through the following derivational steps: (i) a nominative DP is merged as the object of the main verb and an accusative DP is merged as the specifier of the light verb; (ii) Vb moves and adjoins to T^0; (iii) the accusative DP moves overtly to Spec,TP to check the EPP-feature of T and checks its Case against Vb;[10] and (iv) FF(Obj-$_{NOM}$) moves covertly and adjoins to T^0, checking its nominative Case against T.

(35)

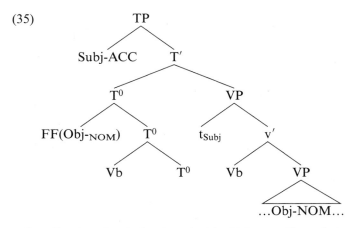

By allowing the derivation sketched above, Chomsky's approach has
the undesirable consequence that it predicts that in a verb movement
language with overt Case morphology, the two sentences corresponding
to the glosses in (36) should be synonymous: (36a) would be derived
along the lines of (33) and (36b) along the lines of (35). That languages
allowing such an ambiguity are unlikely to exist casts even more doubt on
Chomsky's proposal that FF(Obj) can cross the trace of the subject in
Spec,vP.

(36) a. he-NOM kissed her-ACC
     b. he-ACC kissed her-NOM

By contrast, the approach pursued in this chapter, which takes traces to
be accessible to the computational system, successfully excludes (34b) and
(36b): adjunction of FF(Obj) to T in (33) and (35) for purposes of Case
checking is blocked by the intervening Case-feature of the trace of the
subject in Spec,vP.[11] If FF(Obj) cannot skip the trace of the subject
without yielding a minimality violation, as argued above, it remains to be
explained how the object can have its Case checked covertly. The simplest
assumption is that FF(Obj) adjoins to the element that actually checks its
Case-feature, namely, the verbal complex Vb (or its trace, in the case of
overt verb (Vb) movement).[12]

This approach has the advantage of keeping movement as "short" as
possible. Consider languages with no verb movement and no object shift,
such as English. In Chomsky's (1995, 361) analysis, the LF structure of
the T head in these languages is as in (32), with FF(Vb) instead of Vb.
Notice that the alleged impossibility of FF(Obj) adjoining to the traces of

Vb (see note 12) does not necessarily arise in English; the checking of the Case-feature of FF(Obj) could proceed cyclically, with FF(Obj) adjoining to Vb before Vb moved to T. The poverty-of-interpretation conjecture is thus the only motivation for the longer movement of FF(Obj) to Vb. In the analysis pursued here, the shorter movement is the only option available, because the long movement violates the Minimal Link Condition.

It is worth pointing out that the approach explored in this chapter is actually not incompatible with Chomsky's poverty-of-interpretation conjecture. According to this approach, there are only two LF configurations for T and the light verb head across languages, as far as subject and object movement are concerned. Languages with overt subject movement have the subject in the specifier of T and languages without overt subject movement have FF(Subj) adjoined to T; in turn, in languages with overt object movement, the object is in the specifier of Vb and in languages without overt object movement, FF(Obj) is adjoined to (the trace of) Vb.[13]

2.3.4   The θ-Criterion and Economy Computations

Let us finally consider Chomsky's (1995) analysis of the contrast between (37) and (38).

(37) a.   [$_{TP}$ there$_i$ seems [$_{TP}$ t$_i$ to be someone in the room]]
      b. *[$_{TP}$ there seems [$_{TP}$ someone$_i$ to be t$_i$ in the room]]

(38) a.   [$_{TP}$ I$_k$ [$_{vP}$ t$_k$ expect [$_{TP}$ someone$_i$ to be t$_i$ in the room]]]
      b. *[$_{TP}$ I$_k$ [$_{vP}$ t$_k$ expect [$_{TP}$ t$_k$ to be someone in the room]]]

At some point, the derivations of both (37) and (38) reach the step where the structure in (39) is built.

(39) [$_{TP}$ to be someone in the room]

The system then has the option of either satisfying the EPP by merging *there* in (37) and *I* in (38) or moving *someone*. The question is what drives the system to choose Merge over Move in (37), but Move over Merge in (38). Chomsky (1995, 347) proposes that it is the θ-Criterion. If *I* is inserted in Spec,TP in (39), it does not receive a θ-role, causing the derivation to crash. Given that only convergent derivations can be compared for economy purposes, the derivation in (38b) does not block the one in (38a). In (37), on the other hand, the expletive *there* can be inserted in a nonthematic position and therefore the derivation utilizing Merge in (37a) blocks the one in (37b), which resorts to Move.

It should be observed that Chomsky's analysis of the contrast between (37) and (38) is contingent on two assumptions (see Chomsky 1995, sec. 4.6): that θ-roles are not features and are determined configurationally, and that Last Resort does not license movement to thematic positions. However, the analysis of parasitic gaps and across-the-board extraction constructions to be developed in the next chapter rely on exactly the opposite assumptions: that θ-roles are features, and that θ-assignment can indeed license movement operations (see Bošković 1994, Lasnik 1995, Nunes 1995, Bošković and Takahashi 1998, Hornstein 1999, 2001, Ferreira 2000a,b, Rodrigues 2000, 2002, and Hornstein and Nunes 2002, among others). Given the fundamental difference in these sets of assumptions, in this section I consider whether the contrast in (38) is amenable to an alternative analysis (see Nunes 1995, sec. II.16, for further discussion).

Under the assumptions considered here, the unacceptability of (38b) cannot be attributed to a violation of the θ-Criterion, because *I* receives a θ-role when it moves to Spec,vP. It can, however, be straightforwardly accounted for as a violation of the Minimal Link Condition. If *I* is merged in Spec,TP in (39) and moves to the matrix Spec,vP, the Case-feature of its trace will prevent FF(someone) from moving to check its Case against the light verb, causing the derivation to crash. Recall that under the link-checking approach explored in this monograph, the copy of *I* in the embedded TP is not affected by the Case-checking relation involving the highest copy.

Assuming that the expletive *there*, on the other hand, has only a D-feature (see Chomsky 1995, 287), it will induce no intervention effect for the movement of FF(someone) for Case purposes, allowing it to have its Case checked against the light verb of the matrix clause. Thus, at the point where the structure in (39) is built, merger of *there* is the optimal option for checking the EPP-feature; hence the contrast between (37a) and (37b).

2.4   Conclusion

In Chomsky's (1995) system, a trace is taken to be affected by the checking relation affecting the head of its chain (see section 2.2.1). In order to account for the elimination of uninterpretable features of overlapping chains, this chain-checking approach must incorporate several ad hoc amendments, among which is the stipulation that the formal features of traces of A-chains are erased. Once traces of A-chains are stripped of formal features, they are taken to be inaccessible to the computational system.

The alternative to Chomsky's (1995) system developed in this chapter has several advantages, the most important of which is that it assumes no inherent difference between heads of chains and traces. It was shown that the simplest version of the copy theory of movement is the one that makes the correct empirical predictions: traces are accessible to the computational system and may induce minimality effects like any other syntactic objects (see section 2.3).

The alternative approach proposed in section 2.2.2 accounts for the data that are problematic for Chomsky's system in a uniform and principled fashion, with a minimal enrichment of the theoretical apparatus; the only technical innovations are the Feature Uniformity Condition and the operation of Chain Uniformization (see section 2.2.2), which can actually be seen as the implementation of the convention needed in Chomsky's (1995) system to account for uninterpretable features in overlapping chains. Moreover, the simplification of Chomsky's (1995) checking theory with the abandonment of erasure was shown to be empirically justified (see section 2.3): if erasure is adopted, many instances of covert movement are incorrectly ruled in (see Nunes 2000 for further discussion).

The general conclusion is that the null hypothesis concerning the copy theory of movement—namely, that all copies are accessible to the same operations and subject to the same principles—is empirically correct. To the extent that this chapter accounts for the elimination of uninterpretable features of chains and some minimality effects without resorting to intrinsic properties ascribed to traces, it takes further steps toward the elimination of traces as grammatical primitives.

Chapter 3

The Copy + Merge Theory and Sideward Movement

3.1 Introduction: The Copy + Merge Theory of Movement

With the abandonment of D-Structure in the Minimalist Program, the computational system must be provided with means to assemble phrasal syntactic objects. Reviving generalized transformations (see Chomsky 1975), Chomsky (1994, 1995) proposes that Merge is a building operation that takes two syntactic objects α and β (lexical items of the numeration or phrasal objects formed from these items) and forms the complex syntactic object $K = \{\gamma, \{\alpha, \beta\}\}$ or $L = \{\langle \gamma, \gamma \rangle, \{\alpha, \beta\}\}$, where γ is the label of the resulting object indicating its relevant properties. The different labels of K and L respectively encode whether the resulting object is a new category or whether a new segment has been added to an existing category ("substitution" or adjunction, respectively).

The operation Move is accordingly reformulated along the following lines (see Chomsky 1994, fn. 13; 1995, sec. 4.4): given the syntactic object Σ with constituents K and α, Move targets K, raises α, and merges α with K, forming Σ'; the operation is cyclic if $\Sigma = K$ and noncyclic otherwise. Σ' differs from Σ in that K is replaced by $L = \{\gamma, \{\alpha, K\}\}$ or $L = \{\langle \gamma, \gamma \rangle, \{\alpha, K\}\}$, depending on whether movement proceeds by substitution or adjunction. Move also forms the chain $CH = (\alpha, t)$, a two-element pair where t (the trace of α) is a copy of α that is deleted in the phonological component in the case of overt movement, but remains available for interpretation at LF (see Chomsky 1993, 35). Under this view, the inner workings of the operation Move can be described as encompassing the four suboperations in (1).

(1) *Suboperations of Move*
   a. Copy
   b. Merge

    c. Form Chain
    d. Delete Traces for PF purposes

Let us consider each of these suboperations for a moment. As discussed in section 1.2, the copy theory of movement alluded to in (1a) is substantially motivated on both conceptual and empirical grounds: it allows binding theory to be captured without resorting to noninterface levels; it provides the basis for the interpretation of displaced idiom chunks at LF; it allows the operation of reconstruction to be dispensed with; it satisfies the Inclusiveness Condition; it accounts for the shape of phonetically realized traces; and it paves the way for the elimination of traces as grammatical primitives.

As mentioned above, Merge is conceptually motivated by the need to assemble phrasal syntactic objects in a system that does not assume D-Structure. However, it is an odd fact from a conceptual point of view that Merge is an operation in its own right in certain cases, and a suboperation of Move in other cases (see Gärtner 1997 for discussion); this is even more so if Merge and Move are to be compared for economy purposes (see Chomsky 1995, sec. 4.9). In an optimal system, we would in principle expect Merge to have the same theoretical status in every computation.

(1c) is not without problems either. As Brody (1995) has emphatically argued, if chain formation and Move (here understood as the sequence Copy–Merge–Delete Traces) express the same type of relation, a theory that contains both notions is redundant.

Finally, the most obvious problem with the picture outlined in (1) concerns the lack of motivation for deletion of traces in the phonological component (see (1d)). If traces are true copies, why can they not be phonetically realized, behaving like the head of the chain? I argued in chapter 1 that deletion of traces actually reflects optimal applications of the independent operation Chain Reduction, triggered by linearization in the phonological component.

According to the proposal developed in chapter 1, a syntactic object containing a nontrivial chain CH cannot be linearized in accordance with the LCA: since the links of CH are nondistinct, they induce violations of the asymmetry and irreflexivity conditions on linear order, canceling the derivation because no PF object can be formed. To prevent this state of affairs, the phonological component resorts to the operation Chain Reduction, which deletes all but one (visible) link of a nontrivial chain. FF-Elimination then deletes the unchecked formal features (if any) of the link that survives Chain Reduction. Since the head of CH participates in more checking relations, it will always have fewer unchecked formal features (if any) to be deleted by FF-Elimination than the lower links of CH. Thus, a derivation in which Chain Reduction deletes all the links except the head of the chain ends up being more economical than a derivation in which Chain Reduction deletes all of the links of the chain except one trace; the derivation in which the head of the chain survives Chain Reduction requires fewer (if any) applications of FF-Elimination.

Furthermore, as argued in chapter 1, traces may actually be phonetically realized if a given chain link is rendered invisible to the LCA by being reanalyzed as part of a single terminal element, or if the phonetic realization of the head of the chain violates some requirement of the phonological component. This state of affairs shows that there cannot be a suboperation like the one described in (1d), which blindly deletes traces.

Given these considerations, the view of Move as a complex operation along the lines of (1) is substantially weakened. Among the presumed four suboperations of Move, two of them (Chain Reduction and Merge) are arguably independent operations. In addition, we still have the problem that movement and chain formation appear to be redundant in capturing the same types of relations (see Brody 1995).

The overall complexity of the operation Move as formulated by Chomsky (1994, 1995) can be seen as a historical residue of the description of generalized transformations as binary or singulary operations: binary transformations such as Merge target two disconnected syntactic objects, whereas singulary transformations such as Move target two constituents of a single syntactic object (see Chomsky 1975, 1993 and Kitahara 1995). In this chapter, I propose that Move should be understood not as a primitive singulary operation of the computational system, but merely as the description of the interaction of the independent operations Copy, Merge, Form Chain, and Chain Reduction. I refer to this approach as the *Copy+Merge theory of movement*.

(2) *Independent operations of the Copy+Merge theory of movement*
    a. Copy
    b. Merge
    c. Form Chain
    d. Chain Reduction

By decomposing Move into more basic independent operations, the Copy+Merge theory of movement yields a much simpler system that not only overcomes the conceptual problems raised above, but also enjoys broader empirical coverage than the versions of the copy theory explored by Chomsky (1993, 1994, 1995). Under this approach, deletion of traces is derived from optimal applications of Chain Reduction, Merge is always taken to be a full operation of the computational system, and the system allows instances in which the operations Copy and Merge are dissociated from Form Chain and Chain Reduction, rendering the Copy+Merge theory immune to Brody's (1995) criticism about the redundancy between Move and Form Chain.

In particular, the Copy+Merge theory permits constrained instances of what I have called *sideward movement* (see Nunes 1995, 2001),[1] where the computational system copies a given constituent α of a syntactic object K and merges α with a syntactic object L, which has been independently assembled and is unconnected to K, as illustrated in (3).[2] In (3b), no chain can be formed between the two copies of α if we make the standard assumption that the links of a chain must be in a c-command relation.

(3) a. $[_K \ldots \alpha^i \ldots]$ $\alpha^i \xleftarrow{\text{Merge}} [_L \ldots]$

           └─────────┘
                Copy

   b. $[_K \ldots \alpha^i \ldots]$ $[_M \alpha^i [_L \ldots]]$

If evidence for postulating sideward movement can be provided and if sideward movement is constrained enough so that it does not overgenerate, we will then have reasonable grounds to abandon the standard view of movement as a complex singulary operation. This is the approach I will pursue in the following sections, ruling out unwanted instances of sideward movement on the basis of analyses regarding linearization of chains and accessibility of traces developed in chapters 1 and 2, respectively.

The chapter is organized as follows. In section 3.2, I review the conditions on Move, reinterpreting them as conditions on Form Chain. In section 3.3, I outline the general circumstances that allow sideward movement to take place. In sections 3.4 and 3.5, I show that the core properties of parasitic gap and across-the-board-extraction constructions can be derived if they are analyzed in terms of sideward movement. In section 3.6, I analyze some differences between these two constructions, and in section 3.7, I discuss the directionality of sideward movement. In section 3.8, I show that sideward movement provides a cyclic analysis for standard instances of noncyclic movement. In section 3.9, I discuss some extensions of the sideward movement approach, and in section 3.10, I present the conclusions of the chapter.

3.2 Conditions on Chain Formation

In Chomsky's (1995) system, the operation Move is subject to the following conditions: (i) c-command among the chain links (see Chomsky 1995, 235),[3] (ii) Last Resort (see Chomsky 1995, 280), and (iii) the Minimal Link Condition (see Chomsky 1995, 311). In the context of the Copy+Merge theory of movement, where Move is only a taxonomic notion, these conditions will be reinterpreted as holding of the independent operation Form Chain, as stated in (4), where the auxiliary definitions of *sublabel* and *closeness* are given in (5) and (6) (see Chomsky 1995, 268, 356).

(4) *Conditions on Form Chain*
Two constituents α and β can form the nontrivial chain CH $= (\alpha, \beta)$ if
a. α is nondistinct from β;
b. α c-commands β;
c. there is at least one feature F of α such that F enters into a checking relation with a sublabel of the head of the projection with which α merges and for any such feature F of α, the corresponding feature F of β is accessible to the computational system; and
d. there is no constituent γ such that γ has a feature F′ that is of the same type as the feature F of α, and γ is closer to α than β is.

(5) *Sublabel*
σ is a sublabel of the head H iff σ is a feature of H or a feature of some element adjoined to H.

(6) *Closeness*
γ is closer to α than β is iff (a) α c-commands γ and γ c-commands β, and (b) γ is not in the same minimal domain as α or β.

The condition in (4a) states that a chain can only be formed between copies of a given syntactic object (see section 1.5.1); (4c) and (4d) are simply Chomsky's (1995) Last Resort and Minimal Link Condition, restated as conditions on chain formation. For instance, the condition that an inaccessible (erased) feature cannot drive movement in Chomsky's (1995) system is captured in (4c), by taking into consideration the accessibility of the relevant feature F with respect to both α and β. To use Chomsky's (2000) metaphor, in order for a chain to be formed, the features of the copy that undergoes checking probe the structure to find active matching features of the lower copy. As an illustration, let us reconsider the derivation of sentences involving successive-cyclic movement such as (7).

(7) John is likely to be kissed.

As proposed in section 1.5.3.2 (still under the Move-based approach), the checking of interpretable features for PF purposes is optional, but regulated by economy considerations: all things being equal, checking should render the greatest number of features invisible at PF so that applications of FF-Elimination would be minimized. The higher copy of *John* in (8), for instance, has the option of checking its categorial feature for PF purposes when checking the EPP-feature of the embedded clause. If it does, however, it will not be able to move to check the EPP-feature of the matrix clause; in the convergent derivation of (7), the intermediate copy of *John* must then remain unchecked for PF purposes and therefore accessible to the computational system, as represented in (9).

(8) $[_{TP}$ is likely $[_{TP}$ John^i-$_N$ to $[_{vP}$ be kissed John^i-N$]]]$

(9) $[_{TP}$ John^i-$_N$ is likely $[_{TP}$ John^i-N to $[_{vP}$ be kissed John^i-N$]]]$

Under the Copy+Merge approach, on the other hand, there is in principle nothing that prevents the computational system from copying the lower instance of *John* in (8) and merging it in the matrix Spec,TP, as shown in (10), allowing the EPP-feature of the matrix T to be checked.

(10) $[_{TP}$ John^i-$_N$ is likely $[_{TP}$ John^i-$_N$ to $[_{vP}$ be kissed John^i-N$]]]$

The problem that will arise in (10) in the Copy+Merge approach has to do with chain formation: the categorial feature of the highest copy of *John* in (10) participates in a checking relation (it checks the EPP-feature), but according to (4c), such checking is not sufficient to allow chain formation between the two higher copies of *John*, because the categorial feature of the intermediate copy has become inactive after being checked for PF purposes. Using Chomsky's (2000) probe-goal metaphor, when the categorial feature of the highest copy probes the structure, the categorial feature of the intermediate copy is not a suitable goal.

Notice that in terms of accessibility to the computational system, the categorial feature of the lowest copy of *John* is indeed an active goal and would in principle license chain formation between the highest and the lowest copies. However, actual chain formation is blocked by the categorial feature of the intermediate copy. As argued in chapter 2, the null hypothesis of any version of the copy theory of movement is that intermediate traces induce intervention effects like any other syntactic object. Thus, in accordance with (4d), the categorial feature of the intermediate copy in (10), although inactive, induces a minimality effect because it is closer to the highest copy than the lowest copy is.

The only pair of copies that can form a nontrivial chain in (10) is therefore the one involving the two lower copies. An optimal application of Chain Reduction to such a chain would then delete the lowest copy, yielding (11).

(11) $[_{TP}$ John^i-$_N$ is likely $[_{TP}$ John^i-$_N$ to $[_{vP}$ be kissed ~~John^i-N~~$]]]$

Since each of the two higher copies in (11) is treated as a trivial chain, they cannot undergo Chain Reduction. The two copies then induce violations of the asymmetry and irreflexivity conditions on linear order and the derivation is canceled, because the structure cannot be linearized (see section 1.5.2). Thus, the computation must proceed along the lines of (9), where a (linked) chain involving the three copies can be formed, and the optimal reduction of this three-membered chain yields the PF output associated with (7).

As for derivational cost, the preference for Merge over Move in Chomsky's (1995) system is reinterpreted as preference for Merge over Copy (see section 3.6 for further discussion).

To summarize, the conditions regulating movement operations in a Move-based approach and their interpretation as conditions on chain formation under the Copy+Merge approach make the same empirical predictions with respect to standard (upward) movement. However, the two approaches make significantly different predictions with respect to sideward movement, as will be shown in the next sections.

3.3 Sideward Movement

Before examining actual data, let us consider what a legitimate derivation involving sideward movement looks like, under the Copy+Merge approach. The relevant derivational steps are illustrated in (12)–(14). (12) illustrates the instance of sideward movement itself: a given constituent α is copied from K and merges with the independent syntactic object L. At the derivational step represented in (12b), the two copies of α cannot form a chain, because they do not stand in a c-command relation (see (4b)). Further computations may then form a unique syntactic object HP, containing the two copies, as shown in (13). Again, no chain formation can apply to the two copies of α, because of the c-command condition.

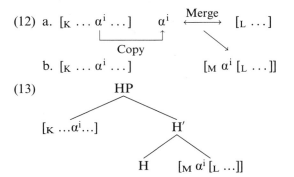

(12) a. [_K ... α^i ...]   α^i $\xleftarrow{\text{Merge}}$ [_L ...]

└──────┘

         Copy

     b. [_K ... α^i ...]   [_M α^i [_L ...]]

(13)   HP

         [_K ...α^i...]   H'

                              H   [_M α^i [_L ...]]

Consider now the stage in (14), where the head Y, which was introduced later in the structure, required an additional copy of α.

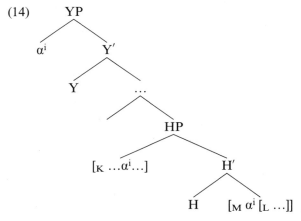

(14)   YP

     α^i   Y'

            Y   ...

                    HP

         [_K ...α^i...]   H'

                              H   [_M α^i [_L ...]]

In (14), the highest copy of α can in principle form a chain with either of the lower copies. Crucially, since neither of the lower copies c-commands the other, neither is closer to the highest copy (see (6)) and no intervention effect should arise (see Brody 1995 and Nunes 1995, 2001). Suppose then that the highest copy does indeed form a distinct chain with each of the lower copies. Optimal applications of Chain Reduction to each of these two-membered chains in the phonological component should delete the lower link of each chain, yielding the structure in (15).

(15)

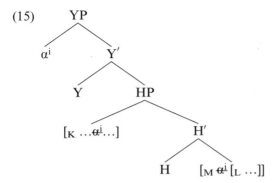

   In the output associated with (15), α appears to have moved from two
different launching sites. Thus, any construction that appears to involve
movement of an element from more than one position "at once" is a
good candidate for a sideward movement analysis. Let us then start the
discussion with two constructions that clearly appear to fit the above
description: parasitic gap and across-the-board constructions.

3.4   Parasitic Gaps

After the first systematic studies of parasitic gap constructions such as
(16) and (17) by Taraldsen (1981), Chomsky (1982), and Engdahl (1983),
a continuously growing literature on the subject has emerged.[4] (18) summarizes some of the properties of parasitic gap constructions discovered
in this literature.[5]

(16) a. Which paper did you file without reading?
   b. $[_{CP}$[which paper]$_i$ did+Q $[_{TP}$ you $[_{vP}[_{vP}$ file $t_i]$ $[_{PP}$ without reading
      PG$_i$]]]]

(17) a. Which politician did critics of upset?
   b. $[_{CP}$[which politician]$_i$ did+Q $[_{TP}$[critics of PG$_i$] upset $t_i]$]

(18) a. Parasitic gaps are licensed at S-Structure (see Chomsky 1982, for
      instance).
   b. Parasitic gaps cannot be c-commanded by the "real" gap (see
      Taraldsen 1981 and Engdahl 1983, for instance).
   c. Parasitic gaps cannot be licensed by A-chains (see Chomsky
      1982, for instance).
   d. Parasitic gaps are "selectively" sensitive to islands; that is,
      although they typically occur within (Condition on Extraction

    Domain) islands, they cannot be separated from their licenser by more than one island (see Kayne 1983, 1984, Contreras 1984, and Chomsky 1986a, for instance).
  e. Parasitic gaps can only be NPs (see Aoun and Clark 1985 and Chomsky 1986a, for instance).
  f. Parasitic gaps cannot be licensed by nonreferential NPs (see Cinque 1990, for instance).

Several different analyses have been put forward to account for the properties listed in (18). Parasitic gaps have been analyzed as (i) traces of across-the-board extraction (see Williams 1990, for instance), (ii) traces of *wh*-phrases that are not the result of movement (see Frampton 1990), (iii) null resumptive pronouns (see Cinque 1990, for instance), and (iv) traces resulting from movement of null operators (see Chomsky 1986a, for instance). The proposal in (iv) in turn has different implementations: for Lasnik and Stowell (1991), the trace of the null operator that appears in parasitic gap constructions is a null epithet; and for Browning (1987), the null operator itself is pro, whereas for Weinberg (1988) it is PRO.

Some of the proposals mentioned above are incompatible with general minimalist guidelines. A minimalist analysis of parasitic gaps should for instance refrain from enriching the technical apparatus with descriptive devices such as the across-the-board formalism (see Williams 1978, 1990). Although I share the intuition already pointed out in Ross 1967 that parasitic gap and across-the-board constructions should be derived along similar lines, I will show that these two constructions can be analyzed within the Copy+Merge theory in terms of the same operations that are responsible for standard instances of movement.

Other proposals mentioned above are specifically incompatible with the copy theory of movement. Take the proposal according to which a parasitic gap is a special kind of trace that does not result from movement (see Frampton 1990), for instance. Within the context of the copy theory, to say that a parasitic gap is a trace that does not arise through movement presumably amounts to saying that it is not introduced into the derivation by Copy. However, if a new term is introduced into the derivation by Select or Merge, it will be interpreted as distinct from every other term in the derivation, thus being unable to form a chain with any other term (see section 1.5.1). In the analysis of parasitic gap constructions to be developed in the following sections, parasitic gaps will be treated as regular traces.

Also at odds with the null hypothesis regarding the copy theory of movement are analyses in which the links of a given chain may be different kinds of syntactic objects. Lasnik and Stowell (1991), for instance, propose that the trace of a nonquantificational null operator, such as the one found in parasitic gap constructions, is a null epithet, a new type of empty category. This proposal attempts to capture the fact that parasitic gaps appear to pattern with epithets in ameliorating weak crossover effects, as illustrated in (19) (Lasnik and Stowell's (20b) and (66b)).

(19) a. [who$_i$ did you stay with t$_i$ [before [his$_i$ wife] had spoken to PG$_i$]]
     b. [which assailant$_i$ did Mary escape from t$_i$ [before [his$_i$ partner] joined up with [the bastard]$_i$]]

Hornstein (1995, chap. 6) shows, however, that the amelioration effect with respect to weak crossover found in (19a) is not restricted to constructions involving nonquantificational null operators and may arise even in constructions involving true quantificational phrases, as illustrated in (20) (Hornstein's (20a) and (20b)).

(20) a. *[[his$_i$ mother] gave [his$_i$ picture] to [every student]$_i$]
     b. [[his$_i$ mother] gave [every student]$_i$ [his$_i$ picture]]

Hornstein (1995, chap. 6) provides a uniform account of data such as (19) and (20) in terms of Higginbotham's (1983, 1985) Linking Theory, according to which the Weak Crossover Condition rules out a pronoun linked to a variable on its right. Under this approach, the reason why (19a), (19b), and (20b) allow a bound reading of the relevant pronoun without inducing a weak crossover effect is that the pronouns need not be linked to a variable on their right in order to be interpreted as bound. The pronouns of (19) can be linked to the variable on their left, and the pronoun inside the subject in (20b) can be linked to the pronoun inside the object, which in turn can be linked to a variable on its left; in (20a), on the other hand, one of the pronouns must be linked to a variable on its right in order for the relevant interpretation to obtain, violating the Weak Crossover Condition.[6]

Also worth mentioning is that the postulated null epithet behaves differently from regular epithets in being able to be associated with non-D-linked *wh*-phrases, as illustrated in (21).

(21) a. [[who the hell]$_i$ should the police arrest t$_i$ [after finding PG$_i$]]
     b. *[[who the hell]$_i$ should the police arrest t$_i$ [after finding [the man]$_i$/[the idiot]$_i$]]

The point of this short digression was to show that data such as (19) do not necessarily require an expansion of the inventory of empty categories or additional assumptions regarding chain formation in order to allow the postulated chain between the null operator and parasitic gap. I will therefore keep to the simplest assumption that two terms can form a chain only if they are nondistinct from one another (see (4a)); a parasitic gap will thus be taken to be nondistinct from any term with which it forms a chain.

Among the proposals mentioned above, the ones that are relevant for a direct comparison with the sideward movement analysis of parasitic gaps to be developed below are therefore the ones that are compatible with general minimalist guidelines and the copy theory, in particular— namely, the proposals that analyze parasitic gaps as (regular) traces of null operators or as null resumptive pronouns. For the sake of discussion, I will take Chomsky 1986a and Cinque 1990 as standard representatives of the null operator and the null resumptive pronoun approaches, respectively.

The discussion is organized as follows. In section 3.4.1, I outline the general analysis of parasitic gaps in terms of sideward movement. In sections 3.4.2 to 3.4.4, I then address each of the properties listed in (18a–d) and compare the sideward movement analysis with the null operator movement and null resumptive pronoun analyses.[7]

3.4.1   General Approach

Let us examine step by step how the parasitic gap construction given in (16a), repeated in (22), can be derived in the Copy+Merge theory of movement.

(22) Which paper did you file without reading?

Suppose the computational system starts with the initial numeration N in (23) and operates until it reaches the derivational stage in (24), where N has been reduced to N' and the two syntactic objects K and L have been assembled.

(23) $N = \{which_1, paper_1, Q_1, you_1, did_1, v_2, file_1, without_1, C_1, PRO_1, T_1, reading_1\}$

(24) a. $N' = \{which_0, paper_0, Q_1, you_1, did_1, v_1, file_0, without_1, C_0, PRO_0, T_0, reading_0\}$

b. K = [$_{CP}$ C [$_{TP}$ PRO$_j$ [$_{T'}$ T [$_{vP}$ t$_j$ [$_{v'}$ v [$_{VP}$ reading [which paper]]]]]]]

c. L = file

Possible continuations of (24) involving merger of L with K or any object formed from the lexical items still available in N' do not converge: the θ-roles of *file* and the remaining *v* in N' still have to be discharged, and there is only one element in N' that could bear a θ-role, namely, *you*. The derivational step sketched in (24) may, however, lead to a convergent result if the computational system makes a copy of *which paper* and merges it with L (an instance of sideward movement) to satisfy the thematic properties of *file* (see Chomsky 2000), as illustrated in (25).

(25) a. K = [$_{CP}$ C [$_{TP}$ PRO$_j$ [$_{T'}$ T [$_{vP}$ t$_j$ [$_{v'}$ v [$_{VP}$ reading [which paper]^i]]]]]]

b. M = [$_{VP}$ file [which paper]^i]

The fact that sideward movement in (25) involves movement to a thematic position should not be at all surprising under the Copy+Merge theory. If we assume, following Chomsky (2000), that applications of Merge must be motivated and that the establishment of a thematic relation can count as an appropriate motivation, an approach that takes movement to be the result of the interaction among Copy, Merge, Form Chain, and Chain Reduction should in principle license copying and merger to satisfy thematic requirements. I will thus assume that movement into thematic positions is indeed a licit operation (see Bošković 1994, Lasnik 1995, Bošković and Takahashi 1998, Hornstein 1999, 2001, Ferreira 2000a,b, and Rodrigues 2000, 2002, among others, for further motivation and discussion).

As the derivation proceeds, other lexical items are pulled out from N' in (24a) and merge with K and M in (25), yielding the objects P and Q in (26).

(26) a. P = [$_{PP}$ without [$_{CP}$ C [$_{TP}$ PRO$_j$ [$_{T'}$ T [$_{vP}$ t$_j$ [$_{v'}$ v [$_{VP}$ reading [which paper]^i]]]]]]]

b. Q = [$_{vP}$ you [$_{v'}$ v [$_{VP}$ file [which paper]^i]]]

(27) represents the next derivational step, where P adjoins to Q (see chapter 1, note 53). In (27), no chain formation between the nondistinct copies of *which paper* can take place, since they are not in a c-command relation (see (4b)).

(27)   vP

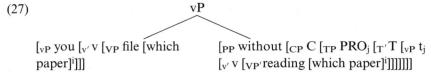

[vP you [v′ v [vP file [which   [PP without [CP C [TP PROj [T′ T [vP tj
paper]ⁱ]]]   [v′ v [vP′ reading [which paper]ⁱ]]]]]]]]

After the remaining lexical items of N′ in (24a) are pulled out and
merge with the structure in (27) and *you* and *did* move, the structure in
(28) is derived (copies irrelevant for the discussion are omitted). Under
the assumption that the interrogative complementizer Q in (28) has a
strong *wh*-feature, another copy of *which paper* is made and merges with
the structure in (28), forming (29).

(28) [CP did+Q [TP you [vP[vP file [which paper]ⁱ] [PP without PRO
    reading [which paper]ⁱ]]]]

(29) [CP[which paper]ⁱ did+Q [TP you [vP[vP file [which paper]ⁱ]
    [PP without PRO reading [which paper]ⁱ]]]]

Given that no further checking relation involves the *wh*-feature of *which*
paper in (29), convergence conditions do not prevent the copy in Spec,CP
from having its *wh*-feature checked for PF purposes when it enters into
a checking relation with the strong feature of the interrogative complementizer Q (see section 1.5.3.2). Economy considerations minimizing
the number of applications of FF-Elimination then ensure that this feature
is so checked, as represented in (30), with the copies numbered for ease of
reference.

(30)   CP

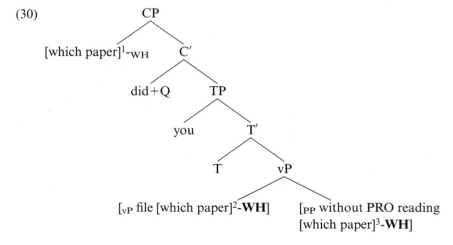

[which paper]¹-WH   C′

                    did+Q   TP

                            you   T′

                                    T   vP

                [vP file [which paper]²-**WH**]   [PP without PRO reading
                                                          [which paper]³-**WH**]

In (30), the copy of *which paper* in Spec,CP can form the chain $CH_1 =$ $(copy^1, copy^2)$ or the chain $CH_2 = (copy^1, copy^3)$ (see Frampton 1990, Brody 1995, and Nunes 1995). In each case, the two instances of *which paper* are nondistinct (see (4a)); $copy^1$ c-commands the other copies (see (4b)); the *wh*-feature of $copy^1$ enters into a checking relation and the corresponding feature of the other copies are accessible to the computational system, in satisfaction of Last Resort (see (4c)); and there is no term containing a *wh*-feature that is closer to $copy^1$ than either of the lower copies is, in compliance with the Minimal Link Condition (see (4d)). Crucially, closeness is defined in terms of c-command (see (6)); thus, given that neither of the lower copies c-commands the other, one is not closer to $copy^1$ than the other is.

Recall that Form Chain is an operation that applies in the course of the mapping from the numeration to LF; although the phonological component is able to differentiate nondistinct terms from terms with identical sets of features (see section 1.5.1), it presumably does not form chains. Let us then consider the situation where $copy^1$ in (30) has not formed a chain with either of the lower copies prior to Spell-Out. In this case, the phonological component will treat each of the instances of *which paper* as a trivial chain. Since these instances are nondistinct, they induce violations of the asymmetry and irreflexivity conditions on linear order, preventing (30) from being linearized in accordance with the LCA (see section 1.5.2). Once no linear order is established, no PF object is formed and the derivation is canceled.

Notice that if two of the *wh*-phrases of (30) were deleted in the phonological component, the derivation could converge at PF even if no *wh*-chain had been formed before Spell-Out. However, as the discussion regarding remnant movement in section 1.6 showed, deletion of constituents is part of the inner workings of Chain Reduction, repeated in (31), which crucially operates with nontrivial chains, not with mere sequences of nondistinct terms.

(31) *Chain Reduction*
   Delete the minimal number of constituents of a nontrivial chain
   CH that suffices for CH to be mapped into a linear order in
   accordance with the LCA.

Thus, if no *wh*-chain has been formed overtly in (30), each *wh*-phrase will be treated by the phonological component as a trivial chain, Chain Reduction will be inapplicable, and the system will fail to linearize the structure.

Let us now consider the case where only the chain $CH_1 = (\text{copy}^1,$ $\text{copy}^2)$ has been formed in (30) before Spell-Out. Since copy^1 requires no application of FF-Elimination targeting its *wh*-feature, the optimal reduction of CH_1 after (30) is shipped to the phonological component involves the deletion of copy^2 (see section 1.5.3.2), as shown in (32).

(32) [$_{CP}$[which paper]^1-$_{WH}$ did+Q [$_{TP}$ you [$_{vP}$[$_{vP}$ file ~~[which paper]^2-**WH**~~] [$_{PP}$ without PRO reading [which paper]^3-**WH**]]]]

The resulting structure in (32) cannot be linearized, however. Since copy^1 and copy^3 did not form a chain before Spell-Out, Chain Reduction is inapplicable; these two nondistinct copies then induce violations of the asymmetry and irreflexivity conditions on linear order, preventing the structure in (32) from being linearized and canceling the derivation. Similar considerations apply to the situation in which only the chain $CH_2 = (\text{copy}^1, \text{copy}^3)$ has been formed before Spell-Out. After CH_2 is reduced in the phonological component as in (33), the two surviving nondistinct copies induce violations of the asymmetry and irreflexivity conditions on linear order, and the derivation is canceled.

(33) [$_{CP}$[which paper]^1-$_{WH}$ did+Q [$_{TP}$ you [$_{vP}$[$_{vP}$ file [which paper]^2-**WH**] [$_{PP}$ without PRO reading ~~[which paper]^3-**WH**~~]]]]

In section 1.6, we saw that the phonetic realization of traces in remnant movement can be adequately accounted for only if Chain Reduction applies "locally," taking into consideration the linearization of a given chain, and not "globally," taking into consideration the linearization of the structure containing the relevant chain. The last scenarios discussed above provide further evidence for this conclusion. If only a single *wh*-chain had been formed in (30) before Spell-Out, a "global" version of Chain Reduction would take into consideration the linearization of the structure of (30) as a whole and would delete both links of the relevant chain, yielding either (34a) or (35a) depending on which *wh*-chain had been formed. However, both derivations yield unacceptable sentences, as shown in (34b) and (35b).

(34) a.   [$_{CP}$~~[which paper]^1-$_{WH}$~~ did+Q [$_{TP}$ you [$_{vP}$[$_{vP}$ file ~~[which paper]^2-**WH**~~] [$_{PP}$ without PRO reading [which paper]^3-**WH**]]]]

   b.   *Did you file without reading which paper?

(35) a.   [$_{CP}$~~[which paper]^1-$_{WH}$~~ did+Q [$_{TP}$ you [$_{vP}$[$_{vP}$ file [which paper]^2-**WH**] [$_{PP}$ without PRO reading ~~[which paper]^3-**WH**~~]]]]

   b.   *Did you file which paper without reading?

If Chain Reduction proceeds "locally" along the lines of (31), as argued in section 1.6, the structure in (30) can only yield a PF object if copy^1 actually forms the chain $CH_1 = (copy^1, copy^2)$ and the chain $CH_2 = (copy^1, copy^3)$. If this happens, the optimal reduction of CH_1 and CH_2 in the phonological component involves the deletion of their lower link, as shown in (36a) and (36b), respectively (see section 1.5.3.2). After (36b) is linearized, further computations in the phonological component finally yield the PF output corresponding to the sentence (22), repeated in (37).

(36) a. [$_{CP}$[which paper]^1-$_{WH}$ did+Q [$_{TP}$ you [$_{vP}$[$_{vP}$ file [which paper]^2-WH] [$_{PP}$ without PRO reading [which paper]^3-WH]]]]]

b. [$_{CP}$[which paper]^1-$_{WH}$ did+Q [$_{TP}$ you [$_{vP}$[$_{vP}$ file [which paper]^2-WH] [$_{PP}$ without PRO reading [which paper]^3-WH]]]]]

(37) Which paper did you file without reading?

The same analysis, mutatis mutandis, extends to "subject" parasitic gaps like (17a), repeated in (38), whose initial numeration N is given in (39).

(38) Which politician did critics of upset?

(39) $N = \{which_1, politician_1, did_1, critics_1, of_1, upset_1, Q_1, v_1\}$

Consider the derivational step in (40), where N has been reduced to N' and the syntactic objects K and L have been formed.

(40) a. $N' = \{which_0, politician_0, did_1, critics_0, of_0, upset_0, Q_1, v_1\}$
b. K = [critics of [which politician]]
c. L = upset

Suppose K and L in (40) merge and the light verb is added to the resulting structure, as represented in the derivational step in (41).

(41) a. $N'' = \{which_0, politician_0, did_1, critics_0, of_0, upset_0, Q_1, v_0\}$
b. [$_{vP}$ v [$_{vP}$ upset [critics of [which politician]]]]

In (41), the light verb has to assign its external θ-role, but no element still available in N'' is a θ-role bearer. This situation could in principle be remedied by movement to Spec,vP (recall that I am assuming that movement to θ-positions is in principle allowed). However, movement of *which politician* is blocked by the Minimal Link Condition owing to the intervention of *critics*, which is also a potential θ-role bearer; in turn, movement of the whole phrase *critics of which politician* should be ruled out by whatever prevents "*John saw," for instance, from yielding an acceptable sentence meaning 'John saw himself', derived by movement of *John* from the internal to the external argument position (see Hornstein 2001 for discussion).[8]

The derivational step in (40) can, however, lead to a convergent result if the computational system copies *which politician* from K and merges it with *upset* (an instance of sideward movement) to satisfy the thematic requirements of the latter, yielding M in (42).

(42) a. $N' = \{which_0, politician_0, did_1, critics_0, of_0, upset_0, Q_1, v_1\}$
      b. $K = [critics\ of\ [which\ politician]^i]$
      c. $M = [upset\ [which\ politician]^i]$

Merger of the light verb with M, followed by merger with K, results in the structure in (43). Merger of the remaining lexical items of the numeration and movement of *critics of which politician* to check the EPP-feature of T and of *which politician* to check the strong *wh*-feature of Q yield the final structure in (44).

(43) $[_{vP}[critics\ of\ [which\ politician]^i]\ [v\ [_{VP}\ upset\ [which\ politician]^i]]]$

(44)

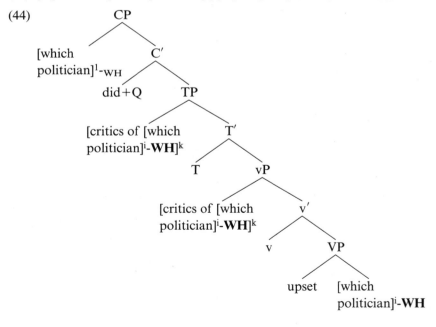

In (44), the two copies of *critics of which politician* form a chain, as in regular instances of movement from Spec,vP to Spec,TP. The interesting case involves the copies of *which politician*. The highest copy can form a different chain with either of the lower copies (crucially, neither is closer to Spec,CP than the other). Assuming that these three chains are formed before Spell-Out, their optimal reduction in the phonological component involves the deletion of the lower link of each chain, yielding (45), which is then converted to the PF output associated with the sentence in (38) after further operations of the phonological component.

(45) $[_{CP}$[which politician]^i did+Q $[_{TP}$[critics of [which politician]^i]^k
      T $[_{vP}$[critics of [which politician]^i]^k upset [which politician]^i]]]

The Copy+Merge theory of movement, which allows constrained instances of sideward movement, thus provides a straightforward analysis of parasitic gaps. Under the approach outlined above, no construction-specific mechanism was employed and the inventory of operations and categories was kept constant. A chain formed before Spell-Out that has a "parasitic gap" as one of its links must undergo Chain Reduction in the phonological component in order to be linearized, like any other chain; hence, a parasitic gap is not phonetically realized for the same reason that traces are not phonetically realized: its deletion is more economical than the deletion of another link of its chain. If the "parasitic gap" copy does not form a chain with another copy before Spell-Out, it will not be deleted by Chain Reduction and will induce violations of the asymmetry and irreflexivity conditions on linear order, preventing the structure from being linearized and canceling the derivation (see section 1.5.2).

According to this approach, the two instances of the *wh*-phrase in the acceptable sentence in (46) must therefore have been distinctively specified in the initial numeration and introduced into the derivation by distinct applications of Select and Merge, and not by the Copy operation. The fact that the two *wh*-phrases cannot be interpreted as covariant suggests that this is indeed the case.

(46) Which paper did you file after reading which paper?

The generalization that emerges is that given the nontrivial chains CH_1 and CH_2, a licit parasitic gap construction can arise only if (i) the links of CH_1 and the links of CH_2 are nondistinct, (ii) CH_1 and CH_2 have been formed before Spell-Out, and (iii) CH_1 and CH_2 have one link in common.

Let us compare these results with the way competing analyses derive the lack of phonetic realization of the "parasitic chain." Since null operator analyses take parasitic gaps to be traces of null operators, they appear to conform with the analysis I proposed above in reducing the lack of phonetic realization of parasitic gaps to the lack of phonetic realization of traces in general. However, there is a crucial difference between these two approaches. In order to completely derive the lack of phonetic realization of the "parasitic chain," the null operator approach must also explain why the null operator of parasitic gap constructions does not alternate with an overt operator. That is, given the alternation between null and overt operators in (47), why can the postulated null operator in the corresponding parasitic gap construction in (48a) not alternate with an overt operator, as shown in (48b)?

(47) a. the paper [O_i that John filed t_i]
     b. the paper [which$_i$ John filed t_i]

(48) a.   the paper [O_i that John [$_{vP}$[$_{vP}$ filed t_i] [without [$_{CP}$ O_k PRO reading t_k]]]]
     b. *the paper [which$_i$ John [$_{vP}$[$_{vP}$ filed t_i] [without [$_{CP}$ which$_k$ PRO reading t_k]]]]

Thus, although the null operator approach may have an answer for why the parasitic gap is not phonetically realized, the reason why the head of the "parasitic chain" in constructions such as (48b) cannot be pronounced still remains to be derived.[9] By contrast, under the sideward movement approach, the parasitic gap in (48b) should be a trace left by sideward movement of the first instance of *which* from the object position of *reading* to the object position of *filed*, as illustrated in (49); once the second instance of *which* binds no variable, the structure violates the ban on vacuous quantification.

(49) *the paper [which$_i$ John [$_{vP}$[$_{vP}$ filed t_i] [without [$_{CP}$ which$_k$ PRO reading t_i]]]]

Analyses that treat parasitic gaps as null resumptive pronouns are subject to a similar criticism. If overt and null resumptive pronouns differ mainly in their set of phonological features, as seems reasonable, a parasitic gap should then freely alternate in being realized as an overt or a null resumptive pronoun. As pointed out by Engdahl (1983), however, there are environments that do not allow overt resumptive pronouns, but do allow parasitic gaps. Thus, the differing behavior of overt and null pronouns in weak crossover configurations such as (50), for instance, poses a potential problem for analyses of parasitic gaps in terms of null resumptive pronouns.

(50) a. Which politician did pictures of upset?
  b. [[which politician]$_i$ did [[pictures of pro$_i$] upset t$_i$]]
  c. *Which politician$_i$ did pictures of him$_i$ upset?
  d. *[[which politician]$_i$ did [[pictures of him$_i$] upset t$_i$]]

I do not intend to claim with the above remarks that it is not possible to assign distinct features to overt and null resumptive pronouns and then obtain different interpretations at LF.[10] All I am saying is that (i) it is not obvious how to do it in a principled fashion and in compliance with minimalist guidelines; and (ii) the analysis I proposed above is exempt from the potential problem of the distribution of overt or null resumptive pronouns, because it derives the lack of phonetic realization of parasitic gaps by treating them as regular traces.

Let us now examine how the analysis of parasitic gaps in terms of sideward movement and linearization of chains that I am proposing here is able to account for the properties listed in (18a–d).

3.4.2 "S-Structure Effects"
Consider (51a–b).

(51) a. Which paper did you file without reading?
  b. *Who filed which paper without reading?

In preminimalist analyses of parasitic gaps, the contrast between these two types of examples was taken to show that a parasitic gap must be licensed at S-Structure (see Chomsky 1982, for instance); otherwise, the parasitic gap in (51b) could be licensed at LF after *which paper* moves in the covert component. Given that the only syntactic levels of representation within the minimalist framework are the interface levels LF and PF, the contrast in (51) presents a challenge for any analysis of parasitic gaps within the Minimalist Program. I will discuss two potential scenarios in which this contrast in (51) should be explained.

Following standard analyses of (51a–b), let us first suppose for the sake of the argument that in the covert component, the *wh*-in situ in (51b) adjoins to the *wh*-phrase in Spec,CP, from which position it should be able to form a chain with the parasitic gap. Such covert movement in no way undermines the analysis of parasitic gaps presented in section 3.4.1. Under the relevant reading, (51b) should be derived by sideward movement of *which paper* from the object of *reading* to the object of *file* (see section 3.4.1), and the (simplified) structure in (52) is the one shipped to the phonological component by Spell-Out.

(52) [who [[filed [which paper]^i] [without PRO reading [which paper]^i]]]

The pair ([which paper]^i, [which paper]^i) in (52) cannot form a chain, because it does not satisfy the c-command condition on Form Chain (see (4b)). As discussed in section 3.4.1, if either instance of the *wh*-phrase in (52) were deleted, the resulting structure could be linearized and eventually converge; however, deletion for purposes of linearization does not involve global computations taking into consideration the whole structure, but is restricted to nontrivial chains (see section 1.6). Thus, after (52) is shipped to the phonological component, each instance of *which paper* is treated as a trivial chain and Chain Reduction is inapplicable. Since neither of the *wh*-copies in (52) is deleted in the phonological component, they induce violations of the asymmetry and irreflexivity conditions on linear order, making it impossible for (52) to be linearized and canceling the derivation. Obviously, this explanation remains intact if Last Resort actually prevents covert movement of the *wh*-in situ in (52) to Spec,CP, as argued by Chomsky (1995, 291). Sideward movement is therefore constrained enough so that it does not incorrectly rule (51b) in.

Let us now assume, in consonance with the discussion in section 3.8.2.3 below, that every movement takes place overtly. The derivation that concerns us here is the one in which the two copies (or their sets of formal features) overtly move to the position where they can check their Case. For the sake of discussion, let us examine the potentially hardest situation, in which the position to which the object of *filed* moves c-commands the other copies in the adjunct clause, as represented in (53) (irrelevant details omitted).

(53)

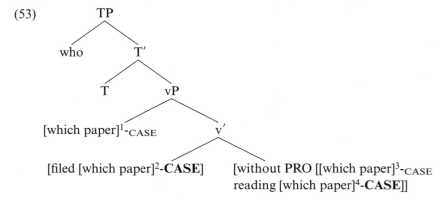

In (53), the only chains that can be formed are $CH_1 = (copy^1, copy^2)$ and $CH_2 = (copy^3, copy^4)$. Crucially, $copy^1$ cannot form a chain with $copy^3$ even if the former c-commands the latter; Last Resort prevents multiple Case checking in a single chain (the Case-feature of $copy^3$ is not accessible to the computational system; see (4c)), and the intervention of PRO, which has a Case-feature, induces a Minimal Link Condition violation (see (4d)). After the structure in (53) is shipped to the phonological component and both CH_1 and CH_2 are reduced, as represented in (54), the links that survive Chain Reduction induce violations of asymmetry and irreflexivity, preventing the structure from being linearized and canceling the derivation.[11] Again, the sentence in (51b) cannot be generated through sideward movement.

(54) [who [[which paper]^1-$_{CASE}$ [$_{vP}$[$_{vP}$ filed [which paper]^2-CASE] [$_{PP}$
      without PRO [[which paper]^3-$_{CASE}$ reading [which paper]^4-
      CASE]]]]]]

While the analyses of the contrast in (51) in terms of resumptive pronouns or traces of null operators must rely on (construction-specific) licensing at a noninterface level (see (18a)), the analysis developed here accounts for (51) on the basis of general considerations regarding linearization in the phonological component. To the extent that the analysis of parasitic gaps in terms of sideward movement and linearization of chains sketched in section 3.4.1 derives "S-Structure effects" without postulating a noninterface level, it gains solid conceptual support from a minimalist perspective. It should be noted again that no new condition or operation was added to the theory. The same reasoning applied to linearization of chains in successive-cyclic movement (see sections 1.5.3.2 and 3.2) derives the "S-Structure effects" on parasitic gap licensing.

3.4.3 Structural Requirements

The licensing of parasitic gaps is also dependent on the structural position of the "real" gap (see Taraldsen 1981 and Engdahl 1983). As shown in (55), a parasitic gap cannot be c-commanded by the licensing gap. (56) further shows that the unacceptability of (55) is not due to some Case incompatibility between the two gaps (see Barss 1986).[12]

(55) a. *I wonder which man called you before you met.
      b. *[I wonder [$_{CP}$[which man]$_i$ [$_{TP}$ t_i [$_{vP}$[$_{vP}$ t_i called you] [$_{PP}$ before
         you met PG$_i$]]]]]

(56) a. I wonder which papers John said were unavailable before
reading.

b. [I wonder [CP[which papers]i [TP John [vP[vP said ti were ti
unavailable] [PP before reading PGi]]]]]]

In this section, I show that the anti-c-command restriction on the distribution of parasitic gaps also follows from the interaction between chain
formation and linearization in the phonological component. Let us start
by examining the derivation of (55a) under the assumption that the temporal PP is adjoined to the light vP shell.[13] Given the simplified derivational step in (57), the computational system may copy *which man* from
K and merge it with L, if there is no other element in the numeration that
could receive the external θ-role of the light verb in L. In such a case,
further computations would then yield the structure in (58), where two
other copies of *which man* are made to check the EPP-feature of T and
the strong *wh*-feature of the embedded interrogative complementizer Q.[14]

(57) a. K = [CP you met [which man]i]
b. L = [vP v [vP called you]]

(58)

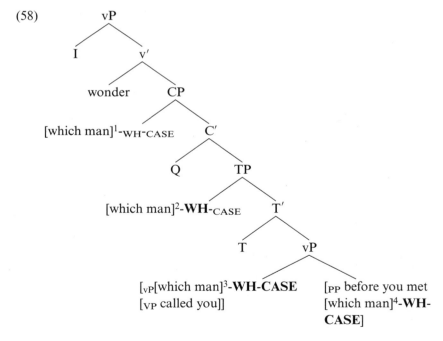

Let us examine which copies of *which man* in (58) can form chains. As in regular *wh*-movement of a subject, $copy^3$ can form a chain with $copy^2$, which in turn can form a chain with $copy^1$; assuming that each of these chains is formed, we obtain the (linked) chain CH = ($copy^1$, $copy^2$, $copy^3$). As for $copy^4$, it cannot form a chain with $copy^3$ because the c-command condition is not satisfied. Furthermore, since $copy^2$ checks Case and there are some nonlocal Case-checking positions and Case-bearing elements between $copy^2$ and $copy^4$, the Minimal Link Condition prevents these two copies from forming a chain. Finally, the Minimal Link Condition also prevents $copy^4$ from forming a chain with $copy^1$, which checks the strong *wh*-feature of Q: $copy^2$ has a *wh*-feature and is closer to $copy^1$ than $copy^4$ is.

If the only nontrivial *wh*-chain formed in (58) is CH = ($copy^1$, $copy^2$, $copy^3$), its optimal reduction in the phonological component will involve the deletion of $copy^2$ and $copy^3$, as shown in (59). The two surviving nondistinct copies of *which man* then induce violations of the asymmetry and irreflexivity conditions on linear order, preventing the structure in (59) from being linearized and canceling the derivation. Therefore, there is no convergent source for the sentence in (55a) under the sideward movement approach to parasitic gap constructions.

(59) [I wonder [$_{CP}$[which man]^1 Q [$_{TP}$[~~which man~~]^2 T [$_{vP}$[$_{vP}$[~~which man~~]^3 [$_{v'}$ v [$_{VP}$ called you]]] [$_{PP}$ before you met [which man]^4]]]]]

For the sake of completeness, suppose we try to circumvent the Minimal Link Condition effect preventing the pair ($copy^2$, $copy^4$) from forming a chain in (58), by placing $copy^4$ in the subject position of the adjunct clause, so that no Case-checking position intervenes between the two copies. Take the case where the adjunct clause is finite, as illustrated in (60) (the irrelevant *wh*-phrases in Spec,vP are omitted).

(60) a. *I wonder which man called you before met you.

b.

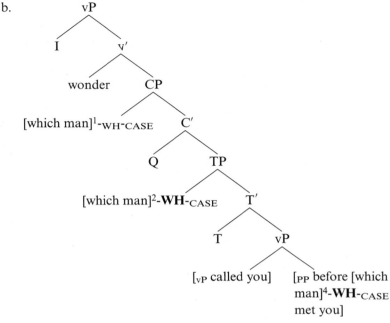

In (60b), the Minimal Link Condition does not prevent copy[4], the "parasitic gap" copy, from forming a chain with copy[2]. However, Last Resort prevents the two copies from forming a chain: when the Case-feature of copy[2] "probes" the structure, the Case-feature of copy[4] has already become inactive after being checked (see (4c)). The presence of multiple *wh*-copies that cannot undergo Chain Reduction will again prevent the structure from being linearized and cancel the derivation.

Consider now the scenario in (61), where the adjunct clause is nonfinite (again, the irrelevant *wh*-phrases in Spec,vP are omitted).

(61) a. I wonder which man called you before meeting you.

b.

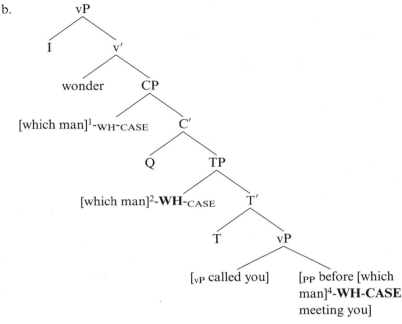

In (61b), the problem of linearization does not arise: Last Resort allows chain formation between copy[2] and copy[4], because the Case-feature of copy[4] has not been checked and is therefore active for the purposes of chain formation. However, the derivation along the lines of (61b) still crashes because the null Case of the nonfinite T head (see Chomsky and Lasnik 1993 and Martin 1996) cannot be checked. The sentence in (61a) is of course acceptable because of the alternative structure in (62), where PRO checks the null Case of the adjunct clause.[15]

(62) [I wonder [CP[which man]i Q [TP[which man]i T [vP[vP called you]
    [PP before [TP PRO meeting you]]]]]]

Let us now return to the acceptable sentence in (56a), repeated in (63). Under the sideward movement approach, the relevant structure of (63) is given in (64), which is derived through sideward movement of *which papers* from within the PP to the thematic position associated with *unavailable* (see section 3.7 for further discussion), followed by successive-cyclic movement to the specifier of the interrogative complementizer.

(63) I wonder which papers John said were unavailable before reading.

(64)

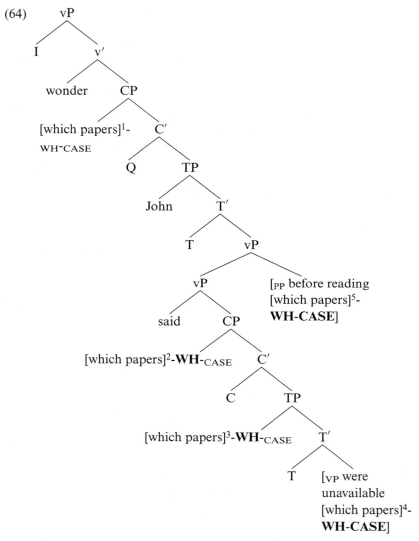

Copy^1 in (64) is the only copy that c-commands copy^5; since there is no intervening element between these two copies that could check the strong *wh*-feature of Q, the chain CH$_1$ = (copy^1, copy^5) is formed. The computational system also forms the chain CH$_2$ = (copy^1, copy^2, copy^3, copy^4). Optimal reduction of CH$_1$ in the phonological component deletes copy^5, yielding the structure in (65), which is then converted into (66) after

CH$_2$ is reduced and its three lower links are deleted. After linearization and remaining operations of the phonological component, the PF output associated with (63) is derived.

(65) [I wonder [$_{CP}$[which papers]^1 Q [$_{TP}$ John [$_{vP}$[$_{vP}$ said [$_{CP}$[which papers]^2 C [$_{TP}$[which papers]^3 T [$_{VP}$ were unavailable [which papers]^4]]]] [$_{PP}$ before reading [which papers]^5]]]]]

(66) [I wonder [$_{CP}$[which papers]^1 Q [$_{TP}$ John [$_{vP}$[$_{vP}$ said [$_{CP}$[which papers]^2 C [$_{TP}$[which papers]^3 T [$_{VP}$ were unavailable [which papers]^4]]]] [$_{PP}$ before reading [which papers]^5]]]]]

The analysis presented above extends straightforwardly to sentences such as (67a) (from Chomsky and Lasnik 1993), which is taken to show that parasitic gaps cannot be licensed by traces of A-movement (see (18c)). Under the relevant reading, (67a) should be derived by sideward movement of *the book* from the object of *reading* to the object of *filed*, yielding the structure in (67b). The copy inside the adjunct clause can form a chain neither with the copy in the object of *filed*, because of lack of c-command, nor with the copy in the matrix subject position, because of the intervention of *my*. Thus, the Copy+Merge theory correctly makes a convergent derivation for (67a) unavailable: copy^3 and the link that survives reduction of the chain CH = (copy^1, copy^2) induce violations of the asymmetry and irreflexivity conditions on linear order, preventing the structure from being linearized.

(67) a. *The book was filed without my reading first.

   b.

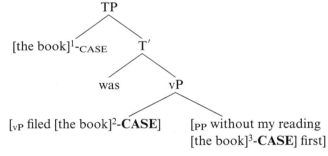

To summarize, the conditions on chain formation (see (4)) prevent a "parasitic gap" from being licensed by a member of an A-chain that c-commands it, yielding a situation where two different chains involving nondistinct copies do not have a link in common. The links of these chains that escape Chain Reduction in the phonological component then induce violations of the asymmetry and irreflexivity conditions on linear order, canceling the derivation because no PF object is formed. The analysis of parasitic gap constructions in terms of sideward movement and linearization of chains thus derives the structural requirements on parasitic gaps (see (18b–c)) without introducing any new principle or operation. The same factors that interact to determine when a "trace" can be deleted are employed to account for why a "parasitic gap" copy cannot be c-commanded by a copy in an A-position.

Competing alternatives, on the other hand, require extra assumptions to account for these structural requirements. Chomsky (1986a, 67), for instance, proposes that the null operator associated with the parasitic gap must be 0-subjacent to the head of the A-chain of the licensing gap, where α is 0-subjacent to β if there are no barriers intervening between them.[16] In turn, in a null resumptive pronoun approach such as Cinque's (1990), the resumptive pronoun in the parasitic gap position must be Ā-bound at S-Structure in order to be licensed; thus, an intervening coindexed gap in an A-position presumably prevents the null resumptive pronoun from being identified.

I will not discuss the adequacy of these proposals in detail. For current purposes, suffice it to note that they either require a considerable enrichment of the theoretical apparatus and/or crucially rely on licensing conditions at S-Structure, an option that is not available within the Minimalist Program.

3.4.4   Island Effects

3.4.4.1   The Puzzles   Perhaps the most interesting questions posed by parasitic gap constructions are related to island effects, especially violations of Huang's (1982) Condition on Extraction Domain (CED), since other island violations may be captured by the Minimal Link Condition or Subjacency. If the copy inside the adjunct clause in (68b) and the copy inside the subject in (69b), for instance, can form a chain with the copy in Spec,CP, why does regular extraction out of an adjunct or a subject yield unacceptable sentences, as illustrated in (70) and (71), respectively?

(68) a. Which paper did you file without reading?
     b. [$_{CP}$[which paper]^i did+Q [$_{TP}$ you [$_{vP}$[$_{vP}$ file [which paper]^i]
        [$_{PP}$ without PRO reading [which paper]^i]]]]

(69) a. Which politician did pictures of upset?

 b. [CP[which politician]^i did+Q [IP[pictures of [which politician]^i]
 upset [which politician]^i]]]

(70) a. *Which book did you review this paper without reading?

 b. [CP[which book]^i did+Q [TP you [vP[vP review this paper]
 [PP without reading [which book]^i]]]]

(71) a. *Which politician did pictures of upset the voters?

 b. [CP[which politician]^i did+Q [[pictures of [which politician]^i]
 upset the voters]]

From a representational point of view, there seems to be no way to capture the distinction between the *wh*-chain involving the copies inside the adjunct and the subject in (68b) and (69b), on the one hand, and the corresponding *wh*-chain in (70b) and (71b), on the other, without additional provisos regarding the "parasitic" chain in (68b) and (69b).[17] Brody (1995, 51), for instance, who develops a representational minimalist approach to parasitic chains, assumes that only "primary" chains are subject to Subjacency.[18]

Another puzzle presented by parasitic gap constructions is that island effects do indeed show up, if the parasitic gap is further embedded in another (CED) island, as illustrated in (72) and (73) (see Kayne 1983, 1984, Contreras 1984, and Chomsky 1986a, among others).

(72) a. *Which book did you borrow after leaving the bookstore
 without finding?

 b. [CP[which book]^i did+Q [TP you [vP[vPborrow [which book]^i]
 [PP after [CP PRO [vP[vP leaving the bookstore] [PP without PRO
 finding [which book]^i]]]]]]]

(73) a. *Which politician did you criticize before pictures of upset the
 voters?

 b. [CP[which politician]^i did+Q [TP you [vP[vPcriticize [which
 politician]^i] [PP before [CP[pictures of [which politician]^i] upset
 the voters]]]]]

Details aside, the null operator analysis of parasitic gaps attributes the contrast between (68a) and (72a) to the barriers crossed by the null operator: it crosses no islands in the derivation in (68a), but it crosses an adjunct island in the derivation of (72a), as shown in (74) and (75).

(74) [CP[which paper]i did+Q [TP you [vP[vP file ti] [PP Oj without PRO reading tj]]]]]

(75) [CP[which book]i did+Q [TP you [vP[vPborrow ti] [PP Oj after [CP PRO [vP[vP leaving the bookstore] [PP without PRO finding tj]]]]]]]

Although the null operator analysis correctly accounts for the contrast between (68a) and (72a), it faces serious difficulties in accounting for parasitic gaps inside subjects such as (69a) (see Chomsky 1986a, 66). In the *Barriers* system, for instance, there is no plausible landing site for the null operator of the structure in (76) that would place it in a position where it would be 0-subjacent to t_i, the head of the A-chain associated with *which politician*.

(76) [CP[which politician]i did+Q [TP[pictures of O] upset ti]]

The null resumptive pronoun approach is not exempt from problems either. In order to account for island effects, Cinque (1990, sec. 3.3.4) proposes (i) that the null resumptive pronoun moves at LF either by itself (see also Haïk 1985) or within a larger phrase under pied-piping, and (ii) that this movement is subject to (a version of) the Connectedness Condition (see Kayne 1984). For reasons internal to his system, LF movement of the null resumptive pronoun or the subject NP in (77) should, however, yield an ill-formed result, contrary to fact.

(77) [CP[which politician]i did+Q [IP[NP pictures of proi] upset ti]]

Cinque (1990, 149) then proposes that neither movement takes place in this kind of parasitic gap construction; rather, the resumptive pronoun is licensed through connectedness by the real gap on its right. If this is so, one wonders why such licensing cannot be extended to the overt pronoun in (78), which, as pointed out earlier, does display a weak crossover effect.

(78) *[[which politician]i did pictures of himi upset ti]

This brief discussion shows that neither the null operator nor the null resumptive pronoun approach successfully treats the island effects found in both "adjunct" and "subject" parasitic gap constructions. I argue in the next section that a uniform account of (68)–(73) can indeed be achieved if the Copy+Merge theory of movement is viewed as part of a derivational model of syntax. The different pattern of acceptability between (68)–(69), on the one hand, and (70)–(73), on the other, will then be seen to follow from their different derivational histories.

3.4.4.2 A Derivational Approach to Island Effects In a derivational system that does not postulate D-Structure and builds syntactic objects in the course of the derivation, the relations 'specifier of' and 'adjunct of' are also established as the derivation proceeds. In other words, a given syntactic object α will become a specifier or an adjunct of β only after α merges with the relevant projection of β. This derivational view leads us to expect that whatever is responsible for the ban on extraction out of specifiers and adjuncts (the CED), it should apply only after the derivational step D, where the relevant relation is established in the derivation. Prior to D, the would-be specifier or adjunct should be completely transparent for extraction. This is the key idea that allows a uniform account of the data discussed in section 3.4.4.1 (see Hornstein 1999, 2001, Nunes and Uriagereka 2000, and Nunes 2001 for discussion).

Let us consider how this idea is explored in Nunes and Uriagereka's (2000) analysis of CED effects. Following Uriagereka's (1999) Multiple Spell-Out system, Nunes and Uriagereka assume that Kayne's (1994) LCA should be simplified along the lines in (79) (without the recursive step of Kayne's original definition).

(79) *Linear Correspondence Axiom*
      A lexical item α precedes a lexical item β iff α asymmetrically
      c-commands β.

According to (79), the head h in (80) should precede the lexical items of its complement WP, because it asymmetrically c-commands them. However, since h does not enter into an asymmetric c-command relation with the lexical items within its specifier YP or the adjunct ZP, no order between h and these lexical items should obtain, contrary to fact. In order to circumvent this linearization problem, Uriagereka (1999) then proposes that Spell-Out independently applies to YP and ZP before they are merged with a projection of h. After YP and ZP are spelled out, they behave like lexical items for the purposes of syntactic computation (a "giant compound" in Uriagereka's terms) and their lexical items are linearized inside their projection in the phonological component.[19] The order between h and the lexical elements of YP and ZP will then be indirectly determined by the order established between h and the wordlike elements YP and ZP.

(80)

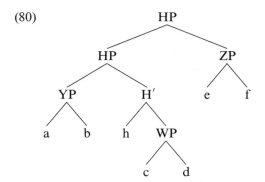

Technical details aside, the gist of Nunes and Uriagereka's proposal is that once a given constituent is spelled out, its terms cannot be copied and consequently cannot undergo movement. The CED effects illustrated by the sentences in (70a) and (71a), repeated in (81), thus receive a straightforward explanation. Assuming that Merge only proceeds cyclically (see section 3.8 for discussion), the relevant derivational steps immediately preceding *wh*-movement in these sentences should be the ones illustrated in (82) and (83), respectively, where the outlined characters represent spelled-out material.

(81) a. *Which book did you review this paper without reading?
     b. *Which politician did pictures of upset the voters?

(82)

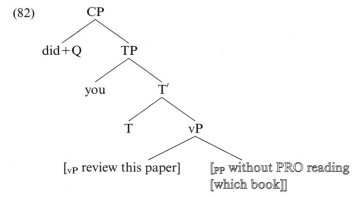

(83)

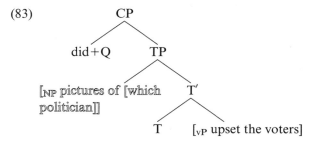

In (82) and (83), the only elements that can check the strong *wh*-feature of the interrogative complementizer Q are *which book* and *which politician*, respectively. However, these phrases have become inaccessible for copying after the adjunct PP in (82) and the subject NP in (83) were spelled out. Hence, the derivation crashes and there is no way to derive the sentences in (81), if derivations unfold in a strictly cyclic fashion (see section 3.8 for further discussion). To put it in general terms, CED effects arise because after a subject or an adjunct is spelled out, its parts behave similarly to bound morphemes: they can be interpreted, but they cannot be copied (moved).

Consider now the derivation of the parasitic gap constructions in (68a) and (69a), repeated in (84), whose relevant derivational steps are repeated in (85) and (86).

(84) a. Which paper did you file without reading?
      b. Which politician did pictures of upset?

(85) a. $K = [_{CP} C [_{TP} PRO_j [_{T'} T [_{vP} t_j [_{v'} v [_{VP} \text{reading} [\text{which paper}]^i]]]]]]$
      b. $L = [_{VP} \text{file} [\text{which paper}]^i]$

(86) a. $M = [\text{pictures of} [\text{which politician}]^i]$
      b. $N = [\text{upset} [\text{which politician}]^i]$

Movement of *which paper* from K to L in (85) and of *which politician* from M to N in (86) takes place while K and M are still independent syntactic objects and their constituents can in principle be copied and merge with other syntactic objects. Sideward movement of *which paper* in (85) and *which politician* in (86) are therefore licit operations. After K and M are spelled out and the derivational steps in (87) and (88) are reached, the *wh*-copy inside the adjunct or the subject patterns like the *wh*-elements in (82) and (83) in being unable to undergo copying to check the strong *wh*-feature of Q.

(87)

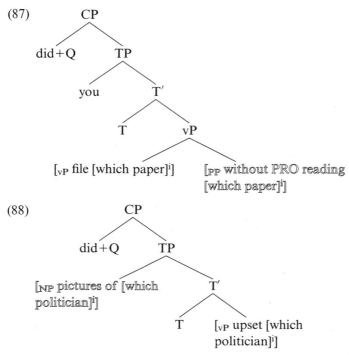

(88)

The difference between (82) and (83), on the one hand, and (87) and (88), on the other, is that the latter contains an additional *wh*-element in the object position of the (main) verb that can perfectly well be copied and check the strong *wh*-feature of Q, as shown in (89) and (90). After the two *wh*-chains of each structure undergo Chain Reduction, the sentences in (84) are derived, as seen in section 3.4.1.

(89) [CP[which paper]^i-WH did+Q [TP you [vP[vP file [which paper]^i-**WH**] [PP without PRO reading [which paper]^i-WH]]]]

(90) [CP[which politician]^i-WH did+Q [IP[pictures of [which politician]^i-WH] upset [which politician]^i-**WH**]]

To put it in general terms, the lack of CED effects in acceptable parasitic gap constructions like the ones in (84) follows from the fact that Last Resort may license sideward movement from within a complex category XP, before XP is spelled out and its constituents become inaccessible to the Copy operation. In other words, sideward movement provides an escape hatch for extraction out of CED islands.[20]

However, such an escape hatch is unavailable for the unacceptable parasitic gap constructions in (72a) and (73a), repeated in (91). At the derivational steps in (92) and (93), where the thematic requirements of *borrow* and *criticize* would license sideward movement of *which book* and *which politician*, respectively, the adjunct PP in K and the subject in M have already been spelled out and their constituents cannot be copied. Thus, from this derivational perspective, the parasitic gap constructions in (91) simply cannot be generated.[21]

(91) a. *Which book did you borrow after leaving the bookstore without finding?
     b. *Which politician did you criticize before pictures of upset the voters?

(92) a. K = [$_{CP}$ PRO [$_{vP}$[$_{vP}$ leaving the bookstore] [$_{PP}$ without PRO finding [which book]^i]]]
     b. L = borrow

(93) a. M = [$_{CP}$ C [$_{TP}$[$_{NP}$ pictures of [which politician]] [$_{T'}$ T [$_{vP}$ upset the voters]]]]
     b. N = criticize

To sum up, the derivational approach explored here accounts for the "selective" sensitivity of parasitic gap constructions with respect to CED effects by relying on the accessibility of the relevant syntactic objects at specific derivational steps. Assuming that derivations proceed in a strictly cyclic fashion (see section 3.8 for detailed discussion), the contrast between unacceptable constructions involving "extraction" from within an adjunct or a specifier such as (81) and (91) and parasitic gap constructions such as (84) follows from their different derivational histories. In the unacceptable cases, the adjunct and the subject containing the *wh*-element have already been spelled out and their constituents are no longer available for copying at the derivational step where Last Resort would license the required copying. In the acceptable parasitic gap constructions, on the other hand, a legitimate instance of copying takes place before the relevant adjunct and subject are spelled out (see (85)–(88)). The Copy+ Merge theory therefore requires no special provisos to account for the "selective" island effects found in parasitic gap constructions. To the extent that it succeeds, this analysis also provides a compelling argument for derivations themselves, for it is not immediately obvious how a representational alternative can fare as well, without imposing restrictions on "parasitic" chains (see Hornstein 1999, 2001 and section 3.9 below for further discussion).

Independent evidence for the approach developed above is provided by Etxepare's (1999) analysis of extraction from conditionals in Spanish. Assuming Cattell's (1978) distinction between stance and nonstance predicates (predicates that do and do not imply the existence of a claim to truth in their finite complement), Etxepare shows that these two classes of predicates behave differently with respect to several properties. For instance, only stance verbs such as *afirmar* 'claim', *asegurar* 'assert', *piensar* 'think', *creer* 'believe', or *decir* 'say' may allow a null complementizer in certain contexts, as illustrated in (94).

(94) *Spanish* (from Etxepare 1999)
    a. *los paquetes que Correos contó/mencionó/interpretó/omitió sus
       empleados enviaron el martes
       'the parcels that the Post Office told/mentioned/interpreted/
       omitted its employees sent on Tuesday'
    b. los paquetes que Correos afirma/asegura/piensa/cree/dice sus
       empleados enviaron el martes
       'the parcels that the Post Office claims/asserts/thinks/believes/
       says its employees sent on Tuesday'

On the basis of these differences, Etxepare argues that the complement of stance verbs involves an extra layer of structure between CP and TP, which he calls FP. What is relevant for our purposes here is that stance and nonstance predicates also pattern differently with respect to extraction in contexts such as the one shown in (95).

(95) *Spanish* (from Etxepare 1999)
    a. *[qué libro]$_i$ mencionaste que [si tu madre ve t$_i$] se armará un
       cirio
       '[Which book]$_i$ did you mention that [if your mother sees t$_i$] she
       will get angry?'
    b. [qué libro]$_i$ dijiste que [si tu madre ve t$_i$] se armará un cirio
       '[Which book]$_i$ did you say that [if your mother sees t$_i$] she will
       get angry?'

The acceptability of (95b) is very surprising, given the standard assumption that conditional clauses are adjunct islands, as (95a) indeed illustrates. Etxepare accounts for this contrast by extending the analysis of parasitic gaps in Nunes 1995 to extractions such as (95b). According to him, the derivation of the sentence in (96), for instance, proceeds along the lines of (97)–(99) (English words are used for purposes of exposition).

(96) *Spanish* (from Etxepare 1999)
[qué libro]$_i$ crees que [si Ricardo lee t$_i$ alguna vez] abandonará la linguística de inmediato
'[Which book]$_i$ do you believe that [if Ricardo ever reads t$_i$] he will give up linguistics immediately?'

(97) a. K = [$_{CP}$ if Ricardo ever reads [which book]]
b. L = [$_{FP}$ F [$_{TP}$ he will give up linguistics immediately]]

(98) a. K = [$_{CP}$ if Ricardo ever reads [which book]^i]
b. M = [$_{FP}$[which book]^i [$_{F'}$ F [$_{TP}$ he will give up linguistics immediately]]]

(99)

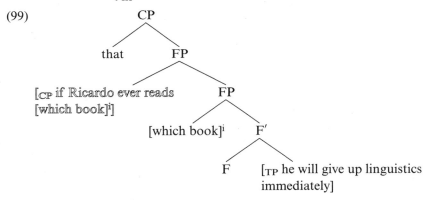

Given the two independent syntactic objects K and L in (97), the computational system copies *which book* from K and merges it with L (an instance of sideward movement) to check a strong feature of F, yielding M in (98). Crucially, at this point of the derivation, K is transparent for movement because it has not yet adjoined to FP (or under Nunes and Uriagereka's (2000) approach, it has not been spelled out yet). After the conditional clause adjoins to FP in (99), it becomes an island and its terms cannot be copied. The copy of *which book* in Spec,FP is, however, available for the Copy operation and may undergo regular successive-cyclic *wh*-movement through the embedded Spec,CP, because the copy inside the conditional clause does not intervene. Further computations then yield the structure in (100). The linked chains CH$_1$ = (copy^1, copy^2, copy^3) and CH$_2$ = (copy^1, copy^2, copy^4) are formed, and their optimal reduction in the phonological component involves the deletion of the lower copies, as shown in (101).

(100)

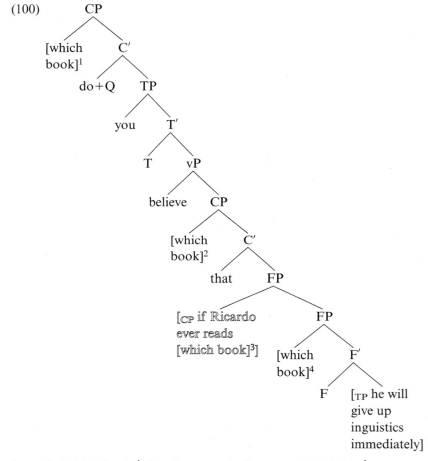

(101) [CP[which book]¹ do+Q [TP you believe [CP~~[which book]²~~ that
[FP[CP if Ricardo ever reads ~~[which book]³~~] [FP~~[which book]⁴~~ F
[TP he will give up linguistics immediately]]]]]]

By contrast, once the complement of nonstance predicates does not involve FP, the derivation of sentences analogous to (96), like (95a), should involve the step abstractly represented in (102), where the conditional clause is adjoined to TP and the *wh*-element is not available for the Copy operation at the point where the intermediate C is introduced into the structure; hence the island effect observed in sentences such as (95a).

(102)

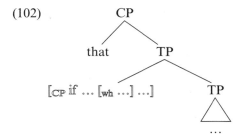

Etxepare's analysis therefore provides compelling evidence not only for sideward movement itself, but also for a derivational approach to islandhood.

3.5 Across-the-Board Extraction

3.5.1 *Wh*-Phrases and Auxiliaries

Let us now consider constructions involving across-the-board (ATB) extraction (see Ross 1967, Williams 1978, and Goodall 1987, among others) such as the one illustrated in (103).

(103) a. Which paper did John file and Mary read?
b. [[which paper]$_i$ did$_j$ John t$_j$ file t$_i$ and Mary t$_j$ read t$_i$]

As originally pointed out by Ross (1967), parasitic gap and ATB constructions are similar in that they appear to involve extraction of the same element from more than one position. This similarity has led researchers to attempt to assimilate one of the two to the other. For example, Haïk (1985) and Williams (1990) have proposed that parasitic gap constructions are to be treated in terms of ATB extraction. Munn (1993) and Postal (1993) have pointed out several problems for this approach, among which are the fact that it requires every structure that allows a parasitic gap to be analyzed as optionally coordinative, and the fact that it crucially relies on the construction-specific ATB operation.

The opposite approach is taken by Munn (1993), who proposes that ATB constructions involve movement of a null operator, as in Chomsky's (1986a) analysis of parasitic gap constructions. This approach has the conceptual advantage of not resorting to the ATB formalism. However, although the proposal is plausible with respect to ATB movement of a *wh*-phrase, ATB extraction of auxiliaries as in (103) or main verbs (see section 3.5.2) does not appear to be amenable to such an approach.

Below, I provide a uniform account of ATB extraction in terms of sideward movement and linearization of chains, with no need to resort to null operators. I will actually show that, despite their apparent differences, ATB and standard movement can receive a uniform treatment under the Copy+Merge theory of movement explored here.

I assume that coordination structures involve hierarchical rather than flat structures and that coordinating conjunctions head their own phrases (see Munn 1987 for an early proposal, among many others). Under this view, *and* in (103b) takes a TP as its complement and another TP as its specifier. Assuming that (104) is the initial numeration underlying (103), the relevant details of the derivation are as follows. At some given derivational step, the initial numeration N has changed to N' in (105a) and the syntactic objects K and L have been formed. Since merger of *file* with either K or any other syntactic object formed from the lexical items still to be selected from the current numeration does not yield a convergent derivation, the computational system makes a copy of the term *which paper* in K and merges it with *file* (an instance of sideward movement), and further applications of Select and Merge form the object M in (106).

(104) $N = \{which_1, paper_1, did_1, Q_1, John_1, v_2, file_1, and_1, Mary_1, read_1\}$

(105) a. $N' = \{which_0, paper_0, did_0, Q_1, John_1, v_1, file_0, and_1, Mary_0, read_0\}$
     b. $K = [_{TP} \text{ did } [_{vP} \text{ Mary v } [_{VP} \text{ read [which paper]]]]}$
     c. $L = file$

(106) a. $K = [_{TP} \text{ did } [_{vP} \text{ Mary v } [_{VP} \text{ read [which paper]}^i]]]$
     b. $M = [_{vP} \text{ John v } [_{VP} \text{ file [which paper]}^i]]$

Given that the only T head available in the initial numeration (namely, *did*) has already been used, the computational system makes a copy of *did* and merges it with M (another instance of sideward movement), yielding O in (107) (see section 3.6 for further discussion).

(107) a. $K = [_{TP} \text{ did}^k [_{vP} \text{ Mary v } [_{VP} \text{ read [which paper]}^i]]]$
     b. $O = [_{TP} \text{ did}^k [_{vP} \text{ John v } [_{VP} \text{ file [which paper]}^i]]]$

The subjects of both K and O in (107) move to their respective Spec,TPs to check the strong feature of each instance of *did*, and the coordinating head *and* merges with one of the resulting structures, forming the (simplified) objects P and R in (108). P and R then merge, and the resulting structure in turn merges with the interrogative complementizer Q, exhausting the numeration and yielding the structure in (109).

(108) a. P = [$_{andP}$ and [$_{TP}$ Mary did^k read [which paper]^i]]
      b. R = [$_{TP}$ John did^k file [which paper]^i]

(109) [$_{CP}$ Q [$_{andP}$ [$_{TP}$ John did^k file [which paper]^i] [$_{and'}$ and [$_{TP}$ Mary did^k read [which paper]^i]]]]

Since the numeration has been exhausted and the complementizer Q in (109) has strong features to be checked, the computational system makes a copy of *did* and adjoins it to Q (see section 3.8.2.2 for further discussion), and then makes another copy of *which paper* and merges it with the resulting structure, yielding the object in (110).

(110)

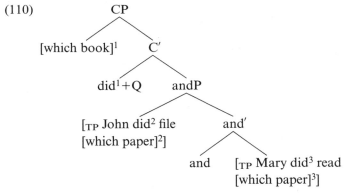

If (110) is spelled out before the *wh*- and T-chains are formed, the nondistinct copies of *which paper* and *did* will induce violations of the asymmetry and irreflexivity conditions on linear order, canceling the derivation. The computational system must therefore form the chains CH$_1$ = ([which paper]^1, [which paper]^2), CH$_2$ = ([which paper]^1, [which paper]^3), CH$_3$ = (did^1, did^2), and CH$_4$ = (did^1, did^3). Each of these chains is then reduced in the phonological component, resulting in the structure in (111), and further computations of the phonological component finally yield the PF output associated with the sentence in (103a).

(111) [$_{CP}$[which paper]^1 did^1+Q [$_{andP}$[$_{TP}$ John ~~did^2~~ file ~~[which paper]^2~~] [$_{and'}$ and [$_{TP}$ Mary ~~did^3~~ read ~~[which paper]^3~~]]]]

It should be clear that the analysis of ATB constructions in terms of sideward movement and linearization of chains that I am proposing is not meant to account for all the properties of extraction out of conjuncts, such as the unacceptability resulting from extraction out of a single conjunct (for relevant discussion, see Ross 1967, Williams 1978, Lakoff 1986, Munn 1993, and Postal 1998, among others). All I am proposing is that the core property of ATB constructions, namely, that a given element appears to be moving from more than one site, is captured very naturally under the Copy+Merge theory of movement, which takes Move to be the description of the interaction among the operations Copy, Merge, Form Chain, and Chain Reduction. To the extent that this analysis succeeds, it allows ATB extraction to be treated as standard cyclic movement (see section 3.8 for further discussion) and to dispense with the ATB formalism.

3.5.2 Main Verbs

In this section, we will see how the sideward analysis discussed above can be extended to ATB movement of verbs out of VP shells (see Larson 1988), with interesting empirical consequences. Consider the Portuguese sentences in (112), for instance.

(112) *Portuguese*
> a. Eu conversei com o João e   com a   Maria.
>   I   talked   with the João and with the Maria
>   'I talked to João and to Maria.'
> b. Eu conversei com o João e   a   Maria.
>   I   talked   with the João and the Maria
>   'I talked to João and Maria.'

Both sentences in (112) may have an interpretation under which there is a single talking event involving three participants. At first sight, the only difference between them seems to be the kind of constituents that are coordinated: PPs in (112a) and DPs in (112b). However, these sentences show an interesting contrast. (112a) also admits a reading under which there are two events with two participants each (the subject and one of the objects), but (112b) does not.[22] This is clear when adverbial expressions modify each of the events, as shown in (113).[23]

(113) a. Eu conversei com o João sábado e com a Maria domingo.
>   'I talked to João on Saturday and to Maria on Sunday.'
>   b. *Eu conversei com o João sábado e a Maria domingo.
>   'I talked to João on Saturday and Maria on Sunday.'

I propose that the ambiguity of (112a) is due to the fact that it may result from two possible convergent derivations starting from the (simplified) initial numeration N given in (114) (English words are used for the sake of exposition).

(114) $N = \{I_1, v_1, talked_1, to_2, João_1, and_1, Maria_1\}$

Under the more obvious derivation, the computational system selects and merges the lexical items of N, yielding the structure in (115), which involves coordination of PPs and movement of *talked* to check the strong feature of the light verb. The verb chain then undergoes Chain Reduction and the lower copy is deleted, as shown in (116).

(115)

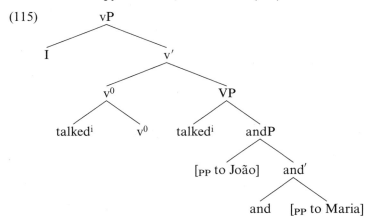

(116) $[_{vP}$ I $[_{v'}$ talked^i+v $[_{VP}$ ~~talked^i~~ $[_{andP}[_{PP}$ to João] $[_{and'}$ and $[_{PP}$ to Maria]]]]]]

Suppose, on the other hand, that the computational system reduces the numeration N in (114) to N′ in (117a) and builds the syntactic objects K and L. Assuming that the general requirement that conjuncts be of the same type is a convergence condition (see section 3.6 for further discussion), there is no convergent continuation for the derivational step in (117), if K merges with L.

(117) a. $N' = \{I_1, v_1, talked_0, to_0, João_0, and_0, Maria_0\}$
　　　b. $K = [_{andP}$ and $[_{VP}$ talked $[_{PP}$ to Maria]]]
　　　c. $L = [_{PP}$ to João]

A convergent result can be obtained, however, if the main verb is copied from K and merges with L (an instance of sideward movement), as illustrated in (118), and the resulting VP merges with K, as shown in (119).

(118) a. K = [$_{andP}$ and [$_{VP}$ talked^i [$_{PP}$ to Maria]]]
      b. M = [$_{VP}$ talked^i [$_{PP}$ to João]]

(119) P = [$_{andP}$[$_{VP}$ talked^i to João] [$_{and'}$ and [$_{VP}$ talked^i to Maria]]]

The next steps of this derivation then involve selection and merger of *I* and the light verb and movement of *talked* to check the strong V-feature of the light verb, yielding the structure in (120).

(120)

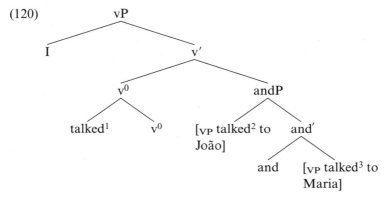

The computational system then forms the chains CH$_1$ = (talked^1, talked^2) and CH$_2$ = (talked^1, talked^3), whose optimal reduction in the phonological component involves the deletion of the lower copies, as shown in (121), yielding what at the surface seems to be a coordination of PPs (see (112a)).

(121) [$_{vP}$[$_{v^0}$ talked^1 [$_{v^0}$ v]] [$_{andP}$[$_{VP}$ ~~talked^2~~ to João] [$_{and'}$ and [$_{VP}$ ~~talked^3~~ to Maria]]]]

By contrast, the sentence in (112b), whose simplified initial derivation is given in (122) (again, English words are used for the sake of exposition), can only result from a derivation involving coordination of DPs, as represented in (123).

(122) N = {I$_1$, v$_1$, talked$_1$, to$_1$, João$_1$, and$_1$, Maria$_1$}

(123)

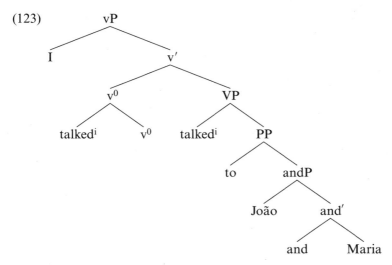

Consider the derivational step in (124), for instance, where the computational system reduces N in (122) to N′ in (124a) and builds K and L.

(124) a. $N' = \{I_1, v_1, \text{talked}_0, \text{to}_0, \text{João}_0, \text{and}_0, \text{Maria}_0\}$
       b. $K = [_{\text{andP}} \text{ and } [_{\text{VP}} \text{ talked } [_{\text{PP}} \text{ to Maria}]]]$
       c. $L = \text{João}$

Merger of K and L does not lead to a convergent result because they are not of the same type. In the case of (112a), this incompatibility was remedied by sideward movement of the verb. However, if that happens in a continuation of (124) and the structure in (125) ends up being built, the derivation crashes because *João* cannot check its Case.

(125)

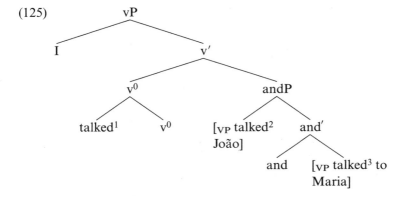

Suppose that we attempt to circumvent this Case problem by allowing sideward movement of both the verb and the preposition in (124), as shown in (126), finally yielding the structure in (127).

(126) a. K = [$_{andP}$ and [$_{VP}$ talked^i [$_{PP}$ to^k Maria]]]
      b. M = [$_{VP}$ talked^i to^k João]

(127)

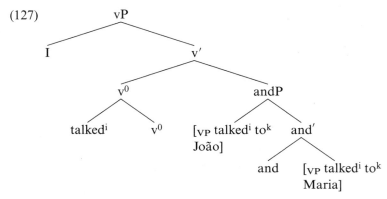

The problem with the structure in (127) is that the two copies of the preposition cannot form a chain and, therefore, cannot undergo Chain Reduction. These nondistinct copies will then prevent the linearization of the structure, canceling the derivation. In other words, (127) is excluded on the basis of the same reasoning used to account for "S-Structure" effects illustrated in (128) (see discussion in section 3.4.2).

(128) a. *Who filed which paper without reading?
      b. [who [[filed [which paper]^i] [without PRO reading [which paper]^i]]]

The contrast in (113) now follows straightforwardly: (113a) can have a derivation along the lines of (115)–(116), with coordination of PPs and a single verb chain, or a derivation along the lines of (117)–(121), with sideward movement of the verb yielding two verb chains, whereas (113b) can only be derived along the lines of (123), with a single verb chain. Under the plausible assumption that each verb chain is to be associated with an event, we can account for the fact that only (112a) and (113a) allow a two-event reading and each event can be independently modified (see Ximenes 2002 for relevant discussion).

To conclude, to the extent that the sideward movement analysis of ATB extraction presented above is able to capture the different readings in (112) without enriching the theoretical apparatus, the Copy+Merge theory of movement gains further conceptual and empirical support.[24]

3.6 Differences between Parasitic Gap and Across-the-Board Extraction Constructions

As seen in sections 3.4 and 3.5, the Copy+Merge theory provides a uniform account of parasitic gap and ATB extraction constructions by allowing constrained instances of sideward movement. However, Postal (1993) has extensively documented restrictions that show up in parasitic gap but not in ATB constructions, which may be taken as an argument against treating the two constructions alike. In this section, I review Hornstein and Nunes's (2002) general approach to the differences between these constructions, which shows that the sideward movement analysis can indeed be maintained.

The data in (129) and (130) illustrate Postal's (1993) observation that parasitic gaps are more restricted than ATB gaps: parasitic gaps cannot be licensed by AdvPs, APs, PPs, nonreferential NPs, or auxiliaries, whereas any of these categories can undergo ATB extraction.[25,26]

(129) a. *how_i did Deborah cook the pork e_i after cooking the chicken e_i
   b. *[how sick]$_i$ did John look e_i without actually feeling e_i
   c. *this is a topic [about which]$_i$ you should think e_i before talking e_i
   d. *[how many weeks]$_i$ did he spend e_i in Berlin without wanting to spend e_i in London
   e. *did_i John e_i call Mary after Paul e_i call Sue

(130) a. how_i did Deborah cook the pork e_i and Jane cook the chicken e_i
   b. [how sick]$_i$ did John look e_i and Betty say he actually felt e_i
   c. this is a topic [about which]$_i$ you should think e_i and I should talk e_i
   d. [how many weeks]$_i$ did you spend e_i in Berlin but want to spend e_i in London
   e. did_i John e_i call Mary and Paul e_i call Sue

If parasitic gap and ATB constructions are both derived along the lines presented in sections 3.4 and 3.5, the question that arises is why sideward movement yields acceptable results in (130), but not in (129). Let us start the discussion by comparing the instance of sideward movement in (132), which is required to yield the acceptable parasitic gap construction in (131), with the instance of sideward movement in (133), which would be required in the derivation of the unacceptable parasitic gap construction in (129a).

(131) Which paper did John file after reading?

(132) a. K = [$_{CP}$ C PRO reading [which paper]^i]
      b. L = [$_{VP}$ file [which paper]^i]

(133) a. K = [after PRO cooking the chicken how^i]
      b. L = [[cook the pork] how^i]

Recall that under the assumption that movement into θ-positions is licensed by Last Resort (see Bošković 1994, Lasnik 1995, Bošković and Takahashi 1998, Hornstein 1999, 2001, Ferreira 2000a,b, and Rodrigues 2000, 2002, among others), sideward movement of *which book* in (132) from K to L is licensed by the θ-requirements of *file* (see section 3.4.1). Given that sideward movement of *how* in (133) is not triggered by either formal feature checking or a θ-relation (*how* is an adjunct in L), Hornstein and Nunes (2002) argue that this movement is not motivated and therefore the parasitic gap construction in (129a) cannot be generated.

With this in mind, let us now consider the relevant instances of sideward movement required to derive the parasitic gap constructions in (129b–d), respectively represented in (134)–(136).

(134) a. K = [without PRO actually feeling [how sick]^i]
      b. L = [look [how sick]^i]

(135) a. K = [before PRO talking [about which]^i]
      b. L = [think [about which]^i]

(136) a. K = [without PRO wanting to PRO spend [how many weeks]^i
         in London]
      b. L = [spend [how many weeks]^i]

At first sight, one could expect that the instances of sideward movement in (134)–(136) should be able to satisfy Last Resort, since the verbs of L select the moved elements. However, as extensively discussed in the literature on the Empty Category Principle (see Cinque 1990, for instance), the moved elements in (134)–(136), although selected, actually behave like adjuncts, thus being unable to move across a weak island, for instance, as illustrated in (137).[27]

(137) a. *how$_i$ do you wonder whether Jane cooked the chicken e$_i$
      b. *[how sick]$_i$ do you wonder whether John felt e$_i$
      c. *this is a topic [about which]$_i$ I wonder whether you want to talk e$_i$
      d. *[how many weeks]$_i$ do you wonder whether he spent e$_i$ in Berlin

Taking the sentences in (137) as evidence that the verbs of L in (134)–(136) do not assign a θ-role to the AP, the PP, and the nonreferential NP with which they merge, Hornstein and Nunes argue that the copying of these elements does not comply with Last Resort. The intuition behind their approach is that although either selection or modification is sufficient to license Merge, Copy can be licensed by Last Resort only under formal feature checking or θ-role assignment. The derivations that could generate the parasitic gap constructions in (129b–d) are therefore canceled at the derivational stages represented in (134)–(136). As Hornstein and Nunes observe, the paradigm in (138) ((138a–b) are from Postal 1993), whose sentences are minimally different, receives a straightforward account under this approach: sideward movement of *what city* in (138a) is licensed by the θ-role assignment of the preposition *in* in the matrix clause, but no θ-relation or feature checking licenses sideward movement of *where* in (138b) or *in what city* in (138c).

(138) a. [what city]$_i$ did Elaine work in e$_i$ without ever living in e$_i$
      b. *where$_i$ did Elaine work e$_i$ without ever living e$_i$
      c. *[in what city]$_i$ did Elaine work e$_i$ without ever living e$_i$

Consider now the sideward movement of the auxiliary in (139), which would be necessary to derive the parasitic construction in (129e).

(139) a. K = [after Paul did^i call Sue]
      b. L = [did^i [$_{VP}$ John call Mary]]

Leaving aside the issue of whether or not the selectional relation between the auxiliary and VP in (139b) involves some sort of θ-role, it is arguably the case that T selects VP and not the opposite. Hornstein and Nunes then argue that sideward movement of *did* in (139) does not satisfy Last Resort because the selectional requirements of *did* were already satisfied within K; hence, the parasitic gap construction in (129e) cannot be generated.

As for the corresponding acceptable ATB extraction constructions in (130a–e), Hornstein and Nunes observe that coordinate structures are independently subject to a Parallelism Requirement (see Chomsky and Lasnik 1993, Chomsky 1995, and Fox 1995 for relevant discussion), which in the specific case of movement operations demands that movement apply to all the conjuncts if it applies to any (Ross's (1967) Coordinate Structure Constraint). Hornstein and Nunes then propose that the Parallelism Requirement is best interpreted as a bare output condition that applies to coordinates, licensing movement operations that would otherwise violate Last Resort.

The two instances of sideward movement shown in (141), which are required in the derivation of the ATB construction in (130a), repeated in (140), for instance, do not satisfy Last Resort, as discussed in the case of analogous parasitic gap constructions. Sideward movement of *how* is licensed by the Parallelism Requirement, however, in that it renders the two VPs parallel, by providing the VP of (141b) with a variable playing the same semantic function as the one in (141a). Sideward movement of *did* also complies with the Parallelism Requirement by making possible the coordination of two like categories (the two TPs).[28] Similar considerations apply to the other ATB constructions in (130b–e).

(140) how_i did_k Deborah e_k cook the pork e_i and Jane e_k cook the chicken e_i

(141) a. K = [and [$_{TP}$ Jane did^k cook the chicken how^i]]
       b. L = [$_{TP}$ Deborah did^k cook the pork how^i]

Hornstein and Nunes's proposal therefore outlines a general approach within which it is possible to capture the similarity between parasitic gap and ATB extraction constructions (their multiple gaps arise through sideward movement), while couching their differences in an independently motivated constraint on coordinate structures (the Parallelism Requirement). We can interpret their results as a tool to distinguish the licensing conditions that Last Resort imposes on the operations Copy and Merge, within the Copy+Merge theory. Given that these are two different operations that are arguably motivated by distinct properties of the architecture of the language faculty, it should come as no surprise that their licensing conditions are not identical. If Hornstein and Nunes's analysis is on the right track, it points to the conclusion that the requirements for Merge to be licensed by Last Resort are less strict than the ones imposed on Copy (see Hornstein and Nunes 2002 for further details and discussion).

3.7 Directionality of Sideward Movement and Cyclic Access to the Numeration

Let us reconsider Nunes and Uriagereka's (2000) account of the CED effect observed in parasitic gap constructions in (142), which was reviewed in section 3.4.2. According to this analysis, the sentences of (142) are unacceptable because sideward movement of *which book* from K to L in (143) and of *which politician* from M to N (144) cannot take place because the embedded subject and the embedded adjunct containing the *wh*-element have been spelled out and all the terms they contain are inaccessible for copying; hence, the sentences in (142) cannot be generated.

(142) a. *Which book did you borrow after leaving the bookstore without finding?
     b. *Which politician did you criticize before pictures of upset the voters?

(143) a. $K = [_{CP} PRO [_{vP}[_{vP}$ leaving the bookstore] $[_{PP}$ without PRO finding [which book]^i]]]
     b. $L =$ borrow

(144) a. $M = [_{CP} C [_{TP}[_{NP}$ pictures of [which politician]] $[_{T'} T [_{vP}$ upset the voters]]]]]
     b. $N =$ criticize

This account of the unacceptability of the parasitic gap constructions in (142) has crucially assumed that the computation proceeds from a "subordinated" to a "subordinating" derivational workspace. In fact, in all the cases of parasitic gap constructions discussed so far, sideward movement has proceeded from within an adjunct or subject to the object position of a subordinating verb. This assumption is by no means innocent. In principle, the computational system could also allow sideward movement to proceed from a "subordinating" to a "subordinated" derivational workspace, while still adhering to cyclicity.[29] Suppose, for instance, that we assemble the matrix VP of (142a), before building the VP headed by *finding*, as represented in (145).

(145) a. $K = [$borrow [which book]]
     b. $L =$ finding

Given the stage in (145), *which book* could undergo sideward movement from K to L and further computations would then yield the (simplified) structure in (146).

(146) [$_{CP}$ did+Q [$_{TP}$ you [$_{vP}$[$_{vP}$ borrow [which book]^i] [$_{PP}$ after [$_{CP}$ PRO [$_{vP}$[$_{vP}$ leaving the bookstore] [$_{PP}$ without PRO finding [which book]^i]]]]]]]

The relevant aspect of (146) is that, although the *wh*-copy inside PP is not accessible to the computational system, the *wh*-copy in the object position of *borrow* is. It could then move to check the strong feature of Q, and deletion of the lower *wh*-copies under Chain Reduction would yield the (simplified) structure in (147), incorrectly ruling in the sentence in (142a).

(147) [$_{CP}$[which book]^i did+Q [$_{TP}$ you [$_{vP}$[$_{vP}$ borrow ~~[which book]^i~~] [$_{PP}$ after [$_{CP}$ PRO [$_{vP}$[$_{vP}$ leaving the bookstore] [$_{PP}$ without PRO finding ~~[which book]^i~~]]]]]]]

Similar considerations apply to the alternative derivation of (142b) sketched in (148)–(150). *Which politician* moves from the object position of *criticize* to the complement position of the preposition in (148); further (cyclic) computations then yield the (simplified) structure in (149), in which the *wh*-copy in the matrix object position is still accessible for copying, thus being able to move and check the strong feature of Q. After this movement takes place, the whole structure is spelled out and the lower copies of *which politician* are deleted by Chain Reduction, as shown in (150), incorrectly ruling in the unacceptable parasitic gap in (142b).

(148) a. X = [criticize [which politician]]
       b. Y = of

(149) [$_{CP}$ did+Q [$_{TP}$ you [$_{vP}$[$_{vP}$ criticize [which politician]^i] [$_{PP}$ before [$_{CP}$[pictures of [which politician]^i] upset the voters]]]]]

(150) [$_{CP}$[which politician]^i did+Q [$_{TP}$ you [$_{vP}$[$_{vP}$ criticize ~~[which politician]^i~~] [$_{PP}$ before [$_{CP}$[pictures of ~~[which politician]^i~~] upset the voters]]]]]

The generalization that arises from this discussion is that sideward movement from a derivational workspace W_1 to a derivational workspace W_2 yields licit results just in case W_1 will be embedded in W_2 at some later derivational step. In the undesirable derivations sketched in (145)–(147) and (148)–(150), sideward movement has proceeded from the "matrix derivational workspace" to a subordinated one. Obviously, the question is how this generalization can be derived from independent considerations.

Nunes and Uriagereka (2000) argue that this problem is actually the same as the one posed by economy computations involving expletive insertion in pairs such as (151), originally noted by Alec Marantz and Juan Romero. The two sentences in (151) arguably share the same initial numeration; thus, if the computational system had access to the whole numeration, economy should favor insertion of *there* at the point where the structure in (152) has been assembled, incorrectly ruling out the derivation of the acceptable sentence in (151b).

(151) a. The fact is that there is someone in the room.
      b. There is the fact that someone is in the room.

(152) [is someone in the room]

Chomsky (2000) proposes that rather than working with the numeration as a whole, the computational system actually works with subarrays of a numeration, each containing one instance of either a complementizer or a light verb. Furthermore, a new subarray may be activated only if the computational system has used up all the lexical items of the currently activated subarray. In the case of (151), competition between insertion of *there* and movement of *someone* arises only if the active subarray feeding the derivation has an occurrence of the expletive at the point where (152) is assembled; if it does not, as would be the case of (151b), movement is the only option and the expletive is inserted later on, when another subarray is selected.

This strongly derivational approach has the relevant components for a principled account of why sideward movement must proceed from embedded to embedding contexts. If the computational system had access to the whole numeration, the derivation of the parasitic gap constructions in (142), for instance, could proceed either along the lines of (143)–(144) or along the lines of (145)–(147) and (148)–(150), yielding an undesirable result because the latter incorrectly predict that the sentences in (142) are acceptable. However, if the computational system works with one subarray at a time and if a given subarray must be exhausted before a new subarray is selected, the unwanted derivations outlined in (145)–(147) and (148)–(150) are correctly excluded. This is in essence the answer Nunes and Uriagereka (2000) provide for the puzzle of why the computational system takes one derivational route and not the other.

Assuming that numerations should be structured in terms of subarrays, the derivation in (145)–(147) should start with the numeration in (153), which contains the subarrays A–F, each determined by a light verb or a complementizer.

(153) $N = \{\{_A\ Q_1, did_1\},$
$\{_B\ you_1, v_1, borrow_1, which_1, book_1, after_1\},$
$\{_C\ C_1, T_1\},$
$\{_D\ PRO_1, v_1, leaving_1, the_1, bookstore_1, without_1\},$
$\{_E\ C_1, T_1\},$
$\{_F\ PRO_1, v_1, finding_1\}\}$

The derivational step in (145), repeated here in (154), which would permit the undesirable sideward movement of *which book*, is actually illicit because it accesses a new subarray (F) before it has used up the lexical items of the active subarray (B).[30]

(154) a. $K = [borrow\ [which\ book]]$
     b. $L = finding$

Similarly, the step in (148), repeated here in (156), illicitly activates subarrays B and D of (155), which is the structured numeration that underlies the derivation in (148)–(150).

(155) $N = \{\{_A\ Q_1, did_1\},$
$\{_B\ you_1, v_1, criticize_1, which_1, politician_1, before_1\},$
$\{_C\ C_1, T_1\},$
$\{_D\ pictures_1, of_1, v_1, upset_1, the_1, voters_1\}\}$

(156) a. $X = [criticize\ [which\ politician]]$
     b. $Y = of$

The problem with the derivations outlined in (145)–(147) and (148)–(150), therefore, is not the instances of sideward movement themselves, but the derivational steps that should allow them. By contrast, lexical access in the derivational routes sketched in (143) and (144), repeated in (158) and (160), may proceed in a cyclic fashion from the structured numerations in (157) and (159), respectively, without improperly activating more than one subarray at a time. However, as discussed above, sideward movement of *which book* in (158) or *which politician* in (160) is impossible because these elements have already been spelled out and are not accessible to the computational system.

(157) $N = \{\{_A\ Q_1, did_1\}$,
$\qquad \{_B\ you_1, finally_1, v_1, borrow_1, after_1\}$,
$\qquad \{_C\ C_1, T_1\}$,
$\qquad \{_D\ PRO_1, v_1, leaving_1, the_1, bookstore_1, without_1\}$,
$\qquad \{_E\ C_1, T_1\}$,
$\qquad \{_F\ PRO_1, v_1, finding_1, which_1, book_1\}\}$

(158) a. $K = [_{CP}\ PRO\ [_{vP}[_{vP}\ leaving\ the\ bookstore]\ [_{PP}\ without\ PRO$
$\qquad$ finding [which book]^i]]]
$\quad$ b. $L = borrow$

(159) $N = \{\{_A\ Q_1, did_1\}$,
$\qquad \{_B\ you_1, v_1, criticize_1, before_1\}$,
$\qquad \{_C\ C_1, T_1\}$,
$\qquad \{_D\ pictures_1, of_1, which_1, politician_1, v_1, upset_1, the_1, voters_1\}\}$

(160) a. $M = [_{CP}\ C\ [_{TP}[_{NP}\ pictures\ of\ [which\ politician]]\ [_{T'}\ T\ [_{vP}\ upset$
$\qquad$ the voters]]]]
$\quad$ b. $N = criticize$

The postulated directionality of movement from more to less embedded domains is further motivated by contrasts such as the one in (161) (based on Postal 1993).

(161) a. This is the book which I was given by Ted after reading.
$\quad$ b. *This is the book which I read before being given by Ted.

The relevant structural difference that seems to underlie the contrast is that in (161a) *read* is in the most embedded domain and *give* is in the subordinating domain, but in (161b) their positions are reversed. Under the analysis developed here, the parasitic gap constructions of (161) should involve the (simplified) derivational steps in (162) and (163), respectively, followed by sideward movement of *which*.

(162) a. $K = [_{CP}\ PRO\ reading\ which]$
$\quad$ b. $L = given$

(163) a. $P = [_{CP}\ PRO\ being\ given\ which\ by\ Ted]$
$\quad$ b. $Q = read$

Assuming with Lasnik (1995) and Chomsky (2000) that what makes an element visible for A-movement is its unchecked *structural* Case, Hornstein and Nunes (2002) argue that sideward movement in parasitic gap constructions must be launched from a position associated with structural rather than inherent Case. Contrasts such as the one in (161) are then accounted for, under the assumption that the theme of *give* in double object constructions is associated with inherent Case (see Larson 1988 for relevant discussion); hence, *which* is visible for copying in (162), but is inert in (163). Glossing over the details of Hornstein and Nunes's analysis, what is relevant for our current discussion is that if *which* could freely move from the object position of *read* to the object position of *give* in the derivation of (161b), we would incorrectly predict that it should be as acceptable as (161a); however, if movement must proceed from more to less embedded domains in a cyclic fashion, this scenario does not arise and (161b) is correctly excluded, because *which* is inert for A-movement in (163), the derivational step that would be required in order for (161b) to be generated (see Hornstein and Nunes 2002 for additional examples and further discussion).

To conclude, the directionality of sideward movement assumed thus far is empirically supported and arguably results as a by-product from the computational system's resorting to cyclic access to the numeration. The fact that the directionality of sideward movement has detectable empirical consequences constitutes in itself an additional argument for a derivational approach to syntactic computations.

3.8   Sideward Movement and Cyclicity of Merge

So far, I have been assuming that operations of merger and movement always apply in a cyclic fashion. In the Copy+Merge theory, this assumption is motivated by island configurations, which, as discussed in sections 3.4.2 and 3.7, are taken to arise in the course of the derivation. If merger and movement could proceed in a noncyclic manner as well, a sentence like (164), for instance, would be incorrectly ruled in by the derivation sketched in (165)–(167). That is, after the computational system built K and L in (165), *which class* could undergo sideward movement to check the strong *wh*-feature of Q, as illustrated in (166); the PP would then noncyclically merge with vP and the lower copy of *which class* would be deleted by Chain Reduction, as shown in (167).

(164) *Which class did Mary call John after?

(165) a. K = [$_{PP}$ after [which class]]
       b. L = [$_{CP}$ did+Q [$_{TP}$ Mary [$_{vP}$ call John]]]

(166) a. K = [$_{PP}$ after [which class]^i]
      b. M = [$_{CP}$[which class]^i did+Q [$_{TP}$ Mary [$_{vP}$ call John]]]

(167) [$_{CP}$[which class]^i did+Q [$_{TP}$ Mary [$_{vP}$[$_{vP}$ call John] [$_{PP}$ after [which ~~class~~]^i]]]]

Crucially, at the derivational step in (165) K is an independent syntactic object and, therefore, not an island for extraction. On the other hand, if the derivation proceeds cyclically, by the time the interrogative complementizer is introduced into the structure, as shown in (168), the PP has already become an adjunct island (in Nunes and Uriagereka's (2000) system, it has already been spelled out) and the *wh*-element is inaccessible for copying; hence the unacceptability of (164).

(168) [$_{CP}$ did+Q [$_{TP}$ Mary [$_{vP}$[$_{vP}$ call John] [$_{PP}$ after [which class]^i]]]]

If the Copy+Merge theory requires that merger and movement always be cyclic, the issue arises of how to analyze cases that have been argued to involve noncyclic operations. Although a full discussion of this topic goes beyond the limits of this monograph, in the following subsections I will examine the exceptional instances of noncyclic movement in Chomsky's (1993, 1995) system, taking them to be representative, and show that they are actually amenable to a cyclic analysis under the Copy+Merge theory of movement.

3.8.1 Noncyclic Movement in Chomsky 1993, 1995

Chomsky (1993, 22) introduces cyclicity into the Minimalist Program by proposing that generalized transformations should be subject to an "Extension Requirement," according to which if a given syntactic object K is targeted by either Merge or Move, the resulting syntactic object should include K as a proper part. Head movement, certain instances of relative clause adjunction, and substitution movement in the covert component are, however, exceptional in this system in that they do not target a root syntactic object.

Such an approach is maintained in its essentials with the development of bare phrase structure. Chomsky (1995, 248) argues that a noncyclic application of Merge embedding α within some already-formed structure β would introduce a serious complication into the system and would require strong empirical motivation; in the absence of such motivation, Chomsky assumes that "Merge always applies in the simplest possible form: at the root" (Chomsky 1995, 248). As for movement, he takes cyclicity to be a property of strong features (see Chomsky 1995, 233); hence, only overt movement must proceed cyclically. The only relevant change from the system developed in Chomsky 1993 is that covert movement by substitution is reanalyzed as adjunction of a set of formal features to a given head (see Chomsky 1995, sec. 4.4.4). With this revision, the distinction between cyclic and noncyclic movement correlates with the difference between movement by substitution and movement by adjunction, the latter not being subject to the Extension Requirement.

This state of affairs is still not satisfactory, however. Move should be subject to the same condition of conceptual simplicity applied to Merge; noncyclic movement should require strong empirical support. Under the Copy+Merge theory of movement, this is even more so, given that Move is not understood as an operation of the computational system, but rather as a reflex of the interaction among the operations Copy, Merge, Form Chain, and Chain Reduction. Let us examine each of the exceptional cases of noncyclic movement mentioned above and see how they can receive a cyclic analysis under the Copy+Merge theory.

3.8.2   Eliminating Noncyclic Movement from the Grammar

3.8.2.1   Relative Clause Adjunction   The sentences in (169), discussed by Chomsky (1993, 36), illustrate the well-known fact that noun complement clauses and relative clauses do not pattern alike as far as reconstruction effects are concerned (see Freidin 1986 and Lebeaux 1988, among others).

(169) a. *Which claim that John$_i$ was asleep was he$_i$ willing to discuss?
     b. Which claim that John$_i$ made was he$_i$ willing to discuss?

Building on the work by Lebeaux (1988), Chomsky (1993) analyzes contrasts such as (169) in terms of the distinction between complements and adjuncts: "[t]he extension property for substitution entails that complements can only be introduced cyclically, hence before *wh*-extraction, while adjuncts can be introduced noncyclically, hence adjoined to the *wh*-phrase after raising to [Spec, CP]" (Chomsky 1993, 37). According to this reasoning, the only possible (convergent) derivation for (169a) is the cyclic one represented in (170), where the complement clause merges with *claim*, before the whole *wh*-phrase is copied and moves to Spec,CP; (169b), on the other hand, may have either the cyclic derivation represented in (171a) or the noncyclic derivation represented in (171b), where the relative clause is adjoined after *which claim* moves to Spec,CP. Although both structures in (170) and (171a) arguably violate Principle C of binding theory, the same is not true of (171b), because *John* is not c-commanded by *he*; hence, the additional derivation in (171b) is the source for the acceptability of (169b), in contrast with (169a).[31]

(170) [[which claim that John$_i$ was asleep]^k was he$_i$ willing to discuss [which claim that John$_i$ was asleep]^k]

(171) a. [[[which claim] [O$_j$ that John$_i$ made t$_j$]]^k was he$_i$ willing to discuss [[which claim] [O$_j$ that John made t$_j$]]^k]
       b. [[[which claim]^k [O$_j$ that John$_i$ made t$_j$]] was he$_i$ willing to discuss [which claim]^k]

Within the Copy+Merge theory of movement, the contrast between (169a) and (169b) can be captured without resort to noncyclic movement. At some point in the (convergent) derivation of (169b) with the relevant interpretation, we have the two unconnected phrase structures in (172), which have been independently assembled. The phrase *which claim* is then copied, but instead of merging with K in (172a), it adjoins to the relative clause in (172b) (an instance of sideward movement), as illustrated in (173).[32] Finally, K and M in (173) merge, yielding the structure in (174) and allowing the interrogative complementizer Q to check its strong *wh*-feature.[33]

(172) a. K = [$_{CP_1}$ was+Q [he$_i$ willing to discuss [which claim]^k]]
       b. L = [$_{CP_2}$ O$_j$ that John$_i$ made t$_j$]

(173) a. K = [$_{CP_1}$ was+Q [he$_i$ willing to discuss [which claim]^k]]
       b. M = [$_{CP_2}$[which claim]^k [$_{CP_2}$ O$_j$ that John$_i$ made t$_j$]]

(174)

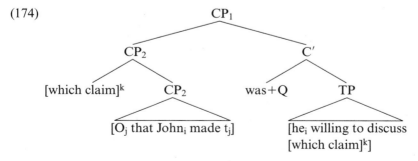

In (174), the upper copy of *which claim* participates in a checking relation with Q, satisfying Last Resort, and c-commands the lower copy (the upper copy is only contained but not dominated by CP$_2$); the Minimal Link Condition is also satisfied because there is no intervening element between the two copies that could participate in the same checking relation as the upper *wh*-copy. Once all conditions on Form Chain are satisfied, the *wh*-copies form the chain CH = ([which claim]^k, [which claim]^k), whose optimal reduction involves the deletion of the lower copy, as shown in (175). (175) then ends up surfacing as (169b) after further operations of the phonological component. Under the Copy+Merge theory, the structure in (174), which allows coreference between *he* and *John*, can therefore be obtained with no need to appeal to noncyclic applications of Merge.

(175) [$_{CP_1}$[$_{CP_2}$[which claim]^k [$_{CP_2}$ O$_j$ that John$_i$ made t$_j$]] [$_{C'}$ was+Q [he$_i$ willing to discuss ~~[which claim]^k~~]]]]

For presentation purposes, I have tacitly assumed a null operator approach to relative clauses in the above discussion. However, the cyclic analysis of (169b) within the Copy+Merge theory of movement is also compatible with a raising analysis of relative clauses (see Vergnaud 1974, Kayne 1994, and Bianchi 1999, among others). A possible implementation of a sideward movement account of (169b) under a raising analysis could proceed as follows.[34] After the "relative" CP in (176a) has been formed through raising and adjunction of *which claim*, the computational system selects the verb *discuss* from the numeration. If there is no convergent derivation that merges L in (176b) with the remaining lexical items of the active subarray of the numeration, the computational system makes a copy of *which claim* and merges it with L (an instance of sideward movement) to satisfy the thematic requirements of *discuss*. After further computations, we reach the derivational step sketched in (177); K and M then merge, forming the structure in (178), which for the purposes of binding theory is identical to (174) in that it allows coreference between *John* and *he*.

(176) a. K = [$_{CP_1}$[which claim]^k [$_{CP_1}$ that John$_i$ made [which claim]^k]]
       b. L = discuss

(177) a. K = [$_{CP_1}$[which claim]^k [$_{CP_1}$ that John$_i$ made [which claim]^k]]
       b. M = [$_{CP_2}$ was+Q [he$_i$ willing to discuss [which claim]^k]]

(178)

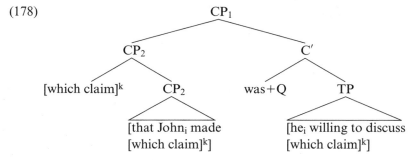

The structure in (178) has the same configuration found in parasitic gap constructions, for the topmost copy of *which claim* may form a different chain with each of the lower copies. Optimal reduction of each chain deletes the lower link, yielding (179), which surfaces as (169b).

(179) $[_{CP_2}[_{CP_1}$ [which claim]^k $[_{CP_1}$ that John$_i$ made ~~[which claim]^k~~]] $[_{C'}$ was+Q $[_{TP}$ he$_i$ willing to discuss ~~[which claim]^k~~]]]

Given the successful cyclic derivation of relative clause adjunction in cases such as (169b), we have to make sure that a sideward movement analysis does not extend to noun complement clauses such as (169a); otherwise, we would incorrectly allow *he* and *John* to be coreferential. Under the proposal explored here that every instance of "movement" (actually Merge in the Copy+Merge theory of movement) is cyclic, the derivational steps sketched in (180)–(181) are excluded by definition: in order for the CP in (180b) to become the complement of the copy of *claim* in (181b), a noncyclic merger between L and M is required.

(180) a. K = [was+Q [he willing to discuss [which^i claim^k]^m]]
      b. L = [that John was asleep]
      c. M = [which^i claim^k]^m

(181) a. K = [was+Q [he willing to discuss [which^i claim^k]^m]]
      b. N = [which^i [claim^k [$_L$ that John was asleep]]]

Suppose, on the other hand, that this problem can be circumvented by having the derivation proceed cyclically, along the lines of (182)–(185). That is, *claim* is copied from K in (182a) and merges with L in (182b), forming N in (183b), which then merges with a copy of *which*, forming P in (184b); finally, K and P in (184) merge, yielding the structure in (185).

(182) a. $K = [was+Q [he willing to discuss [which^i claim^k]]]$

   b. $L = [that John was asleep]$

   c. $M = [claim^k]$

(183) a. $K = [was+Q [he willing to discuss [which^i claim^k]]]$

   b. $N = [claim^k [_L that John was asleep]]$

   c. $O = [which^i]$

(184) a. $K = [was+Q [he willing to discuss [which^i claim^k]]]$

   b. $P = [which^i [claim^k [that John was asleep]]]$

(185) $[[_P which^i [claim^k [that John was asleep]]] [_K was+Q [he willing to discuss [which^i claim^k]]]]$

The problem with the derivation outlined in (182)–(185) is that no chain involving the two copies of *claim* or the two copies of *which* can be formed: a potential chain $CH_1 = (which^i claim^k, which^i claim^k)$ cannot be formed because the first link is not a constituent in (185); the other potential chains $CH_2 = (claim^k, claim^k)$ and $CH_3 = (which^i, which^i)$ cannot be formed either, because there is no c-command between their links. Once Chain Reduction is inapplicable, the nondistinct copies of *claim* and *which* in (185) induce violations of the asymmetry and irreflexivity conditions on linear order, canceling the derivation.

The only other relevant cyclic derivation for (169a) that would allow coreference between *John* and *he* is outlined in (186)–(188), where a copy of *which claim* merges with L in (186b) and the resulting syntactic object M in (187b) merges with K, forming the structure in (188).

(186) a. $K = [was+Q [he willing to discuss [which claim]^i]]$

   b. $L = [that John was asleep]$

(187) a. $K = [was+Q [he willing to discuss [which claim]^i]]$

   b. $M = [[which claim]_i [_L that John was asleep]]$

(188) $[[_M[which claim]^i [_L that John was asleep]] [_K was+Q [he willing to discuss [which claim]^i]]]$

In order for a chain involving the two copies of *which claim* in (188) to be formed, the upper copy must have merged with L in (187b) by adjunction; otherwise, the upper copy would not be able to c-command the lower one. If this is the case, however, L cannot be interpreted as the complement of *claim* in (188), because it does not fall within the internal domain of *claim* (see Chomsky 1993, 12). The derivation involving the steps in (186)–(188), if convergent at all, should then receive a deviant interpretation at the interface.

To sum up, the Copy+Merge theory of movement is able to account for the differences between relative clauses and noun complement clauses as far as reconstruction effects are concerned, without resorting to non-cyclic movement. Unwanted instances of sideward movement in the derivations involving noun complement clauses are excluded by the independently motivated conditions on linearization of chains in the phonological component.[35]

3.8.2.2 Head Movement As mentioned in section 3.8.1, head movement is exceptional in Chomsky's (1993, 1995) systems in not being subject to the Extension Requirement. It should be noted that this assumption is motivated only for theory-internal reasons, having to do with the view of Move as a complex singulary transformation. If it is assumed that Move must relate constituents of a single phrase marker, a verb can adjoin to a T head, for instance, only after a projection of T containing the verb has been formed.

Once the displacement property of human languages is interpreted as the interaction of the independent primitive operations Copy, Merge, Form Chain, and Chain Reduction, overt head movement can always proceed in a cyclic fashion. Verb movement to T, for instance, can proceed as illustrated in (189)–(191) (see Bobaljik 1995a, Nunes 1995, Bobaljik and Brown 1997, and Uriagereka 1998).

(189) a. $K = [_{VP} \ldots V \ldots]$
      b. $L = T$

(190) a. $K = [_{VP} \ldots V^i \ldots]$
      b. $M = [_{T^0} V^i [_{T^0} T]]$

(191) a. $[_{TP}[_{T^0} V^i [_{T^0} T]] [_{VP} \ldots V^i \ldots]]$
      b. $[_{TP}[_{T^0} V^i [_{T^0} T]] [_{VP} \ldots \underline{V^i} \ldots]]$

Given the VP and the T head in (189), the computational system makes a copy of the verb and adjoins it to T (an instance of sideward movement) to check the strong V-feature of T, as shown in (190); after K and M in (190) merge, as shown in (191a), the two copies of the verb form the chain $CH = (V^i, V^i)$. In the phonological component, CH undergoes Chain Reduction and the copy of the verb inside the VP is deleted, as shown in (191b).

Recall from the discussion of (127), repeated in (192), that if the copies
resulting from sideward movement of heads cannot undergo Chain Reduction, the structure cannot be linearized and the unwanted movement
is correctly excluded.

(192)

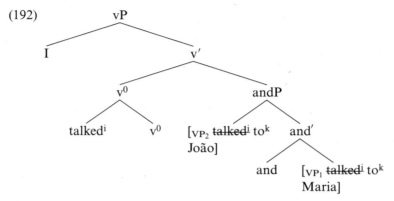

In the case of (192), sideward movement of *talked* from VP$_1$ to VP$_2$, followed by cyclic adjunction to v^0 through sideward movement, yields a
structure in which two verb chains can be formed and their lower links
can be deleted by Chain Reduction. Sideward movement of *to*, on the
other hand, does not yield a configuration where a preposition chain can
be formed. The two nondistinct instances of *to* then prevent the structure
from being linearized, blocking the two-event reading for the corresponding Portuguese sentence in (193) (see discussion in section 3.5.2). In other
words, sideward movement of heads does not to lead to overgeneration,
because copy deletion only applies under Chain Reduction.

(193) *Portuguese*
       Eu conversei com o   João e   a   Maria.
       I   talked   with the João and the Maria
       'I talked to João and Maria.'

The Copy+Merge theory of movement, therefore, not only can provide
a cyclic derivation for standard overt head movement, but also can exclude unwanted instances of "sideward head movement," on the basis of
reasoning independently required to explain why chains in general cannot
have more than one link phonetically realized (see section 1.5.2).

3.8.2.3 Covert Movement   Covert movement is the last instance of noncyclic movement required in Chomsky's (1993) system. If overt move-

ment can only be triggered by strong features (see Chomsky 1993, 30; 1995, 233), movement in the covert component to check weak uninterpretable features will invariably target a nonroot syntactic object. This is also true of Chomsky's (1995) system, where covert movement is reinterpreted as movement of formal features.

Several approaches to the copy theory have, however, attempted to eliminate covert movement, while still maintaining a derivational model (see Bobaljik 1995b, Groat and O'Neil 1996, and Gärtner 1997, for instance). These analyses share the following assumptions: (i) every movement operation takes place before Spell-Out; and (ii) the standard difference between overt and covert movement is expressed in terms of whether the head or the tail of the chain is phonetically realized, in accordance with some notion of optimality of copies or positions (see section 1.5.3). If any of these approaches is on the right track, operations traditionally analyzed as covert movement of phrases may proceed cyclically without any problems (the same is true of Kayne 1998).[36] On the other hand, if covert movement actually involves movement of sets of formal features in the covert component, as proposed by Chomsky (1995), it seems bound to proceed noncyclically.

Since my goal in this section is only to show that noncyclic movement may be eliminated from the grammar if sideward movement is assumed, I will not attempt to choose among these various derivational ways of dealing with "covert movement." Rather, I will show that even if Chomsky's Move F approach proves to be the correct one, it is still amenable to a cyclic analysis. For the sake of the reasoning, let us then assume that every movement takes place overtly and that strong features trigger overt movement of categories, whereas weak features trigger overt movement of sets of formal features.[37]

We have seen in section 3.8.2.2 that overt head movement can proceed cyclically under the Copy+Merge theory owing to the possibility of sideward movement in this system. Given that movement of any set of formal features FF to check a feature of the head H must involve adjunction of FF to H, as argued by Chomsky (1995, 271), "covert feature movement" can be reanalyzed as overt sideward movement of FFs. Given the derivational step in (194) in a language where T has a weak V-feature, for instance, the computational system copies the formal features of the verb and adjoins them to T (an instance of sideward movement), as shown in (195), and later merges the VP and the complex T head, as shown in (196), allowing the chain $CH = (FF(V^i), FF(V^i))$ to be formed.

(194) a. $K = [_{VP} \dots V \dots]$
      b. $L = T$

(195) a. $K = [_{VP} \dots V^i \dots]$
      b. $M = [_{T^0} FF(V^i) [_{T^0} T]]$

(196) $[_{TP}[_{T^0} FF(V^i) [_{T^0} T]] [_{VP} \dots V^i \dots]]$

Assuming the null hypothesis that reduction of FF-chains such as $CH = (FF(V^i), FF(V^i))$ in the phonological component does not differ from reduction of category chains, the same linearization considerations that ruled out the structure resulting from sideward movement of *to* in (192) should also rule out corresponding derivations where nondistinct copies of FFs do not form a chain and, consequently, are not subject to Chain Reduction. By relying on sideward movement, the Copy+Merge theory is therefore able to analyze Chomsky's Move F approach in cyclic terms.[38]

3.8.3 Summary

There are basically three motivations for postulating noncyclic movement in Chomsky's (1993, 1995) systems. The first one is theory internal. If it is assumed that Move is a complex singulary operation that targets constituents of a single phrase marker, head movement can proceed only after the projections of the landing site and the target of movement are constituents of the same phrase marker; hence, head movement is bound to be noncyclic. The second motivation, also theory internal, is related to the format of the computational system. If it is assumed that movement operations may proceed before and after Spell-Out, covert movement invariably targets a part of the whole syntactic object formed overtly. Finally, the postulation of noncyclic movement is also empirically motivated by some reconstruction effects associated with relative clauses in contrast with noun complement clauses (but see note 35).

In section 3.8.2.3, I showed that, under the assumption that every movement operation takes place overtly, Chomsky's (1995, sec. 4.4.4) proposal regarding covert movement can be interpreted as overt adjunction of sets of formal features to the relevant heads. The lack of cyclicity of "covert movement" inherent to the Move F approach should then be reduced to the lack of cyclicity in overt head movement. Such a reduction allows us to dispense with noncyclic movement motivated by theory-internal reasons, for the Copy+Merge theory of movement is successful in providing a cyclic analysis for head movement in terms of sideward movement (see section 3.8.2.2). A cyclic analysis in terms of sideward movement for the relevant cases of relative clause adjunction (see section 3.8.2.1) is also tenable. Moreover, unwanted instances of sideward movement are prevented by the same considerations that are independently required to explain why in general not all the links of a chain are phonetically realized (see section 1.5.2): a syntactic object with visible instances of nondistinct copies cannot be linearized in accordance with the LCA.

To the extent that the Copy+Merge theory of movement is able to eliminate noncyclic movement operations for the three cases discussed above and constrain sideward movement without enriching the theoretical apparatus, it constitutes a substantial conceptual improvement over an approach that takes Move as a complex singulary operation such as the one in Chomsky 1993, 1994, 1995. It remains to be seen if other constructions that are taken to involve noncyclic movement are subject to the same analysis (see Stepanov 2000 for relevant discussion).

3.9   Further Extensions

Hornstein (1999, 2001) develops an analysis that dispenses with the control module and treats controlled PRO as a trace (a copy), by allowing movement into thematic positions. A subject control sentence such as (197a), for instance, is derived along the lines of (197b): *John* is generated in the embedded Spec,vP and moves to check the EPP-feature of the embedded T; assuming that the embedded T does not assign Case, *John* then moves to the matrix Spec,vP, where it receives another θ-role, and finally moves to the matrix Spec,TP, where it gets its Case checked (see Hornstein 1999, 2001 for details and discussion).

(197) a. John tried to solve the problem.
       b. $[_{TP}$ John^i $[_{T'}$ T $[_{vP}$ John^i $[_{vP}$ tried $[_{CP}$ C $[_{TP}$ John^i $[_{T'}$ to $[_{vP}$ John^i $[_{vP}$ solve the problem]]]]]]]]]]

At first sight, adjunct control structures such as (198) should present problems for such an analysis, for it should require movement of *John* from within the adjunct clause, yielding a CED violation.

(198) John greeted everybody before leaving the room.

Extending the approach taken in Nunes 1995, Hornstein proposes that (198) is derived by sideward movement and that the relevant movement of *John* takes place before the embedded clause is adjoined to the matrix vP. Details of technical implementation aside, the derivation of (198) can thus proceed along the lines of (199)–(201).

(199) a. K = [$_{TP}$ John^i [$_{vP}$ John^i leaving the room]]
     b. L = [$_{vP}$ greeted everybody]

(200) a. K = [$_{CP}$ C [$_{TP}$ John^i [$_{vP}$ John^i leaving the room]]]
     b. M = [$_{vP}$ John^i [$_{v'}$ greeted everybody]]

(201)

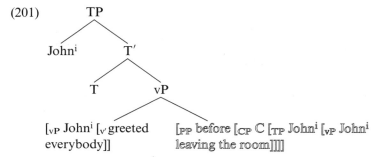

After checking the EPP-feature of the nonfinite T in (199a), *John* is copied and merges with L (an instance of sideward movement) to receive the external θ-role of the light verb of L, yielding M in (200b). Further computations then build the TP in (201), where another copy of *John* is made to check the EPP-feature of the matrix T. The structure in (201) has the same relevant properties as parasitic gap and ATB extraction constructions in that an upper copy can form a different chain with each of the lower copies. Deletion of the lower copies of *John* then yields the PF output associated with (198).

Hornstein's elimination of the control module therefore provides further conceptual and empirical evidence for sideward movement and for a derivational approach to islands.[39] Additional evidence comes from Ferreira's (2000a,b) and Rodrigues's (2000, 2002) analyses of null subjects in Brazilian Portuguese. Technical differences aside, they both propose that null subjects in Brazilian Portuguese arise from movement to θ-positions, much like Hornstein's (1999, 2001) reanalysis of control theory. Under this perspective, a Brazilian Portuguese sentence like (202), whose matrix and embedded subjects must be interpreted as coreferential, is derived by movement of *o João* from the embedded Spec,vP all the way up to the matrix Spec,TP, as illustrated in (203) (English words are used for convenience), followed by deletion of the lower copies.[40]

(202) *Brazilian Portuguese*
    O João disse que comprou o   livro.
    the João said that bought   the book
    'João$_i$ said that he$_i$ bought the book.'

(203) [$_{TP}$ João^i [$_{vP}$ João^i [$_{v'}$ said [$_{CP}$ that [$_{TP}$ João^i [$_{vP}$ João^i [bought the book]]]]]]]]

What is relevant for our purposes is that null subjects cannot appear inside relative clauses, for instance, but can appear inside adjunct clauses, as respectively shown in (204a–b).

(204) *Brazilian Portuguese*
    a. ??O João não leu o   livro que comprou.
        the João not read the book that bought
        'João$_i$ didn't read the book that he$_i$ bought.'
    b. O João saiu depois que comprou o   livro.
        the João left after   that bought   the book
        'João$_i$ left after he$_i$ bought the book.'

According to Ferreira's (2000a,b) and Rodrigues's (2000, 2002) analyses, the relevant steps that should yield the sentences in (204) are as represented in (205) and (206) (again, English words are used for convenience).

(205) [$_{vP}$ read [[the book] [O$_i$ that João bought t$_i$]]]

(206) a. K = [$_{CP}$ C [$_{TP}$ João^i [$_{vP}$ João^i [$_{v'}$ bought the book]]]]
     b. L = left

In (205), the relative clause has already become an island at the derivational step where *João* should raise to check the external θ-role of the matrix light verb; the unacceptability of (204a) is therefore due to a CED violation. In (206), on the other hand, *João* can move from K and merge with *left* (an instance of sideward movement) before K becomes an adjunct; in other words, (204b) is analyzed along the lines of Hornstein's analysis of control into adjunct clauses.

The "selective" island effects exhibited by null subjects in Brazilian Portuguese therefore present strong evidence not only for a derivational view of island effects, but also for the cyclicity of Merge advocated here. Suppose for instance that the relative clause in (205) could have merged noncyclically. *João* could then undergo sideward movement to the matrix Spec,vP prior to the noncyclic adjunction of the relative clause and (204a) should be as acceptable as (204b), contrary to fact.

3.10 Conclusion

As discussed in chapter 1, one of the key features of the analysis of movement operations in the Minimalist Program is its commitment to the copy
theory. The adoption of the copy theory of movement is conceptually
justified in that it allows interpretive phenomena having to do with binding theory and idioms to be accounted for without resorting to noninterface levels (see Chomsky 1993); it is also empirically justified by instances
of phonetically realized traces such as the ones discussed in section 1.5.3.
This difference aside, the Minimalist Program as formulated in Chomsky
1993, 1994, 1995 essentially follows the traditional analysis of movement
as a complex singulary transformation. More specifically, movement under the copy theory is taken to involve the suboperations of copying,
merger, and chain formation, coupled with the operation of trace deletion
for PF purposes (if the movement is overt).

This analysis of movement faces several conceptual problems: Merge
is taken to be either a "full" operation or a suboperation of Move (see
Gärtner 1997); Move must proceed noncyclically in instances involving
head movement, covert movement, and certain cases of relative clause
adjunction; movement and chain formation capture the same type of relation (see Brody 1995); and there is no motivation for deletion of traces.
The last point also leads to empirical problems in that it is not obvious
why some traces can escape deletion (see chapter 1).

In this chapter, I have argued instead that Move is not a primitive
operation of the computational system, but merely a description of the
interaction among the independent operations Copy, Merge, Form Chain,
and Chain Reduction. Under this conception of movement, which I referred to as the Copy+Merge theory of movement, all the conceptual
problems are overcome.

Starting with the last one mentioned above, deletion of traces is taken
to be triggered by linearization in the phonological component (see
chapter 1). Assuming that copies count as nondistinct for interpretation
at LF, as well as for "syntactic" computations in the phonological component, a structure containing copies cannot be linearized in accordance
with Kayne's (1994) LCA because the copies induce violations of the
asymmetry and irreflexivity conditions on linear order. In order to allow
a structure containing a chain to be linearized, the phonological component employs the operation Chain Reduction, which in general has the

effect of deleting all but one link of a chain. The choice of the link to be kept is determined by economy considerations regarding the elimination of formal features in the phonological component. In the standard case, that means that only the head of the chain survives Chain Reduction; however, if a given chain link becomes invisible to the LCA in virtue of being reanalyzed as part of a terminal element, it will also survive Chain Reduction (see section 1.5.3.3). The Copy+Merge theory of movement thus meets both conceptual and empirical demands regarding deletion of traces in the phonological component.

By taking Copy, Merge, Form Chain, and Chain Reduction to be independent operations, the system argued for here crucially differs from the standard analysis of movement within the Principles-and-Parameters Theory in that it allows instances of sideward movement, where a given constituent of a syntactic object is copied and merges with an independent syntactic object. In these cases, applications of Copy and Merge are dissociated from Form Chain and Chain Reduction, eliminating the redundancy between chain formation and movement that exists in standard approaches. Once sideward movement is permitted in the system, head movement, adjunction of formal features, and adjunction of relative clauses can always proceed cyclically, paving the way for the elimination of noncyclic movement in the theory of grammar. Thus, Merge is always a "full" operation concatenating root syntactic objects.

Unwanted applications of sideward movement are ruled out by the linearization considerations that trigger deletion of traces: if two copies do not form a chain or if the independent chains containing them do not have a link in common, these copies cannot be targeted by Chain Reduction and end up preventing the structure from being linearized by violating the asymmetry and irreflexivity conditions on linear order.[41]

The Copy+Merge theory of movement also broadens the empirical coverage of standard analyses of movement by deriving the core properties of parasitic gap and across-the-board constructions from the analysis independently motivated by instances of "regular" movement. In particular, sideward movement is responsible for the possibility of multiple gaps, and potential unwanted instances of multiple gaps either do not arise given the cyclic derivational nature of the computation or are excluded by general linearization considerations. To the extent that parasitic gap and across-the-board extraction are handled without construction-specific operations or the introduction of principles that are not independently needed, they lend strong conceptual and empirical support to the Copy+Merge theory of movement and the proposal regarding linearization of chains.

Finally, the reanalysis of Move in terms of Copy, Merge, Form Chain, and Chain Reduction also provides strong evidence for a derivational approach to syntactic computations in that syntactic objects become islands at specific steps of the derivation and sideward movement proceeds from more to less embedded domains.

Conclusion

In this monograph, I have explored the null hypothesis under the copy theory of movement, namely, that traces are not grammatical primitives and that their properties follow from deeper features of the system. In particular, I argued that it is not an intrinsic property of traces that they are not phonetically realized. The phonetic realization of traces is determined by a convergence condition—the requirement that the result of the syntactic computations be linearized in the phonological component—and economy conditions regarding the elimination of formal features in the phonological component. The analysis developed in chapter 1 thus accounted not only for the standard case, in which the head of the chain is pronounced, but also for instances in which different parts of the chain are phonetically realized (scattered deletion), instances where traces (lower copies) are pronounced instead of the head of the chain, and instances where more than one chain link is phonetically realized.

The null hypothesis also proved empirically correct with respect to the role of traces in minimality computations. I showed in chapter 2 that traces are accessible to the computational system and do induce minimality effects, like any other syntactic objects.

In chapter 3, I explored the copy theory to its limits, arguing that Move is not a theoretical primitive, but rather a taxonomic description of the interaction among more basic operations. This new perspective on the displacement property of human languages, which I referred to as the Copy+Merge theory, is different from standard analyses in that it allows restricted instances of sideward movement (movement from one syntactic tree to another). Besides paving the way for the elimination of noncyclic movement in the grammar, the Copy+Merge theory enjoys a significantly broader empirical coverage in that it accounts for standard properties of multiple gap constructions such as parasitic gap and ATB constructions, without construction-specific operations or principles that are not independently motivated. Under this view, multiple gap constructions do not differ from standard instances of (upward) movement.

By rethinking movement operations under minimalist guidelines, we thus end up with the interesting result that the minimalist search for conceptual elegance does indeed meet empirical demands.

Notes

Chapter 1

1. Chomsky 1993 was republished as chapter 3 of Chomsky's *The Minimalist Program*, and much of Chomsky 1994 is included in chapter 4 of that book. From now on, I will refer to chapter 4 simply as Chomsky 1995 and will specifically refer to Chomsky 1993, 1994, 2000, 2001 only if the relevant content differs substantially from Chomsky 1995. For a general introduction to the Minimalist Program, see Uriagereka 1998 and Hornstein, Nunes, and Grohmann, forthcoming.

2. For relevant discussion, see Chomsky 1973, 1981, 1982, 1986b, Fiengo 1977, Aoun et al. 1987, Rizzi 1990, and Epstein 1991, among others.

3. Assuming that traces are copies, it must be the case that binding theory applies only to coindexation between distinct elements and not between copies; otherwise, the structure in (ib), which underlies the sentence in (ia), would incorrectly induce a Principle C violation.

(i) a. John was arrested.
    b. [John^i was arrested John^i]

4. Note that it is not the introduction of objects in the course of the derivation by itself that is problematic, for both traces and copies are introduced in this way. The difference is that while the copy theory creates an object by manipulating material that is available in the numeration that feeds the computation (the same applies to the structure-building operation Merge), the trace theory introduces a completely new element.

5. At first sight, the unacceptability of (19b) has an obvious explanation within Chomsky's (1995) system: the strong feature of T has not been checked. Although this is a straightforward account of one potential derivation of (19b), it does not extend to the derivation outlined in (18). After the copy of *John* merges with the structure in (18a), becoming the specifier of T, it can check the strong feature of T. The unacceptability of (19b) therefore cannot be reduced to a problem of strong feature checking.

6. A derivation is said to be *canceled* if an illegitimate operation is performed during the computation, if the pair (PF, LF) is not formed, or if the numeration is not exhausted (see Chomsky 1995, 225–226).

7. For evidence that this kind of construction is sensitive to island effects, see McDaniel 1986 and Fanselow and Mahajan 1995, among others.

8. For morphological effects of the Parallelism Requirement, see Ximenes 2002.

9. See Merchant 2001 for further discussion of the proposed correlation between low-flat intonation and ellipsis.

10. But see Zocca 2003. Within Chomsky's (2000, 2001) Agree-based framework, Zocca proposes that the relevant items in cases such as (24b) are indeed identical before Agree takes place.

11. This is made explicit by Groat and O'Neil (1996), who propose a system where every movement operation takes place overtly:

> While MPLT [Chomsky 1993] must stipulate some means to ensure that the tail of a chain is marked in some way as not pronounced (perhaps in the PF component), we instead enrich the principle Form-chain with respect to the COPY THEORY.... This enrichment of Form-chain replaces whatever mechanism is stipulated to mark the tail of a chain as phonologically null. (Groat and O'Neil 1996, 135)

12. For instance, the optimality-theoretic assumptions of Pesetsky (1997, 1998) may be more successful in permitting sentences such as (ia), where only the trace is phonetically realized (see section 1.5.3.2 for details), whereas the formulation of Speak Up in (31) faces an additional problem with remnant movement, illustrated in (iia): its structure arguably involves five copies of *John*, as shown in (iib), and the copy that is realized is not the topmost/leftmost one (see section 1.6 for further discussion).

(i) *Serbo-Croatian* (from Bošković 2000, 2001)
   a. Šta   uslovljava šta?
      what conditions what
      'What conditions what?'
   b. [šta ~~šta^i~~ uslovljava šta^i]

(ii) a. I wonder how likely to win John is.
    b. [I wonder [how likely ~~John^i~~ to ~~John^i~~ win]^k John^i is [~~how likely John^i to John^i win~~]^k]

13. Brody (1995) actually outlines a conceptual justification for the principle of Transparency in (29), on the grounds that "the grammar is designed in such a way that where possible PF makes the (L)LF chain relations explicit" (Brody 1995, 107). It is not obvious, however, how this line of argumentation explains the unacceptability of (iia), given the structure in (i); the chain relation between the two copies of (i) seems to be more explicit in (iia) than in (iib). It is also unclear how contrasts such as the one between (20) and (21), on the one hand, and (22) and (23), on the other, can be accounted for under this view.

(i) [John^i [was [kissed John^i]]]

(ii) a. *John was kissed John.
    b. John was kissed.

14. The motivation for treating terms related by the Copy operation as nondistinct rather than identical has to do with feature checking. If (34) has been

formed by movement, for instance, the higher copy of *John* checks its Case-feature against T, whereas the Case-feature of the lower copy is still unchecked. In this scenario, the two instances of *John* in (34), although nondistinct in terms of the initial numeration, are not identical.

15. As Chomsky (1995, 227) observes, this proposal is at odds with the Inclusiveness Condition on the mapping from the numeration to LF, because the identification marks are not present in the numeration. It might be possible to determine whether or not a term is a copy of another term in compliance with the Inclusiveness Condition, if we keep track of the history of the derivation. If two contiguous derivational steps S_1 and S_2 differ in that a new term T is introduced into the computation, two possibilities arise: if from S_1 to S_2 the numeration has been reduced, T is to be interpreted as distinct from all the other syntactic objects available at S_2; if the numerations of S_1 and S_2 are the same, T must be a copy of some syntactic object available at S_1. In case there is more than one element at S_1 with the same set of features as T, independent conditions on chain formation could then determine which candidate is the only option that yields a convergent derivation. In a structure such as (i), for instance, only the pairs $(John^4, John^3)$ and $(John^2, John^1)$ could in principle form a chain; forming a chain with the pair $(John^4, John^1)$, for instance, would violate the Minimal Link Condition because the other two instances of *John* intervene, whereas forming a chain with the pair $(John^3, John^2)$ would violate Last Resort because $John^2$ has its Case-feature checked and is inert for the computational system (see Lasnik 1995, Chomsky 2000, 2001, and the discussion in section 3.2 below).

(i) $[_{TP}$ John^4 T $[_{vP}$ John^3 $[_{v'}$ said $[_{CP}$ that $[_{TP}$ John^2 was $[_{vP}$ kissed John$^1]]]]]]$

Whether or not it is desirable that the recognition of copies by the computational system proceeds along these lines remains to be determined. For expository purposes, I will adopt Chomsky's (1995, 227) proposal mentioned in the text.

16. See section 1.5.3.3 for the reason why this assumption is invalid for a restricted set of cases.

17. Here I put aside the question of how two heads in a mutual c-command relation can be linearized; I will return to it in section 1.5.3.3.

18. The unacceptability of the sentence in (ib) with two distinct instances of *John*, resulting from the structure in (ia), has nothing to do with linearization. The ill-formedness of (ia) is due to the fact that the lower instance of *John* cannot have its Case-feature checked (see section 2.2.2 for relevant discussion).

(i) a. $[_{TP}$ John^i $[_{T'}$ was+T $[_{vP}$ kissed John$^k]]]$
    b.   *John was kissed John.

19. Borrowing a metaphor suggested by Bob Frank (personal communication), it is as if deletion paints features blue and the interface is unable to see deleted features because it wears blue glasses.

20. Chomsky's (1995) proposal regarding feature deletion under checking is actually more complex in that it also resorts to an additional operation of erasure, which "is a 'stronger form' of deletion, eliminating the element entirely so that it is inaccessible to any operation, not just to interpretability at LF" (Chomsky

1995, 280). In this monograph, I will assume the gist of Chomsky's idea regarding the relation between interpretability at LF and accessibility to the computational system, but not its technical implementation in terms of erasure. All that is necessary for present purposes is to assume that a deleted feature cannot participate in a checking relation. For arguments against erasure, see Nunes 2000 and chapter 2 below.

21. Similarly to the case of Chain Reduction, the specification of the number of features to be deleted by FF-Elimination may follow from economy considerations concerning derivational length: all things being equal, a derivation in which a given feature F is unnecessarily deleted by FF-Elimination will be longer than a derivation in which F is not deleted. As before, I will keep the description of FF-Elimination in (57) for expository purposes.

22. Notice that this extension does not prevent Morphology from accessing deleted features. According to Chomsky's (1995, 280) definition of deletion, which is adopted here, a feature that is deleted through a checking operation becomes invisible at LF but is accessible to the computation (see note 19). The proposal in the text only extends invisibility at LF to invisibility at PF, as well. For relevant discussion of these issues, see Nunes 2000.

23. The issue of how the unchecked uninterpretable features of traces are eliminated in the covert component is addressed in chapter 2.

24. As formulated in (57), FF-Elimination applies after a given syntactic object is linearized and, therefore, after Chain Reduction has applied. This is crucial in the reasoning; otherwise, if FF-Elimination could for instance apply to the DP chain in (58) before Chain Reduction, there would be no principled basis for distinguishing (59a) from (59b) and (59c). More generally, the account of why heads of chains are usually the optimal candidates for phonetic realization would be lost.

The required order of application between Chain Reduction and FF-Elimination may, however, be determined without stipulation (see Nunes 1999b for further discussion). According to the notion of derivational cost proposed by Chomsky (1995, 226), an operation is costless if it is required as a defining property of a derivation and costly if it is required to yield a convergent derivation. In the case at hand, if the DP chain in (58), for instance, is not reduced, the structure containing it cannot be linearized and no PF object can be formed. Since a computation that does not yield the pair ⟨PF, LF⟩ does not count as a derivation (see Chomsky 1995, 225–226), Chain Reduction is required for a derivation to be obtained; as a defining property of a derivation, Chain Reduction is therefore costless. If FF-Elimination does not apply to (58), on the other hand, an illegitimate PF object may eventually be formed; hence, by being associated with PF convergence, FF-Elimination is derivationally costly. Thus, at the derivational step where a chain can in principle undergo either Chain Reduction or FF-Elimination, economy considerations will ensure its reduction.

I leave this discussion pending further research on the interactions of Chain Reduction and FF-Elimination with other operations of the phonological component. For relevant discussion, see Santos 2002. Santos suggests that prosodic parsing follows Chain Reduction and precedes FF-Elimination, citing the fact that in Brazilian Portuguese, traces do not block stress retraction, whereas pro does.

25. Consider the structure of the sentences in (i) within Chomsky's (1995) system, as represented in (ii).

(i) a. I believe John to be likely to be kissed.
   b. What did John say that Mary bought?

(ii) a. [$_{TP}$ I believe [$_{TP}$ John^i-**N** to be likely [$_{TP}$ John^i-**N** to be kissed John^i-**N**]]]
    b. [$_{CP}$ what^i-**WH** did+Q John say [$_{CP}$ what^i-**WH** that Mary bought what^i-**WH**]]

In each step of both instances of successive-cyclic movement, it is the categorial feature (an interpretable feature) of the moved element that enters into a checking relation with a feature of the target (an EPP-feature in (iia) and a strong *wh*-feature in (iib)). If interpretable features remain unaffected by checking operations, as Chomsky (1995, 280) proposes, the links of DP chains and *wh*-chains should be identical with respect to the only checking relation that takes place overtly, as represented in (ii), providing no principled basis for why deletion of traces should be the optimal solution in the analysis we are entertaining.

Notice that this potential problem does not arise if an exceptional Case-marking subject occupies a Case position (see Postal 1974, Lasnik and Saito 1992, Koizumi 1993, and Lasnik 1999b, among others) or if *wh*-phrases have an uninterpretable feature to be checked against an interrogative complementizer (see Chomsky 2000, 2001). Under these assumptions, both the head of the DP chain associated with *John* in (ia) and the head of the *wh*-chain in (iib) would have checked more features, thus being the optimal links for phonetic realization, as desired.

Within the confines of the assumptions in Chomsky 1995, the technical problem posed by (i) can be circumvented if my proposal that uninterpretable features become invisible at PF after being checked is extended to interpretable features, as well. Chomsky's (1995, 280) proposal that an interpretable feature is able to participate in multiple checking relations can then be reinterpreted in the following way. When participating in an overt checking relation, an interpretable feature can optionally be deleted with respect to PF, becoming invisible at this level. If it is deleted with respect to PF, it patterns with deleted uninterpretable features in not being able to enter into any further checking relation; if it is not deleted, it is allowed to enter into another checking relation. Under this view, the sentences in (i) are derived after Chain Reduction deletes the lower copies of the structure in (iii), where the subscript convention is now generalized to mean 'invisible at the relevant interface' (PF for interpretable features, and LF and PF for uninterpretable features).

(iii) a. [$_{TP}$ I believe [$_{TP}$ John^i-$_N$ to be likely [$_{TP}$ John^i-**N** to be kissed John^i-**N**]]]
     b. [$_{CP}$ what^i-$_{WH}$ did+Q John say [$_{CP}$ what^i-**WH** that Mary bought what^i-**WH**]]

26. The facts are attributed by Franks (1998) to Radanović-Kocić 1988 and Sandra Stjepanović in personal communication, respectively.

27. Bošković (2000, 2002) attributes the observation regarding the contrast between (63a) and (63b) to Wayles Browne (personal communication).

28. Bošković (2000, 2002) shows that the same reasoning accounts for the contrast in (i) in Bulgarian, which was observed by Billings and Rudin (1996). As Bošković (1997) argues, only the highest *wh*-phrase in Bulgarian is subject to the Superiority Condition; the order between the other *wh*-phrases is free, as (ii) illustrates. The unacceptability of (ib) should thus be due to the occurrence of two adjacent identical *wh*-elements.

(i) *Bulgarian* (from Billings and Rudin 1996)
   a. Koj kogo na kogo e pokazal?
       who whom to whom is pointed-out
       'Who pointed out whom to whom?'
   b. *Koj na kogo kogo e pokazal?
       who to whom whom is pointed-out

(ii) *Bulgarian* (from Bošković 2000, 2002)
   a. Koj kogo kak e tselunal?
       who whom how is kissed
       'Who kissed whom how?'
   b. Koj kak kogo e tselunal?
       who how whom is kissed

29. I am thankful to Max Guimarães for having brought the relevance of Golston's (1995) work to my attention.

30. See also Bobaljik 1995b, 1999, where it is proposed that a shifted object may be pronounced in the lower position if adjacency between I and the verb is disrupted, and Stjepanović 1999, where free word order in Serbo-Croatian is analyzed as resulting from the phonetic realization of different chain links, depending on stress assignment.

31. Franks (1998, 31) hints that "[p]resumably, the fact that all but the highest copy usually deletes is an economy property of PF, trying to preserve as much as possible of what the overt syntax provides it with at Spell Out," but he does not elaborate further on the precise nature of such an economy property. This suggestion is similar to Brody's (1995, 107) conceptual justification for the principle of Transparency (see note 13) and, as such, it is not obviously applicable to cases where multiple copies are phonetically realized (see section 1.5.3.3).

32. This led me in Nunes 1995 to attempt (unsuccessfully) to analyze the identical elements in (70)–(74) as distinct elements. The current analysis builds on and expands the account offered in Nunes 1999a.

33. Evidence that the LCA may not determine the order of morphemes in words formed in the course of the derivation is provided by the European Portuguese sentence in (ia), which is arguably derived from (ib) after the preposition *de* adjoins to the auxiliary *hei* and the resulting X^0 adjoins to C^0. If the LCA applied word-internally, we would incorrectly predict that in (ia) *de* should precede rather than follow *hei*, given that the preposition asymmetrically c-commands the auxiliary in the final structure. Thanks to Ana Maria Martins for helpful discussion.

(i) a. O que hei-de eu fazer?
what have.1SG-to I do
'What can I do?'
b. [$_{CP}$ C^0 [$_{TP}$ eu [hei [de [fazer [o que]]]]]]

34. Elements adjoined to a head H are in the checking domain of H (see Chomsky 1995, 268); hence, *wh*-movement via adjunction to C^0 in (80) is able to license whatever feature checking takes place in intermediate C positions. On the optimality of adjunction to heads versus movement to specifiers, see Nunes 1998.

35. Under this view, sentences such as (70) or (i) should involve fusion between the preposition and the *wh*-word, followed by fusion with the intermediate C^0.

(i) *German* (from McDaniel 1986)
Mit wem glaubst du *mit wem* Hans spricht?
with whom thinks you *with whom* Hans talks
'With whom do you think Hans is talking?'

36. Fanselow and Mahajan (1995) propose that in German, intermediate traces may cliticize to C^0 in the phonological component, thereby becoming invisible to deletion. Although this proposal can explain why full *wh*-traces cannot be phonetically realized in intermediate trace positions, it does not have a principled explanation for why traces in general cannot be phonetically realized.

37. Clitic duplication is also found in other varieties of South American Spanish, with a very intriguing dialectal variation. I am thankful to Mónica Zoppi-Fontana for discussion of the data in (84)–(86) and to Marcela Depiante for discussion of the data in (88)–(91).

38. I am assuming that deletion of the lower or the upper clitic copy in (87) yields the sentences in (84) only for the sake of discussion. Whatever turns out to be the appropriate analysis of clitic placement in these sentences, the important point is that only one copy of the clitic surfaces at PF.

39. See Galves 2000 for evidence that enclitics in Romance have a tighter morphological relationship with their hosts than proclitics.

40. Notice that I am not assuming that every head adjunction leads to morphological reanalysis; otherwise, standard verb movement to T, for example, would necessarily involve verb duplication (phonetic realization of both the moved verb and its trace). The fact that clitic duplication in (85a) and (86a) does not allow concomitant verb duplication indicates that the moved verb is still visible to the LCA after restructuring. Three possibilities come to mind that would derive the correct results: (i) the clitic and the verb are adjoined to different functional categories; (ii) the clitic adjoins to V and the two-segment V category is the one that is restructured; and (iii) the category resulting from restructuring the three-segment F^0 structure in (87) is actually V, rather than F. I leave the choice among these alternatives pending further research.

41. See Oroz 1966 and Silva-Corvalán 1989 for this pattern in Chilean Spanish.

42. I am thankful to Héctor Campos (personal communication), who called my attention to contrasts such as the one in (90) in Chilean Spanish.

43. Koopman (1984) also discusses predicate clefting in Gbadi, which exhibits the same general pattern as Vata.

44. More precisely, "the focused verb merely consists of the segmental specification of the verb, without its tonal specification. Since the elements with no associated tone surface carrying mid tone ..., the focused verb invariably surfaces with mid tone" (Koopman 1984, 155).

45. Koopman (1984, chap. 6) analyzes Vata predicate clefting in terms of verb movement to C, with a resumptive verb left behind in order to circumvent a potential Empty Category Principle violation. From this perspective, it is not clear why the resumptive verb should be subject to the morphological restrictions discussed below.

46. Notice that movement of the verb to Foc^0 skipping T^0 in (92b) is incorrectly ruled out by the Head Movement Constraint (see Travis 1984) but correctly allowed by the Minimal Link Condition (see Chomsky 1995): assuming that movement to Foc^0 is triggered to check the focus feature of the verb, the auxiliary in T^0 should not induce minimality effects, because auxiliaries in Vata cannot undergo clefting (see Koopman 1984, 79).

47. As suggested by Esmeralda Negrão (personal communication), it may also be the case that the change of tonal specification of the focused verb (see note 44) results from the proposed morphological reanalysis.

48. Another interesting case of verb reduplication was pointed out to me by David Adger (personal communication). In some varieties of English, the auxiliary verb *have* may be duplicated if the higher copy is reduced, as shown in (ia), and if the two copies are not adjacent, as shown in (ib).

(i) a.   They might've not have left.
    b.   *They might've have left.

According to the approach explored here, the phonological reduction of the higher copy of *have* in (ia) may be seen as the reflex of the morphological reanalysis that renders it invisible for the purposes of the LCA. In turn, the unacceptability of (ib) suggests that the restriction against adjacent homophonous morphemes (see section 1.5.3.2) may be checked prior to the proposed morphological reanalysis.

49. See Abels 2001 for verb duplication in Russian predicate cleft constructions and Bastos 2001 for verb duplication in constructions involving topicalization of verbal constituents in Brazilian Portuguese.

50. Luciana Dourado (personal communication) has pointed out to me that the alternative with standard incorporation in Panara is generally found in the speech of old informants. This indicates that the morphological reanalysis may have become obligatory for the younger generations. As suggested to me by Max Guimarães (personal communication), it is plausible that a similar diachronic reanalysis may have happened in Romance, where apparent cases of preposition duplication could have given rise to a new set of verbal prefixes. This would explain why the specific preposition a verb selects is partially determined by its prefix, as illustrated in (i) with Portuguese.

(i) *Portuguese*
   a. *cons*tituir *com* 'constitute with'
   b. *des*tituir *de* 'deprive of'
   c. *com*por *com* 'compose with'
   d. *de*por *de* 'depose from'
   e. *as*cender *a* 'ascend to'
   f. *des*cender *de* 'descend from'

51. The data discussed in this section involved morphological reanalysis of the head of the chain, as in the case of duplication of clitics, verbs, and postpositions, or reanalysis of intermediate traces, as in the cases of *wh*-movement. However, nothing in principle prevents tails of the chains from being morphologically reanalyzed. A potential example of such a case is auxiliary doubling in English child grammar, as illustrated in (i). If children allow the complex formed by negation and the tail of the auxiliary chain to be morphologically restructured, only the copy of the auxiliary in C will be visible to the LCA and Chain Reduction will not be necessary (for an alternative analysis, see Hiramatsu 1999).

(i) *English child grammar* (from Guasti, Thornton, and Wexler 1995)
   a. What *did* he *did*n't wanna bring to school?
   b. What kind of bread *do* you *do*n't like?
   c. Why *could* Snoopy *could*n't fit in the boat?

52. This section develops the analysis proposed in Nunes 2003.

53. The issue of whether adjuncts are linearized by the procedure that linearizes specifiers and complements or by a different procedure seems to be orthogonal to the analysis to be developed below (see Kayne 1994 and Chomsky 1995, for relevant discussion). Thus, regardless of the specific linearization procedure for adjuncts, *before* in (102), for instance, should be preceded by [bought it^i] and precede [saw it^i]; given that the two instances of *it* in this case are nondistinct, we end up with the contradictory requirement that *before* should precede and be preceded by the same element, which prevents the structure from being linearized. For expository purposes, I will henceforth assume that right-adjunction is available in the grammar.

54. To be explicit, given that [elected John^3] in (106b) should precede X, which in turn should precede *John^2*, and that these two instances of *John* are nondistinct, we obtain the contradictory requirements that X should precede and be preceded by *John* and that *John* should precede itself.

55. Here I will not attempt to characterize the conditions under which remnant movement is allowed (see Müller 1998 and Kayne 1998 for relevant discussion). My only purpose is to provide an account of the phonetic realization of the chains involved in remnant movement.

56. The same result would also obtain if Chain Reduction had first applied to CH_2, yielding (ia), and then to CH_1, yielding (ib). Crucially, *John^3* in (ia) satisfies the description of the chain link of CH_1 that is to be deleted (see (107a)).

(i) a. [$_{XP}$[$_{VP}$ elected John^3]^k [$_{X'}$ X [$_{TP}$ John^2 [$_{T'}$ was [$_{VP}$ ~~elected John^1~~]^k]]]]
   b. [$_{XP}$[$_{VP}$ elected ~~John^3~~]^k [$_{X'}$ X [$_{TP}$ John^2 [$_{T'}$ was [$_{VP}$ ~~elected John^1~~]^k]]]]

57. Thanks to Fumi Niinuma (personal communication), who brought these constructions to my attention. *con* in the glosses of (111) and (112) stands for *contrastive particle*. As Mary Kato (personal communication) has observed, given the semantics of these constructions (see Bastos 2001) and the topic marker *wa* in (112), it is more reasonable to analyze (111) and (112) as involving predicate topicalization, rather than predicate clefting. If this turns out to be the correct analysis, the FocP projection in (114) should be replaced by a TopP projection.

58. The issue of whether Foc^0 in (114) is head initial or head final is orthogonal to the point under discussion.

59. The same kind of contrast holds in ASL, as illustrated in (i) (see Petronio 1993, Petronio and Lillo-Martin 1997, and Nunes and Quadros, in preparation, for analysis and further discussion).

(i) *American Sign Language* (from Petronio and Lillo-Martin 1997)
    a.   ANN CANNOT READ CANNOT
    b.   *ANN CANNOT READ CANNOT READ
        'Ann CAN'T read.'
    c.   NANCY HATE ICE-CREAM HATE
    d.   *NANCY HATE ICE-CREAM HATE ICE-CREAM
        'Nancy HATES ice cream.'

60. I am thankful to Norbert Hornstein (personal communication), who brought this issue to my attention.

Chapter 2

1. See also Hornstein's (1995) All For One Principle.

2. The stipulation is restricted to A-chains, because the formal features of *wh*-traces may be required for further checking relations (see Chomsky 1995, 302–303). In (ia) and (ib), for instance, the formal features of the *wh*-trace must move in the covert component in order to check Case, whereas in (ic) the formal features of the verb should raise covertly and check its ϕ-features against the *wh*-trace in Spec,TP.

(i) a. [what$_i$ did John see t$_i$]
    b. [guess what$_i$ there is t$_i$ in the room]
    c. [who$_i$ do you think [$_{TP}$ t$_i$ [$_{vP}$ t$_i$ works hard]]]

3. It is also not obvious that when the head of a nontrivial chain CH raises, the new chain involves the newly created position and the tail of CH, as proposed by Chomsky (1995, 300). As I will show in sections 3.2 and 3.4.3, there is actually evidence related to the anti-c-command restriction on parasitic gap licensing that indicates that the Minimal Link Condition prevents a copy C^1 from forming a chain with a copy C^3 over a copy C^2 such that C^2 c-commands C^3.

Moreover, if formal features are relevant for the computations of binding and scope, the stipulated erasure of the formal features should rule out interpretations related to binding and scope that are arguably associated with intermediate links of A-chains (see Lebeaux 1991, Aoun and Li 1993, and Hornstein 1995, among others, for evidence for the interpretive role of A-traces, and Lasnik 1999a for evidence against it). A possible way out, although undeveloped, is found in Chomsky's (1995, 387 n. 75) suggestion that "[d]epending on exactly how interface operations are understood, the semantic features of intermediate traces could be accessible to interpretive operations before they become invisible for further interpretation, possibly allowing implementation of ideas about the interpretive role of intermediate traces."

4. Given that unaccusative verbs have ϕ-features and presumably do not make use of the light verb shell (see Hale and Keyser 1993 and Chomsky 1995), the main verb should in principle be the element that carries ϕ-features.

5. Recall that, since the categorial and ϕ-features of the higher link are interpretable, they are deleted with respect to PF, but not with respect to LF (see section 1.5.3.2).

6. Similar to the case of Chain Reduction and FF-Elimination (see sections 1.5.3.1 and 1.5.3.2), it is actually unnecessary to specify that Chain Uniformization deletes as few features as possible; the exact number of features to be deleted is indirectly determined by economy considerations regarding derivational length. However, I will use the formulation in (13) for expository purposes.

7. Notice that we need not impose a specific order for chains to be inspected with respect to feature composition (in a top-down or bottom-up fashion). In instances such as (16) and (18), at least one sequence of applications of Chain Uniformization allows the derivation to converge, which is enough for the conceptual-intentional interface to assign the relevant interpretation to the structure obtained.

8. The reasoning is the same used by Chomsky and Lasnik (1993, 547) to prevent deletion of starred traces (traces marked [−γ] in Lasnik and Saito's (1984) system) of adjunct chains violating the ECP: "[W]e now regard the operation of deletion, like movement, as a 'last resort' principle, a special case of the principle of economy of derivation (make derivations as short as possible, with links as short as possible). . . . Deletion is impermissible in a uniform chain, since these are already legitimate."

9. Under Chomsky's (1995, 281) analysis, the categorial feature of an expletive is deleted but not erased, therefore being accessible to the computational system. See Nunes 2000 for discussion.

10. Given that θ-role assignment and feature checking are in complementary distribution in Chomsky's (1995) system, the subject in (35) could not check its Case in situ because Spec,vP is involved in a thematic relation.

11. As Eduardo Raposo (personal communication) calls to my attention, object clitic placement in Romance must check features other than Case in order to skip the trace of the subject without inducing minimality effects.

12. The assumption that traces cannot be targets of movement (see Chomsky 1995, 304) is an extension of the assumption that traces are irrelevant for computing locality. Once the latter are dropped on conceptual and empirical grounds, as argued above, there is no reason to keep the former. For evidence that traces may be targets for movement, see Bošković and Franks 2000.

13. See Aoun and Nunes 2002 for further evidence in favor of the adjunction of FF(Obj) to Vb, based on vehicle change effects (in the sense of Fiengo and May 1994). The gist of Aoun and Nunes's proposal is that what is copied in the second conjunct of (i), for instance, is not the whole predicate of the first conjunct, but the verb with the adjoined FF(John), which has moved for Case-checking purposes. Assuming that for the purposes of binding theory, FF(John) is equivalent to the pronoun *him*, copying *admire*+FF(John) to the second conjunct induces a Principle B effect in (ia), but not in (ib).

(i) a. *Mary admires John$_i$, but he$_i$ doesn't.
     b. Mary admires John$_i$, but he$_i$ doesn't think Susan does.

Chapter 3

1. The sequence of derivational steps described in (3) is referred to as an *interarboreal operation* by Bobaljik (1995a) and Bobaljik and Brown (1997) and as *paracyclic movement* by Uriagereka (1998, chap. 4).

2. With the elimination of D-Structure in the Minimalist Program, assembly of unconnected phrase markers is independently required for any phrase involving a complex specifier or a complex adjunct. For instance, consider the partial derivation of (ia), after the verb has already been merged with the object, forming K in (ib). Suppose that we merge *man* with K, yielding the object L in (iia), and then we merge *the* with L, forming the object M in (iib). In this derivation, *the* and *man* do not form a constituent. Thus, in order for the correct structure to be formed in a cyclic fashion (see section 3.8 for discussion), *the* and *man* should merge independently of K, as shown in (iiia), and the resulting object should then merge with K, as shown in (iiib).

(i) a. The man saw the woman.
     b. K = [saw [the woman]]

(ii) a. L = [man [saw [the woman]]]
      b. M = [the [man [saw [the woman]]]]

(iii) a. N = [the man]
       b. O = [[the man] [saw [the woman]]]

3. As discussed in section 1.6.1, given that no element can check a feature against itself, the c-command requirement is actually restricted to *asymmetric* c-command.

4. For relevant discussion, see Kayne 1983, 1984, Contreras 1984, Aoun and Clark 1985, Haïk 1985, É. Kiss 1985, Chomsky 1986a, Browning 1987, Safir 1987, Weinberg 1988, Cinque 1990, Frampton 1990, Williams 1990, Lasnik and Stowell 1991, Postal 1993, 1994, Manzini 1994, Munn 1994, and Brody 1995, among others.

5. Chomsky (1986a), citing Kearney 1983, takes the absence of reconstruction in the parasitic gap position in constructions such as (i) as evidence for the parasitic nature of the empty category in the object of *read*. The reverse pattern found in parasitic gaps inside relative clauses adjoined to subjects, as illustrated in (ii)

(from Munn 1994), shows that reconstruction in either gap is in principle possible and that other factors are responsible for the pattern exhibited below (see Williams 1990, Munn 1994, and Nissenbaum 1998 for relevant discussion).

(i) a. Which books about himself did John file before Mary read?
    b. *Which books about herself did John file before Mary read?

(ii) a. *Which picture of herself did every boy who saw say Mary liked?
    b. Which picture of himself did every boy who saw say Mary liked?

6. See Hornstein 1995, chaps. 6 and 7, for additional data, alternative formulations of the Weak Crossover Condition, and a detailed discussion of Lasnik and Stowell's (1991) null epithet proposal.

7. The discussion of the properties in (18e) and (18f) will be delayed until section 3.6, where parasitic gap and across-the-board extraction constructions will be contrasted.

8. In section 2.3.3, I proposed that accusative Case checking involves either movement of the object DP to the outer Spec,vP or adjunction of the formal features of the object DP to the light verb; furthermore, as we will see in section 3.8.2.3, under the Copy+Merge theory FF-movement takes place overtly and in a cyclic fashion through sideward movement. Thus, under the Copy+Merge theory the structure under discussion should be derived along the lines of (i)–(iii): FF([critics of which politician]) undergoes sideward movement from K to L in (i), yielding M in (ii), which then merges with K, followed by movement of *critics of which politician*, yielding (iii). It is arguably the case that (iii) is not a licit syntactic object, though. The light verb ends up with two nondistinct elements in its checking domain and, even more problematic, the set of formal features of [critics of which politician] within Spec,vP ends up within the domain of the nondistinct FF([critics of which politician]) adjoined to the light verb. That is, this configuration should be ruled out along with vacuous projections and structures resulting from self-adjunction.

(i) a. $K = [_{VP}$ upset [critics of which politician]]
    b. $L = v$

(ii) a. $K = [_{VP}$ upset [critics of which politician]^i]
    b. $M = [_{v^0}$ FF([critics of which politician]^i) [$_{v^0}$ v^0]]

(iii)

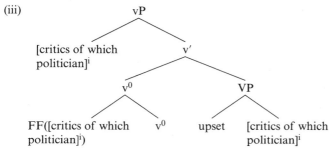

9. Munn's (1994) analysis of parasitic gaps, in which the null operator is a copy of the element that licenses it, may be immune to this criticism, if the "null operator" copy forms a chain with the element that licenses it.

10. Cinque (1990, 155), for instance, suggests that overt resumptive pronouns give rise to (stronger) weak crossover effects, as opposed to null resumptive pronouns (see also Chomsky 1982, 44).

11. The same reasoning holds if the overt object movement in (53) actually involves overt movement of sets of formal features (see section 3.8.2.3).

12. Languages may vary in this regard (see É. Kiss 1985, for instance). The contrast between the Russian sentences in (i) (from Franks 1993, 525), for example, shows that a "real" gap and a "parasitic" gap may differ in Case specification in Russian only if a syncretic form compatible with both Cases is employed.

(i) a. mal'çik, [*kotoromu/*kotorogo]$_i$ Maša   davala den'gi t$_i$
       boy   who(DAT)/(GEN)   Masha(NOM) gave   money
       do togo, kak (ona) stala   izbegat' PG$_i$, . . .
       until   she   started to-avoid
       'the boy who Masha gave money to until she started to avoid him'

   b. devuška, [kotoroj]$_i$ Ivan   daval den'gi t$_i$ do togo, kak (on)
       girl   who(DAT-GEN) Ivan(NOM) gave   money until   he
       stal   izbegat' PG$_i$
       started to-avoid
       'the girl who Ivan gave money to until he started to avoid her'

Similar considerations extend to the sideward analysis of across-the-board *wh*-movement to be discussed in section 3.5 (see Dyła 1984 and Franks 1993 for a discussion of contrasts like that in (i) in Polish across-the-board constructions). It is plausible that the parameter at stake can be stated in terms of lexical specification: nouns are generically specified for Case in languages like English, but specified for a particular kind of Case in languages like Russian. Thus, the possibility of sideward movement of DPs may be restricted by Case conflict in Russian (see (i)), but not in English (see (56)).

13. According to the analysis to be developed in section 3.4.4.2, if the PP in (55b) had adjoined to VP rather than vP, the constituents of the PP would have become inert after adjunction and there would be no source for the copy of *which man* at the derivational step where the light verb would merge with the two-segment VP.

14. A technical question arises regarding the potential source for the copy in Spec,CP in (58). If Copy targets the *wh*-phrase in Spec,vP, for instance, FF-Elimination will have to delete the unchecked Case-feature of the newly created copy in the phonological component; if Copy targets the *wh*-phrase in Spec,TP, on the other hand, FF-Elimination will not be required to delete the Case-feature of the resulting copy, because its source has already checked its Case-feature. Economy considerations therefore require that Copy target the *wh*-phrase in the Spec,TP in (58). To put it generally, given a derivation with two nondistinct terms as potential targets for the Copy operation, Copy will target the term with more features checked, up to convergence (see Nunes 1995, sec. IV.2.3, for further discussion).

15. Hornstein's (1999, 2001) analysis of controlled PRO as a trace (a copy) actually takes a sentence like (61a) to be derived along the lines of (61b), with sideward movement of *which paper* from the embedded Spec,TP to the matrix Spec,vP. Crucially, Hornstein does not assume null Case. See section 3.9 for more details about Hornstein's analysis.

16. Chomsky (1986a, 63) also raises the possibility that the "licensing chain" and the "parasitic chain" are connected by a process of chain composition and that a subchain of the composed chain will violate the Chain Condition if the parasitic gap is c-commanded by the real gap.

17. This problem also arises in Munn's (1994) analysis, according to which null operators are copies of the elements that license them. Under this view, a sentence such as (68a) has the structure in (i), with the "null operator" copy occupying the embedded Spec,CP.

(i) $[_{CP}[\text{which paper}]^i \text{ did+Q } [_{TP} \text{ you } [_{vP}[_{vP} \text{ file [which paper}]^i] [_{PP} \text{ without}$
$[_{CP}[\text{which paper}]^i \text{ C } [_{TP} \text{ PRO reading [which paper}]^i]]]]]]$

Munn's proposal would be compatible with the analysis of copy deletion developed in chapter 1 if the "null operator" copy in (i), for instance, formed a chain with the element that licenses it; otherwise, the nondistinct copies that do not form a chain should induce violations of the asymmetry and irreflexivity conditions on linear order, making it impossible for a PF object to be formed and canceling the derivation. However, if a (linked) chain between the copy in the matrix Spec,CP and the two copies inside the adjunct clause in (i) can be formed, there is no explanation for the unacceptability of (70a), since it could be assigned the analogous structure in (ii), with a "null operator" copy in the specifier of the adjunct clause.

(ii) $[_{CP}[\text{which book}]^i \text{ did+Q } [_{TP} \text{ you } [_{vP}[_{vP} \text{ review this paper] } [_{PP} \text{ without}$
$[_{CP}[\text{which paper}]^i \text{ C } [_{TP} \text{ PRO reading [which paper}]^i]]]]]]$

18. However, I will have nothing to say here on the connectedness effects displayed by *wh*-in-situ in English and negative quantifiers in Italian, which Brody analyzes in terms of secondary chains, on the basis of work by Kayne (1984) and Longobardi (1991).

19. For the linearization of heads in a mutual c-command relation such as *c* and *d* in (80), for instance, see Chomsky 1995, 337, and the discussion in section 1.5.3.3.

20. I should point out that although the sideward movement analysis can successfully account for the acceptability of parasitic gaps inside simple subjects, as in (84b), it affords only a partial account of constructions involving a parasitic gap inside a relative within the subject, as illustrated in (i) (from Frampton (1990, 21), who attributes it to Richard Kayne; see also Williams 1990, among others, for discussion).

(i) a. a guy that every joke we told to delighted
   b. $[[\text{a guy}]_k [O_k \text{ that } [[\text{every joke}]_i [O_i \text{ we told } t_i \text{ to } PG_k] \text{ delighted } t_k]]]$

According to the discussion above, O_k in (ib) could move from the position of the object of *to* and merge with *delighted* before the relative clause headed by *every joke* is spelled out and becomes an island for extraction. In order for the structure to be linearized, the "null operator" copy of O_k and its "parasitic gap" copy should then form a chain; however, the relevant checking relation involving the relative null operator O_i should induce a minimality effect, since in principle it participates in the same kind of checking relation as O_k. I leave this problem pending further research on the relevant checking involving relative clause formation.

21. The reader may have noted that a crucial aspect of this proposal is that (sideward) movement always proceeds from a subordinated to a subordinating domain. If the computational system could first start building the matrix derivational workspace before building an embedded derivational workspace, the sentence in (91a), for instance, would be incorrectly ruled in by a derivation where sideward movement proceeded from the object of *borrow* to the object of *finding*. This issue will be discussed in detail in section 3.7.

22. I am thankful to Ricardo Etxepare for helpful discussion about the relevant readings.

23. At this point, I have no account of why English also allows the two-event reading for constructions such as (112b). It should be observed that this contrast between English and Portuguese also shows up in constructions involving a ditransitive verb (see Pesetsky 1995), as illustrated in (i).

(i) a. John gave flowers to her yesterday and (to) him on Sunday.
    b. João deu flores pra ela ontem e *(pra) ele domingo.

24. Apparent counterexamples to the elimination of the ATB formalism involve *wanna*-contraction constructions such as (ia–c), which were pointed out to me by David Lightfoot (personal communication). These cases appear to indicate that *wanna*-contraction is possible only if both instances of *to* cliticize in an ATB fashion. This conclusion is not forceful, though. The pattern in (i) may follow from the two possibilities of conjunction represented in (ii); only (iib) seems to permit contraction, apparently yielding an ATB effect. See Ximenes 2002 for clearer cases of contraction in coordinate structures triggered by the Parallelism Requirement.

(i) a. I want to dance and to sing.
    b. I wanna dance and sing.
    c. I wanna dance and (*to) sing.

(ii) a. [want [$_{andP}$[to dance] [$_{and'}$ and [to sing]]]]
     b. [want to [$_{andP}$[dance] [$_{and'}$ and [sing]]]]

25. Recall that the properties of parasitic gaps listed in (18e–f), repeated in (i), were left unexplained in section 3.4.1.

(i) a. Parasitic gaps can only be NPs (see Aoun and Clark 1985 and Chomsky 1986a, for instance).
    b. Parasitic gaps cannot be licensed by nonreferential NPs (see Cinque 1990, for instance).

26. (129a–c) and (130a–c) are from Postal 1993 and (129d) is from Cinque 1990. Munn (1993) judges (130d) as "*"; the judgment reported here is from Hornstein and Nunes 2002.

27. Also see Schein 1993, sec. 5.1, for a discussion of the relation between being selected and being an argument.

28. Movement of *did* in (141) is therefore analogous to movement of the verb from K to L in (i), discussed in section 3.5.2.

(i) a. $N' = \{I_1, v_1, talked_0, to_0, João_0, and_0, Maria_0\}$
   b. $K = [_{andP}$ and $[_{VP}$ talked $[_{PP}$ to Maria]]]
   c. $L = [_{PP}$ to João]

29. This was actually what I suggested in Nunes 1995.

30. Nunes and Uriagereka (2000) follow Chomsky (2000) in assuming that the maximal projection determined by a subarray is either vP or CP (a *phase* in Chomsky's (2000) terms). In convergent derivations, prepositions that select clausal complements must then belong to the "subordinating" array, and not to the array associated with the complement clause (otherwise, we would have a PP phase). Hence, the prepositions *after* and *without* in (153) and *before* in (155) belong to subarrays determined by a light verb, and not by a complementizer.

31. Semantic restrictions may, however, rule out structures resulting from noncyclic adjunction. As discussed by Heycock (1995, 558), the "nonreferential" *wh*-phrase in (ia) requires reconstruction, as opposed to the "referential" *wh*-phrase in (ib) (see Fox 1999 for relevant discussion). Since my purpose here is only to provide a cyclic analysis for the cases where reconstruction is not required, I will not discuss cases such as (ia), which arguably involve a derivation along the lines of (171a).

(i) a. *[how many lies aimed at exonerating Clifford$_i$]$_k$ is he$_i$ planning to come up with t$_k$
   b. [which lies aimed at exonerating Clifford$_i$]$_k$ did he$_i$ expect t$_k$ to be effective

32. Sideward movement of *which claim* in (172)–(173) takes place from the matrix to an embedded derivational workspace, apparently contradicting the proposal regarding cyclic access to the numeration discussed in section 3.7. There is, however, one difference that may explain why the movement in (172)–(173) is permitted. In the undesirable case illustrated in (i)–(ii), for instance, the computational system activates the subarray D before having integrated all of the lexical items of the active subarray B into the structure being built; crucially, the preposition *before* can only be integrated into the structure after merging with a complement.

(i) $N = \{\{_A Q_1, did_1\}$,
   $\{_B you_1, v_1, file_0, which_0, book_0, before_1\}$,
   $\{_C C_1, T_1\}$,
   $\{_D PRO_1, v_1, reading_0\}\}$

(ii) a. $K = [file [which book]]$
    b. $L = reading$

Thus, in an instance of licit sideward movement such as the one illustrated in (iii)–(iv), for instance, the computational system must first build the CP based on subarrays C and D, which *before* can then take as its complement when the subarray B is activated.

(iii) $N = \{\{_A \, Q_1, did_1\},$
$\{_B \, you_1, v_1, file_0, before_1\},$
$\{_C \, C_0, T_0\},$
$\{_D \, PRO_0, v_0, reading_0, which_0, book_0\}\}$

(iv) a. $K = [_{CP} \, C \, [_{TP} \, PRO \, [_{T'} \, T \, [_{vP} \, v \, [_{vP} \, reading \, [which \, book]]]]]]$
b. $L = file$

In the case of (172)–(173), on the other hand, there is no selector for the relative clause in the subarrays corresponding to the matrix clause; rather, the licensing of the null operator may be conceived of as a selecting feature that triggers sideward movement of *which claim*. Below, we will see that under a raising analysis of relative clauses, movement actually proceeds in the expected direction, from the relative clause to the object position of the main verb.

33. In Chomsky's (1993) system, an element adjoined to a maximal projection HP or to the specifier of HP is in the checking domain of the head of HP (see Chomsky 1993, 11–19, for definitions and discussion). In the case of (174), the higher *wh*-phrase is adjoined to the relative clause, which is itself in the specifier of the matrix clause; thus, the *wh*-phrase is in the checking domain of both the head of the relative clause and the head of the matrix clause. See Kato and Nunes 1998 for further discussion.

34. Since an adequate discussion of the correct analysis of relative clauses is beyond the scope of this monograph, I leave for another occasion the choice between the two traditional analyses and a full exploration of the raising analysis to be suggested below.

35. A reviewer of Nunes 2001 observes that the cyclic analysis of relative clause adjunction presented here cannot account for the possibility of coreference in a sentence such as (i), which involves adjunction within a complement clause. The amelioration effect noted by the reviewer also shows up when a noun complement clause is embedded in another noun complement clause as in (iia–b), or when the relevant nominal expression is within the specifier of a complement as in (iic) (see Safir 1999, among others, for relevant discussion).

(i) Which claim that a woman that John$_i$ met was asleep was he$_i$ willing to discuss?

(ii) a. Whose claim that the rumors that John$_i$ acted illegally are true was he$_i$ willing to discuss?
b. Whose attempts to prove the accusation that John$_i$ was guilty was he$_i$ unaware of?
c. Which picture of John$_i$'s mother did he$_i$ like?

What the data in (i)–(ii) appear to show is that the level of embedding of the relevant nominal expression is an extra factor in allowing (marginal) coreference with the pronoun. At this point, I have nothing to say about whether this amelioration effect should be captured in grammatical terms by somehow imposing lack of reconstruction in the most embedded position in cases of multiple embedding or whether it should be explained by parsing considerations. I would like to point out, however, that if it turns out that the complement/relative clause reconstruction asymmetry is illusory (see Lasnik 1998) or that a relative clause cannot modify a single chain link for independent reasons, the main point of this section remains essentially unaltered. The reasoning used here to provide a sideward movement analysis for relative but not for complement clauses was the same employed to derive the core properties of parasitic gap constructions (see section 3.4) and to exclude unwanted instances of sideward movement of heads (see section 3.5.2).

36. Chomsky (2000) also attempts to eliminate covert movement by analyzing "covert dependencies" in terms of overt applications of Agree. For empirical arguments for treating covert movement in terms of Move F rather than Agree, see chapter 2, note 13, and Aoun and Nunes 2002.

37. A similar proposal was independently developed by Oishi (1997), who also observes that under this view, the effects of Procrastinate regarding covert versus overt movement are locally derived from feature strength.

38. Both Chomsky's (1995, sec. 4.4.4) covert movement of formal features and its reinterpretation above in terms of overt sideward movement of formal features need to assume that the set of formal features of a given lexical item is accessible to the Copy operation, and that the computational system may form a chain $CH = (FF^i, FF^i)$ relating two copies of a given set of formal features. If Copy and Form Chain can only operate with terms (constituents), which are defined in (i) (from Chomsky 1995, 247), a lexical item LI should then have the format $LI = \{\gamma, \{FF, SF, PF\}\}$, where FF is a set of formal features, SF is a set of semantic features, PF is a set of phonological features, and γ is a label specifying the relevant properties of LI much like the label of phrasal syntactic objects (see Chomsky 1995, 243).

(i) *Term*

For any structure K, (a) K is a term of K; and (b) if L is a term of K, then the members of the members of L are terms of K.

Notice that although SF and PF also end up being terms under this view, Last Resort correctly prevents them from moving outside LI, because they do not participate in checking relations. See Nunes and Thompson 1998 for relevant discussion and definitions.

39. See Hornstein 2001 for an extension of this analysis to purpose clause and *tough*-movement constructions.

40. See Ferreira 2000a,b and Rodrigues 2000, 2002 for different proposals regarding how the Case-feature of the embedded T head is checked.

41. For relevant discussion, see Hornstein 2001 and Kayne 2002, where certain instances of pronouns are analyzed as saving devices for constructions formed from illicit sideward movement, and Boeckx 2001, where donkey pronouns are treated as residues of sideward movement.

References

Abels, Klaus. 2001. The predicate cleft construction in Russian. In *Formal Approaches to Slavic Linguistics 10: The Indiana meeting 2000*, ed. by Steven Franks, Tracy King, and Michael Yadroff, 1–19. Ann Arbor: Michigan Slavic Publications.

Aoun, Joseph, and Robin Clark. 1985. On non-overt operators. In *Studies in syntax*, ed. by Gary Gilligan, Mohammad Mohammad, and Ian Roberts, 17–85. Southern California Occasional Papers in Linguistics 10. Los Angeles: University of Southern California, Department of Linguistics.

Aoun, Joseph, Norbert Hornstein, David Lightfoot, and Amy Weinberg. 1987. Two types of locality. *Linguistic Inquiry* 18, 537–577.

Aoun, Joseph, and Yen-hui Audrey Li. 1993. *Syntax of scope*. Cambridge, Mass.: MIT Press.

Aoun, Joseph, and Jairo Nunes. 2002. Vehicle change effects: An argument for Move-F. Ms., University of Southern California, Los Angeles, and Universidade Estadual de Campinas.

Ausin, Adolfo, and Marcela Depiante. 1999. On the syntax of *parecer* with and without an experiencer. Paper presented at the 3rd Hispanic Linguistics Symposium, Georgetown University, October.

Barss, Andrew. 1986. Chains and anaphoric dependencies. Doctoral dissertation, MIT, Cambridge, Mass.

Bastos, Ana. 2001. *Fazer, eu faço!* Topicalização de constituintes verbais em português brasileiro. Master's thesis, Universidade Estadual de Campinas.

Bianchi, Valentina. 1999. *Consequences of antisymmetry: Headed relative clauses*. Berlin: Mouton de Gruyter.

Billings, Loren, and Catherine Rudin. 1996. Optimality and superiority: A new approach to multiple *wh*-ordering. In *Formal Approaches to Slavic Linguistics: The College Park meeting 1994*, ed. by Jindřich Toman, 35–60. Ann Arbor: Michigan Slavic Publications.

Bobaljik, Jonathan. 1995a. In terms of Merge: Copy and head movement. In *Papers on minimalist syntax*, ed. by Rob Pensal fini and Hiroyuki Ura, 41–64.

MIT Working Papers in Linguistics 27. Cambridge, Mass.: MIT, Department of Linguistics and Philosophy, MITWPL.

Bobaljik, Jonathan. 1995b. Morphosyntax: The syntax of verbal inflection. Doctoral dissertation, MIT, Cambridge, Mass.

Bobaljik, Jonathan. 1999. A-chains at the interfaces: Copies, agreement, and "covert" movement. Ms., McGill University, Montreal.

Bobaljik, Jonathan, and Samuel Brown. 1997. Interarboreal operations: Head movement and the Extension Requirement. *Linguistic Inquiry* 28, 345–356.

Boeckx, Cedric. 2000. Raising and experiencers, cross-linguistically. Ms., University of Connecticut, Storrs.

Boeckx, Cedric. 2001. (In)direct binding. Ms., University of Connecticut, Storrs.

Bošković, Željko. 1994. D-Structure, Theta-Criterion, and movement into theta-positions. *Linguistic Analysis* 24, 247–286.

Bošković, Željko. 1997. Superiority effects with multiple *wh*-fronting in Serbo-Croatian. *Lingua* 102, 1–20.

Bošković, Željko. 2000. What is special about multiple *wh*-fronting? In *NELS 30*, ed. by Mako Hirotani, Andries Coetzee, Nancy Hall, and Ji-Yung Kim, 83–107. Amherst: University of Massachusetts, GLSA.

Bošković, Željko. 2001. *On the nature of the syntax-phonology interface: Cliticization and related phenomena*. Amsterdam: Elsevier Science.

Bošković, Željko. 2002. On multiple *wh*-fronting. *Linguistic Inquiry* 33, 351–383.

Bošković, Željko, and Steven Franks. 2000. Across-the-board movement and LF. *Syntax* 3, 107–128.

Bošković, Željko, and Daiko Takahashi. 1998. Scrambling and Last Resort. *Linguistic Inquiry* 29, 347–366.

Britto, Helena. 1997. Deslocados à esquerda, resumptivo-sujeito, ordem SV: A expressão do juizo categórico e tético no português do Brasil. Doctoral dissertation, Universidade Estadual de Campinas.

Brody, Michael. 1995. *Lexico-Logical Form: A radically minimalist theory*. Cambridge, Mass.: MIT Press.

Browning, M. A. 1987. Null operator constructions. Doctoral dissertation, MIT, Cambridge, Mass.

Cardinaletti, Anna, and Michal Starke. 1999. The typology of structural deficiency: A case study of the three classes of pronouns. In *Clitics in the languages of Europe*, ed. by Henk van Riemsdijk, 145–233. EALT/EUROPTYP 20-5. Berlin: Mouton de Gruyter.

Cattell, Ray. 1978. On the source of interrogative adverbs. *Language* 54, 61–77.

Ćavar, Damir, and Gisbert Fanselow. 1997. Split constituents in Germanic and Slavic. Paper presented at International Conference on Pied-Piping, Friedrich-Schiller Universität Jena, June.

Chierchia, Gennaro. 1991. Functional *wh* and weak crossover. In *Proceedings of the Tenth West Coast Conference on Formal Linguistics*, ed. by Dawn Bates, 75–90. Stanford, Calif.: CSLI Publications.

Chomsky, Noam. 1973. Conditions on transformations. In *A festschrift for Morris Halle*, ed. by Stephen Anderson and Paul Kiparsky, 232–286. New York: Holt, Rinehart and Winston.

Chomsky, Noam. 1975. *The logical structure of linguistic theory*. New York: Plenum.

Chomsky, Noam. 1976. Conditions on rules of grammar. *Linguistic Analysis* 2, 303–351.

Chomsky, Noam. 1981. *Lectures on government and binding*. Dordrecht: Foris.

Chomsky, Noam. 1982. *Some concepts and consequences of the theory of government and binding*. Cambridge, Mass.: MIT Press.

Chomsky, Noam. 1986a. *Barriers*. Cambridge, Mass.: MIT Press.

Chomsky, Noam. 1986b. *Knowledge of language: Its nature, origin, and use*. New York: Praeger.

Chomsky, Noam. 1993. A minimalist program for linguistic theory. In *The view from Building 20: Essays in linguistics in honor of Sylvain Bromberger*, ed. by Kenneth Hale and Samuel Jay Keyser, 1–52. Cambridge, Mass.: MIT Press.

Chomsky, Noam. 1994. Bare phrase structure. MIT Occasional Papers in Linguistics 5. Cambridge, Mass.: MIT, Department of Linguistics and Philosophy, MITWPL.

Chomsky, Noam. 1995. Categories and transformations. In *The Minimalist Program*, 219–394. Cambridge, Mass.: MIT Press.

Chomsky, Noam. 2000. Minimalist inquiries: The framework. In *Step by step: Essays on minimalist syntax in honor of Howard Lasnik*, ed. by Roger Martin, David Michaels, and Juan Uriagereka, 89–155. Cambridge, Mass.: MIT Press.

Chomsky, Noam. 2001. Derivation by phase. In *Ken Hale: A life in language*, ed. by Michael Kenstowicz, 1–52. Cambridge, Mass.: MIT Press.

Chomsky, Noam, and Howard Lasnik. 1993. The theory of principles and parameters. In *Syntax: An international handbook of contemporary research*, ed. by Joachim Jacobs, Arnim von Stechow, Wolfgang Sternefeld, and Theo Vennemann, 506–569. Berlin: Walter de Gruyter.

Cinque, Guglielmo. 1990. *Types of Ā-dependencies*. Cambridge, Mass.: MIT Press.

Contreras, Heles. 1984. A note on parasitic gaps. *Linguistic Inquiry* 15, 704–713.

Dourado, Luciana. 2002. Construções aplicativas em Panará. *Revista de Documentação de Estudos em Lingüística Teórica e Aplicada (D.E.L.T.A.)* 18, 67–86.

du Plessis, Hans. 1977. *Wh*-movement in Afrikaans. *Linguistic Inquiry* 8, 723–726.

Dyła, Stefan. 1984. Across-the-board dependencies and Case in Polish. *Linguistic Inquiry* 15, 701–705.

Engdahl, Elisabet. 1983. Parasitic gaps. *Linguistics and Philosophy* 6, 5–34.

Epstein, Samuel David. 1991. *Traces and their antecedents*. Oxford: Oxford University Press.

Etxepare, Ricardo. 1999. On null complementizers in Spanish. Ms., Lengoaiarako Euskal Herriko Ikergune Aniztuna (Basque Center for Language Research), Vitoria-Gasteis, and Centre National de la Recherche Scientifique, Paris.

Fanselow, Gisbert, and Anoop Mahajan. 1995. Partial movement and successive cyclicity. In *Papers on wh-scope marking*, ed. by Uli Lutz and Gereon Müller, 131–161. Arbeitspapiere des Sonderforschungsbereichs 340, Sprachtheoretische Grundlagen für die Computer Linguistik, Bericht Nr. 76. University of Stuttgart and University of Tübingen.

Ferreira, Marcelo. 2000a. Argumentos nulos em português brasileiro. Master's thesis, Universidade Estadual de Campinas.

Ferreira, Marcelo. 2000b. Hyperraising and null subjects in Brazilian Portuguese. Ms., Universidade Estadual de Campinas.

Ferreira, Marília. 1999. Cópia pronominal em um dialeto do português brasileiro: Uma abordagem minimalista. Generals paper, Universidade Estadual de Campinas.

Fiengo, Robert. 1977. On trace theory. *Linguistic Inquiry* 8, 35–61.

Fiengo, Robert, and Robert May. 1994. *Indices and identity*. Cambridge, Mass.: MIT Press.

Fox, Danny. 1995. Economy and scope. *Natural Language Semantics* 3, 283–341.

Fox, Danny. 1999. Reconstruction, binding theory, and the interpretation of chains. *Linguistic Inquiry* 30, 157–196.

Frampton, John. 1990. Parasitic gaps and the theory of *wh*-chains. *Linguistic Inquiry* 21, 49–77.

Franks, Steven. 1993. On parallelism in across-the-board dependencies. *Linguistic Inquiry* 24, 509–529.

Franks, Steven. 1998. Clitics in Slavic. Paper presented at the Comparative Morphosyntax Workshop, Bloomington, Ind.

Freidin, Robert. 1986. Fundamental issues in the theory of binding. In *Studies in the acquisition of anaphora*, vol. 1, ed. by Barbara Lust, 151–188. Dordrecht: Reidel.

Galves, Charlotte. 2000. Agreement, predication and pronouns in the history of Portuguese. In *Portuguese syntax: New comparative studies*, ed. by João Costa, 143–168. Oxford: Oxford University Press.

Gärtner, Hans-Martin. 1997. Generalized transformations and beyond: Reflections on minimalist syntax. Doctoral dissertation, Johann-Wolfgang-Goethe Universität, Frankfurt.

Gärtner, Hans-Martin. 1998. Review of "The copy theory of movement and linearization of chains in the Minimalist Program." *GLOT International* 8.3, 16–20.

Golston, Chris. 1995. Syntax outranks phonology: Evidence from Ancient Greek. *Phonology* 12, 343–368.

Goodall, Grant. 1987. *Parallel structures in syntax.* Cambridge: Cambridge University Press.

Groat, Erich, and John O'Neil. 1996. Spell-Out at the interface: Achieving a unified syntactic computational system in the minimalist framework. In *Minimal ideas: Syntactic studies in the minimalist framework*, ed. by Werner Abraham, Samuel David Epstein, Höskuldur Thráinsson, and C. Jan-Wouter Zwart, 113–139. Amsterdam: John Benjamins.

Guasti, Maria Teresa, Rosalind Thornton, and Kenneth Wexler. 1995. Negation in children's questions: The case of English. In *BUCLD 19: Proceedings of the 19th Annual Boston University Conference on Language Development*, ed. by Dawn MacLaughlin and Susan McEwen, 228–239. Somerville, Mass.: Cascadilla Press.

Haïk, Isabelle. 1985. The syntax of operators. Doctoral dissertation, MIT, Cambridge, Mass.

Hale, Kenneth, and Samuel Jay Keyser. 1993. On argument structure and the lexical expression of syntactic relations. In *The view from Building 20: Essays in linguistics in honor of Sylvain Bromberger*, ed. by Kenneth Hale and Samuel Jay Keyser, 53–109. Cambridge, Mass.: MIT Press.

Halle, Morris, and Alec Marantz. 1993. Distributed Morphology and the pieces of inflection. In *The view from Building 20: Essays in linguistics in honor of Sylvain Bromberger*, ed. by Kenneth Hale and Samuel Jay Keyser, 111–176. Cambridge, Mass.: MIT Press.

Heycock, Caroline. 1995. Asymmetries in reconstruction. *Linguistic Inquiry* 26, 547–570.

Hiemstra, Inge. 1986. Some aspects of *wh*-questions in Frisian. *North-Western European Language Evolution (NOWELE)* 8, 97–110.

Higginbotham, James. 1983. Logical Form, binding, and nominals. *Linguistic Inquiry* 14, 395–420.

Higginbotham, James. 1985. On semantics. *Linguistic Inquiry* 16, 547–593.

Hinterhölzl, Roland. 1999. Licensing movement and stranding in the West Germanic OV languages. In *The derivation of VO and OV*, ed. by Peter Svenonius, 293–326. Amsterdam: John Benjamins.

Hiramatsu, Kazuko. 1999. What Move didn't delete? In *UConn Working Papers in Linguistics 10*, ed. by David Braze, Kazuko Hiramatsu, and Yutaka Kudo, 75–110. Cambridge, Mass.: MIT, Department of Linguistics and Philosophy, MITWPL.

Hornstein, Norbert. 1984. *Logic as grammar.* Cambridge, Mass.: MIT Press.

Hornstein, Norbert. 1995. *Logical Form: From GB to minimalism*. Oxford: Blackwell.

Hornstein, Norbert. 1999. Movement and control. *Linguistic Inquiry* 30, 69–96.

Hornstein, Norbert. 2001. *Move! A minimalist theory of construal*. Oxford: Blackwell.

Hornstein, Norbert, and Jairo Nunes. 2002. On asymmetries between parasitic gap and across-the-board constructions. *Syntax* 5, 26–54.

Hornstein, Norbert, Jairo Nunes, and Kleanthes Grohmann. To appear. *Understanding minimalism: An introduction to minimalist syntax*. Cambridge: Cambridge University Press.

Huang, C.-T. James. 1982. Logical relations in Chinese and the theory of grammar. Doctoral dissertation, MIT, Cambridge, Mass.

Kato, Mary, and Jairo Nunes. 1998. Two sources for relative clause formation in Brazilian Portuguese. Paper presented at the Eighth Colloquium on Generative Grammar, Universidade de Lisboa, April.

Kayne, Richard. 1983. Connectedness. *Linguistic Inquiry* 14, 223–249.

Kayne, Richard. 1984. *Connectedness and binary branching*. Dordrecht: Foris.

Kayne, Richard. 1991. Romance clitics, verb movement, and PRO. *Linguistic Inquiry* 22, 647–686.

Kayne, Richard. 1994. *The antisymmetry of syntax*. Cambridge, Mass.: MIT Press.

Kayne, Richard. 1998. Overt vs. covert movement. *Syntax* 1, 128–191.

Kayne, Richard. 2002. Pronouns and their antecedents. In *Derivation and explanation in the minimalist program*, ed. by Samuel David Epstein and T. Daniel Seely, 133–166. Oxford: Blackwell.

Kearney, Kevin. 1983. Governing categories. Ms., University of Connecticut, Storrs.

É. Kiss, Katalin. 1985. Parasitic chains. *The Linguistic Review* 5, 41–74.

Kitahara, Hisatsugu. 1995. Target α: Deducing strict cyclicity from derivational economy. *Linguistic Inquiry* 26, 47–78.

Koizumi, Masatoshi. 1993. Object agreement phrases and the split VP hypothesis. In *Papers on Case and agreement I*, ed. by Jonathan David Bobaljik and Colin Phillips, 99–148. MIT Working Papers in Linguistics 18. Cambridge, Mass.: MIT, Department of Linguistics and Philosophy, MITWPL.

Koopman, Hilda. 1984. *The syntax of verbs*. Dordrecht: Foris.

Lakoff, George. 1986. Frame semantic control of the Coordinate Structure Constraint. In *Papers from the Parasession on Pragmatics and Grammatical Theory*, ed. by Anne Farley, Peter Farley, and Karl-Erik McCullough, 152–167. Chicago: University of Chicago, Chicago Linguistic Society.

Larson, Richard. 1988. On the double object construction. *Linguistic Inquiry* 19, 335–391.

Lasnik, Howard. 1995. Last Resort and Attract F. In *Papers from the 6th Annual Meeting of the Formal Linguistics Society of Mid-America*, ed. by Leslie Gabriele, Debra Hardison, and Robert Westmoreland, vol. 1, 62–81. Bloomington: Indiana University, Indiana University Linguistics Club.

Lasnik, Howard. 1998. Some reconstruction riddles. In *Proceedings of the 22nd Annual Penn Linguistics Colloquium*, ed. by Alexis Dimitriadis, Hikyoung Lee, Christine Moisset, and Alexander Williams, 83–98. University of Pennsylvania Working Papers in Linguistics 5.1. Philadelphia: University of Pennsylvania, Penn Linguistics Club.

Lasnik, Howard. 1999a. Chains of arguments. In *Working minimalism*, ed. by Samuel David Epstein and Norbert Hornstein, 189–215. Cambridge, Mass.: MIT Press.

Lasnik, Howard. 1999b. *Minimalist analysis*. Oxford: Blackwell.

Lasnik, Howard, and Mamoru Saito. 1984. On the nature of proper government. *Linguistic Inquiry* 15, 235–289.

Lasnik, Howard, and Mamoru Saito. 1992. *Move α*. Cambridge, Mass.: MIT Press.

Lasnik, Howard, and Tim Stowell. 1991. Weakest crossover. *Linguistic Inquiry* 22, 687–720.

Lebeaux, David. 1988. Language acquisition and the form of the grammar. Doctoral dissertation, University of Massachusetts, Amherst.

Lebeaux, David. 1991. Relative clauses, licensing, and the nature of the derivation. In *Perspectives on phrase structure: Heads and licensing*, ed. by Susan Rothstein, 209–239. Syntax and Semantics 25. San Diego, Calif.: Academic Press.

Lightfoot, David. 2002. The form of innateness claims. Ms., Georgetown University, Washington, D.C.

Longobardi, Giuseppe. 1991. In defense of the correspondence hypothesis: Island effects and parasitic gaps in Logical Form. In *Logical structure and linguistic theory*, ed. by C.-T. James Huang and Robert May, 149–196. Dordrecht: Kluwer.

Manzini, Maria Rita. 1994. Locality, minimality, and parasitic gaps. *Linguistic Inquiry* 25, 481–508.

Martin, Roger. 1996. A minimalist theory of PRO. Doctoral dissertation, University of Connecticut, Storrs.

McDaniel, Dana. 1986. Conditions on *wh*-chains. Doctoral dissertation, City University of New York.

Merchant, Jason. 2001. *The syntax of silence*. Oxford: Oxford University Press.

Müller, Gereon. 1998. *Incomplete category fronting: A derivational approach to remnant movement in German*. Dordrecht: Kluwer.

Munn, Alan. 1987. Coordinate structures and X-bar theory. In *McGill working papers in linguistics 4*, ed. by Zofia Laubitz and Eithne Guilfoyle, 121–140. Montreal: McGill University, Linguistics Department.

Munn, Alan. 1993. Topics in the syntax and semantics of coordinate structures. Doctoral dissertation, University of Maryland, College Park.

Munn, Alan. 1994. A minimalist account of reconstruction asymmetries. In *NELS 24*, ed. by Mercè Gonzàlez, 397–410. Amherst: University of Massachusetts, GLSA.

Nishiyama, Kunio, and Eun Cho. 1997. Predicate cleft constructions in Japanese and Korean: The role of dummy verbs in TP/VP preposing. In *Japanese/Korean Linguistics 7*, ed. by Noriko Akatsugu, Hajime Hoji, Shoichi Iwasaki, Sung-Ock Sohn, and Susan Strauss, 463–479. Stanford, Calif.: CSLI Publications.

Nissenbaum, Jon. 1998. Movement and derived predicates: Evidence from parasitic gaps. In *The interpretive tract*, ed. by Uli Sauerland and Orin Percus, 247–295. MIT Working Papers in Linguistics 25. Cambridge, Mass.: MIT, Department of Linguistics and Philosophy, MITWPL.

Nunes, Jairo. 1995. The copy theory of movement and linearization of chains in the Minimalist Program. Doctoral dissertation, University of Maryland, College Park.

Nunes, Jairo. 1998. Bare X-bar theory and structures formed by movement. *Linguistic Inquiry* 29, 160–168.

Nunes, Jairo. 1999a. Linearization of chains and phonetic realization of chain links. In *Working minimalism*, ed. by Samuel David Epstein and Norbert Hornstein, 217–249. Cambridge, Mass.: MIT Press.

Nunes, Jairo. 1999b. Some notes on Procrastinate and other economy matters. *Revista de Documentação de Estudos em Lingüística Teórica e Aplicada (D.E.L.T.A.)* 15, 27–55.

Nunes, Jairo. 2000. Erasing erasure. *Revista de Documentação de Estudos em Lingüística Teórica e Aplicada (D.E.L.T.A.)* 16, 415–429.

Nunes, Jairo. 2001. Sideward movement. *Linguistic Inquiry* 32, 303–344.

Nunes, Jairo. 2003. Head movement, remnant movement, and phonetic realization of chains. In *Head movement and syntactic theory*, ed. by Anoop Mahajan, 161–177. UCLA/Potsdam Working Papers in Linguistics, Syntax at Sunset 3. Los Angeles: UCLA, Department of Linguistics.

Nunes, Jairo, and Ronice Quadros. In preparation. Focus duplication in Brazilian Sign Language. Ms., Universidade Estadual de Câmpinas and Universidade Federal de Santa Catarina.

Nunes, Jairo, and Ellen Thompson. 1998. Appendix. In Juan Uriagereka, *Rhyme and reason: An introduction to minimalist syntax*, 497–521. Cambridge, Mass.: MIT Press.

Nunes, Jairo, and Juan Uriagereka. 2000. Cyclicity and extraction domains. *Syntax* 3, 20–43.

Oishi, Masayuki. 1997. Reducing Procrastinate to feature strength. *Interdisciplinary Information Sciences* 3, 65–70.

Oroz, Rodolfo. 1966. *La lengua castellana en Chile*. Santiago: Universidad de Chile, Facultad de Filosofia y Educacion.

Pesetsky, David. 1995. *Zero syntax*. Cambridge, Mass.: MIT Press.

Pesetsky, David. 1997. Optimality Theory and syntax: Movement and pronunciation. In *Optimality Theory: An overview*, ed. by Diana Archangeli and D. Terence Langendoen, 134–170. Malden, Mass.: Blackwell.

Pesetsky, David. 1998. Some optimality principles of sentence pronunciation. In Pilar Barbosa, Danny Fox, Paul Hagstrom, Martha McGinnis, and David Pesetsky, eds., *Is the best good enough?*, 337–383. Cambridge, Mass.: MIT Press.

Petronio, Karen. 1993. Clause structure in American Sign Language. Doctoral dissertation, University of Washington, Seattle.

Petronio, Karen, and Diane Lillo-Martin. 1997. *Wh*-movement and the position of Spec-CP: Evidence from American Sign Language. *Language* 73, 18–57.

Postal, Paul. 1974. *On raising: One rule of English grammar and its theoretical implications*. Cambridge, Mass.: MIT Press.

Postal, Paul. 1993. Parasitic gaps and the across-the-board phenomenon. *Linguistic Inquiry* 24, 734–754.

Postal, Paul. 1994. Parasitic and pseudoparasitic gaps. *Linguistic Inquiry* 25, 63–117.

Postal, Paul. 1998. *Three investigations on extraction*. Cambridge, Mass.: MIT Press.

Quadros, Ronice. 1999. Phrase structure of Brazilian Sign Language. Doctoral dissertation, Pontifícia Universidade Católica do Rio Grande do Sul.

Radanović-Kocić, Vesna. 1988. The grammar of Serbo-Croatian clitics: A synchronic and diachronic perspective. Doctoral dissertation, University of Illinois, Urbana-Champaign.

Rizzi, Luigi. 1990. *Relativized Minimality*. Cambridge, Mass.: MIT Press.

Rodrigues, Cilene. 2000. Deriving Brazilian Portuguese referential subjects from movement. Generals paper, University of Maryland, College Park.

Rodrigues, Cilene. 2002. Morphology and null subjects in Brazilian Portuguese. In *Syntactic effects of morphological change*, ed. by David Lightfoot, 160–178. Oxford: Oxford University Press.

Ross, John R. 1967. Constraints on variables in syntax. Doctoral dissertation, MIT, Cambridge, Mass.

Rudin, Catherine, Christina Kramer, Loren Billings, and Matthew Baerman. 1999. Macedonian and Bulgarian *li* questions: Beyond syntax. *Natural Language and Linguistic Theory* 17, 541–586.

Safir, Ken. 1987. The anti-c-command condition on parasitic gaps. *Linguistic Inquiry* 18, 117–171.

Safir, Ken. 1999. Vehicle change and reconstruction in Ā-chains. *Linguistic Inquiry* 30, 587–620.

Santos, Raquel. 2002. Categorias sintáticas vazias e retração de acento em português brasileiro. *Revista de Documentação de Estudos em Lingüística Teórica e Aplicada (D.E.L.T.A.)* 18, 67–86.

Schein, Barry. 1993. *Plural and events.* Cambridge, Mass.: MIT Press.

Silva-Corvalán, Carmen. 1989. *Sociolingüística: Teoría e análisis.* Madrid: Alhambra.

Stepanov, Arthur. 2000. The timing of adjunction. In *NELS 30*, ed. by Mako Hirotani, Andries Coetzee, Nancy Hall, and Ji-Yung Kim, 597–611. Amherst: University of Massachusetts, GLSA.

Stjepanović, Sandra. 1999. What do second position cliticization, scrambling and multiple *wh*-fronting have in common? Doctoral dissertation, University of Connecticut, Storrs.

Taraldsen, Knut Tarald. 1981. The theoretical implications of a class of marked extractions. In *Theory of markedness in generative grammar*, ed. by Adriana Belletti, Luciana Brandi, and Luigi Rizzi, 475–516. Pisa: Scuola Normale Superiore.

Thornton, Rosalind. 1990. Adventures in long-distance moving: The acquisition of complex *wh*-questions. Doctoral dissertation, University of Connecticut, Storrs.

Travis, Lisa. 1984. Parameters and effects of word worder variation. Doctoral dissertation, MIT, Cambridge, Mass.

Uriagereka, Juan. 1995. Aspects of the syntax of clitic placement in Western Romance. *Linguistic Inquiry* 26, 79–124.

Uriagereka, Juan. 1998. *Rhyme and reason: An introduction to minimalist syntax.* Cambridge, Mass.: MIT Press.

Uriagereka, Juan. 1999. Multiple Spell-Out. In *Working minimalism*, ed. by Samuel David Epstein and Norbert Hornstein, 251–282. Cambridge, Mass.: MIT Press.

Vergnaud, Jean-Roger. 1974. French relative clauses. Doctoral dissertation, MIT, Cambridge, Mass.

Weinberg, Amy. 1988. Locality principles in syntax and parsing. Doctoral dissertation, MIT, Cambridge, Mass.

Wilder, Chris. 1995. Rightward movement as leftward deletion. In *On extraction and extraposition in German*, ed. by Uli Lutz and Jürgen Pafel, 273–309. Amsterdam: John Benjamins.

Williams, Edwin. 1978. Across-the-board rule application. *Linguistic Inquiry* 9, 31–43.

Williams, Edwin. 1990. The ATB theory of parasitic gaps. *The Linguistic Review* 6, 265–279.

Ximenes, Cristina. 2002. Contração de preposição em estruturas coordenadas. Master's thesis, Universidade Estadual de Campinas.

Zocca, Cynthia. 2003. O que não está lá? Um estudo sobre morfologia flexional em elipses. Master's thesis, Universidade Estadual de Campinas.

Index